D1267938

The Hungarian Experience

in Economic Planning

A THEORETICAL AND EMPIRICAL STUDY

by Bela A. Balassa

New Haven

YALE UNIVERSITY PRESS, 1959

© *1959 by the Yale University Press, Inc.*
Set in Baskerville type and
printed in the United States of America by
Vail-Ballou Press, Inc., Binghamton, N.Y.
All rights reserved. This book may not be
reproduced, in whole or in part, in any form
(except by reviewers for the public press),
without written permission from the publishers.
Library of Congress catalog card number: 59-13443

Preface

THERE is a considerable amount of literature on the theoretical problems of economic planning, and the number of books dealing with the achievements of Soviet-type economies is growing from year to year. Less attention has been paid to integrating the two areas: studying the way theoretical blueprints work in practice. The present book deals with the latter problem: it presents a theoretical model of central planning based on physical allocation of resources, and examines the functioning of this model in Hungarian practice. It endeavors, furthermore, to evaluate the performance of the Hungarian economy by means of a set of success indicators.

The analysis of the Hungarian experience in planning is based essentially on the situation prevailing before the Hungarian Revolution (October 23, 1956), though where information is available reference is also made to later developments. In addition to a liberal use of published Hungarian material, I have drawn on my own experience.

Since this study is primarily concerned with planning methods and their application in the Hungarian economy rather than with factual description, no extensive coverage of the economic structure is attempted; banking, transportation, and commerce, for example, are not dealt with. Also, in areas widely covered, such as industry, the objective of the study is to show the inner working of the mechanism rather than supply factual information on particular industries. The reader interested in such information is referred to the studies of Spulber and Helmreich.* In appraising the achievements of the Hungarian economy I have used official national income data, with appropriate corrections. Problems of two sectors of special importance—agriculture and foreign trade —are dealt with separately in appendices.

* Nicolas Spulber, *The Economics of Communist Eastern Europe*, Cambridge, Technology Press of M.I.T., 1957; and Ernst C. Helmreich, ed., *Hungary*, New York, Praeger, 1957. Both books present official Hungarian statistical data.

v

The nonprofessional reader may wish to skim the first chapter and return to it occasionally when it is referred to in the text. Those not acquainted with the concepts of scarcity prices, equilibrium, and efficiency are urged to read Appendix A before proceeding to Chapter 3.

Books written in Hungarian are cited first by their Hungarian titles, followed by the English translation of these titles; subsequent citations are by the English form. Articles published in Hungarian periodicals and newspapers are cited by their English title, followed by the abbreviated name of the periodical or newspaper. For a list of these abbreviations, which incorporates also the most frequently cited books, see page xi. A list of cited Hungarian periodicals and newspapers and of books dealing with the Hungarian economy is appended at the end of the book (page 277).

I would like to express my gratitude to John M. Montias and Geoffrey Shepherd for their detailed and painstaking criticism of an earlier draft of the book. A later draft was ready by William J. Fellner, Lloyd G. Reynolds, and Robert Triffin. I am heavily indebted to them for their useful advice on many points. Egon Sohmen made valuable suggestions on Chapters 1 and 7. I also want to thank David Horne for his patience in editing the manuscript and for his valuable help in matters of presentation. Elinor Horne and Elaine Sprenkle did an excellent typing job.

The present version of this book was awarded the John Addison Porter Prize of Yale University in 1959. The first version was written while I was a Rockefeller fellow. Most of the research and writing was undertaken under a grant from the Relm Foundation, which also gave financial assistance to publication. The last part of the work was carried out under the tenure of a Ford fellowship. To all three of these foundations I am under particular obligation.

B. A. B.

New Haven, Connecticut
April 1959

Contents

Tables

Abbreviations

ASH	*Annuaire statistique hongrois*, 1938, Budapest, 1940
AT	*Agrártudomány (Agricultural Science)*
DE	*Demográfia (Demography)*
EH	*Esti Hirlap (Evening Gazette)*
Facts and Figures	*Adatok és adalékok a népgazdaság fejlödésének tanulmányozásához (Facts and Figures for the Examination of the Development of the National Economy)*, Budapest, 1957
GF	*Gazdasági Figyelö (Economic Observer)*
GT	*Gazdaságstatisztikai Tájékoztató (Bulletin of Economic Statistics)*
Kornai	J. Kornai, *A gazdasági vezetés tulzott központositása (The Excessive Centralization of Economic Management)*, Budapest, 1957
KSz	*Közgazdasági Szemle (Economic Review)*
ME	*Müszaki Élet (Technical Life)*
MGIH	*A Magyar Gazdaságkutató Intézet Helyzetjelentései (Economic Reports of the Hungarian Institute for Economic Research)*
MSzKSz	*Magyar-Szovjet Közgazdasági Szemle (Hungarian-Soviet Economic Review)*
National Accounts	*Népgazdasági mérlegek, reáljövedelmek (National Accounts, Real Incomes)*, 1956, Budapest, 1957
NSz	*Népszabadság (Freedom of the People)*
PESz	*Pénzügy és Számvitel (Finances and Accounting)*
Péter	G. Péter, *A gazdaságosság és jövedelmezöség jelentösége a tervgazdálkodásban (The Importance of Efficiency and Profitability in Planning)*, Budapest, 1956
Prices	*Áralakulás Magyarországon 1938-ban és 1949–1955-ben (Prices in Hungary in 1938 and 1949–1955)*, Budapest, 1957
PSz	*Pénzügyi Szemle (Financial Review)*

SE	Statisztikai évkönyv (Statistical Yearbook), 1949–55, Budapest, 1957
SHK	Statisztikai Havi Közlemények (Monthly Bulletin of Statistics)
SSz	Statisztikai Szemle (Statistical Review)
ST	Statisztikai Tájékoztató (Statistical Bulletin)
SzA	Századok (Centuries)
SzF	Szabad Föld (Free Land)
SzN	Szabad Nép (Free People)
TSz	Társadalmi Szemle (Social Review)
Yearbook	A Magyar Tudományos Akadémia Közgazdaságtudományi Intézetének Évkönyve (Yearbook of the Economic Institute of the Hungarian Academy of Science), 1, 1957, Budapest, 1957

1. Socialism versus Capitalism: the Economist's Case

SETTING THE STAGE

THE PROBLEM of socialism versus capitalism has a long history. We may consider, however, that the period of modern controversy begins with the publication of E. Barone's famous article "The Ministry of Production in the Collectivist State." [1] Examining the question of whether centralized decision-making can replace the free market, Barone concludes that such a solution— although theoretically possible—would encounter practical difficulties because of the gigantic task of collecting data and the continual change of technological coefficients.

Barone, then, ignited the fire of discussion; others have supplied fuel to keep it blazing. It is not our purpose here to evaluate the debate or even to summarize it,[2] but it will be useful to state the position of some of the participants. Among the many shadings of opinion, we can distinguish four main groups.

1. L. von Mises flatly maintains that economic calculation in a socialist economy is impossible.[3] He is equipped with arguments even against those who cite the Soviet Union and Nazi Germany as cases of successful planning, contending that "these socialist states base the calculations on which they make their decisions on the prices established abroad. Without the help of these prices their actions would be aimless and planless. . . . socialism will result in complete chaos . . . if it is applied in the greater part of the world." [4]

1. Originally published in 1908 in Italian, English translation in F. A. Hayek, ed., *Collectivist Economic Planning* (London, Routledge, 1935), pp. 245–90.

2. See Abram Bergson, "Socialist Economics," in *A Survey of Contemporary Economics* (2 vols. Homewood, Illinois, Irwin, 1948–52), Vol. 1 (ed. H. S. Ellis, 1948), 412–48.

3. His position was originally stated in a German article in 1920, the English translation of which was published in *Collectivist Economic Planning* under the title "Economic Calculation in the Socialist Commonwealth," pp. 87–130.

4. *Omnipotent Government* (New Haven, Yale University Press, 1944), p. 55.

2. The leading theorists belonging to the second group are F. A. Hayek and L. Robbins; a brief but apt description of their views has been given by O. Lange: "They do not deny the *theoretical* possibility of a rational allocation of resources in a socialist economy; they only doubt the possibility of satisfactory *practical* solution of the problem." [5]

Robbins has occupied himself with Barone's problem of centralized decision-making, envisaged as the mathematical solution of "a system of simultaneous equations . . . whose solution would show the equilibrium distribution of factors and the equilibrium production of commodities," where the equations should contain consumers' and resource-holders' preferences and the technological possibilities of production. According to Robbins, "in practice this solution is quite unworkable." [6] The words "unworkable" and "unpracticable" appear frequently in Robbins' and Hayek's writings. I suspect that for many people these expressions have emotional connotations implying that there is *no* solution; yet Hayek at one place gives a perfectly clear statement interpreting them as meaning inefficient:

> It was not the possibility of planning as such which has been questioned on the grounds of general considerations, but the possibility of successful planning, of achieving the ends for which planning was undertaken. . . . There is no reason to expect that production would stop, or that the authorities would find difficulty in using all the available resources somehow, or even that output would be permanently lower than it had been before planning started. What we should anticipate is that output, where the use of the available resources was determined by some central authority, would be lower than if the price mechanism of a market operated freely under otherwise similar circumstances.[7]

Hayek considers primarily the allocation of given resources among alternative ends at a certain point of time, and argues that

Recently a similar argument was offered in a revised edition of *Socialism* (New Haven, Yale University Press, 1951), p. 119.

5. "On the Economic Theory of Socialism," in B. E. Lippincott, ed., *On the Economic Theory of Socialism* (Minneapolis, University of Minnesota Press, 1938), p. 62. Italics in original.

6. *The Great Depression* (London, 1934), p. 151.

7. "The Present State of the Debate," in *Collectivist Economic Planning*, pp. 203–4.

a socialist economic system is less efficient than free enterprise because of lack of incentives, the need for bureaucracy, and the abrogation of consumer sovereignty.

3. On the socialist side the so-called "market solution" is represented by Lange,[8] H. D. Dickinson,[9] and, in his earlier writings, A. P. Lerner.[10] According to advocates of the market solution, a socialist economy can work in basically the same way as a freely competitive system if production decisions are decentralized and the Planning Board assumes the price-determining function of the market mechanism. Prices are determined by trial and error, the right prices being those at which demand and supply balance. The managers act according to rules essentially corresponding to profit maximization. Free consumers' choice and free choice of occupation are presupposed. The principal analytical differences between the workings of the free competitive market and the socialist market solution are that in the latter the amount of saving and investment for the whole economy (but not the direction of investment into industries and firms) and the rate of interest are determined by the planning authorities; interrelationships in production (cost-reducing economies of the firm resulting from the expansion of the industry, such as cross-fertilization of ideas on new technology, the growth of a skilled labor force, etc.) are taken into account in determining prices; and property-income claims are abolished.

Another form of the market solution, the so-called Yugoslav solution, dispenses with the price-fixing function of the Planning Board. Prices are determined on a competitive market, which consists of socialist firms. This solution was foreseen by Dickinson.[11]

4. Another group of socialist economists, including M. Dobb [12] and P. M. Sweezy,[13] favor centralized planning. Whereas the

8. "On the Economic Theory of Socialism," pp. 57–129. At present Lange professes different views.

9. *Economics of Socialism,* Oxford University Press, 1939.

10. "Economic Theory and Socialist Economy," *Review of Economic Studies,* 2 (1934–35), 51–61, and "Statics and Dynamics in Socialist Economics," *Economic Journal,* 47 (1937), 253–70.

11. *Economics of Socialism,* pp. 104–5.

12. *On Economic Theory and Socialism,* New York, International Publishers, 1954; and *Political Economy and Capitalism,* New York, International Publishers, 1945, esp. chap. 8.

13. *Socialism,* New York, McGraw-Hill, 1949.

Planning Board in the original form of the market solution is essentially a price-fixing agency acting according to the rules of the competitive market, in the centralist scheme this Board makes all or most of the essential production and investment decisions. The proponents of centralized planning usually postulate the physical allocation of resources by the central authorities instead of use of the price-mechanism, and maintain the necessity for overruling consumers' preferences. A form of centralized planning is used in Soviet-type economies.

Although the debate [14] on the issues of socialism versus capitalism has raged for about four decades, many of the participants (with some exceptions, like Lerner, who now favors a mixed system) stick to their original views. Two quotations chosen at random reflect the inflexibility in their thinking. Mises contends: "The intellectual bankruptcy of the socialist doctrine can no longer be disguised. . . . The avowal of socialist ideas is to-day the proof of complete ignorance of the basic problems of economics." [15] On the other side, in the foreword to Douglas Jay's *The Socialist Case*, the former British prime minister Clement Attlee asserts: "I believe myself that these [i.e. the socialist] arguments are unanswerable . . ." [16]

But where is truth to be found? In Bergson's opinion the controversy boils down to the question, which is more efficient, socialism or capitalism? He continues: "As we see it, it is now the only issue outstanding. The discussion in the preceding sections, it is hoped, will provide a partial basis for judgment on this important matter. For the rest . . . we leave this issue too for the reader to decide." [17]

In the opinion of the present writer the question first to be answered is whether there is any possibility of devising an objective test which can be used in comparing the efficiency of economic systems. Bergson also suggests that some kind of efficiency test should be agreed upon, but he does not go further. The fundamental problem remains: Is there a test or formula that can serve in reaching scientifically reasoned conclusions? This question will be taken up in the remaining part of the chapter.

14. It was throughout restricted in the Western world; Soviet authors, professing the official views of the Communist party, have not taken much cognizance of it.

15. *Socialism*, p. 586.

16. London, Faber and Faber (1946), p. vii.

17. "Socialist Economics," p. 447.

CHOICE IN A DYNAMIC WORLD

Economists have long been concerned with the definition of an economic optimum and with the ways it can be achieved. In the first decade of this century V. Pareto defined an optimum (efficient) position by the requirement that there should not exist any possible reallocation of resources which could make anybody better off without making somebody worse off.[18] One of the conditions of a Pareto optimum is that there should be no possibility of increasing the production of one commodity without reducing the production of another. It has been pointed out that this Pareto optimum is not a single point, that there are many possible positions fulfilling the above criteria. All these optima are positions of general equilibrium.

Pareto optima indicate efficient allocation of resources among alternative uses. It can be shown that—within certain simplifying assumptions—efficient allocation of resources is achieved in pure competition, where the so-called marginal equivalences are fulfilled.[19] But the distribution of income resulting from pure competition may not be considered desirable. It is conventionally assumed that the distribution of income can be changed without impairing efficiency by so-called lump-sum redistributions.[20]

In a static system the fulfillment of the conditions for Pareto optima would supply us with a test of efficiency on the basis of which the performance of different economic systems could be evaluated. Since we do not live in a static world, such a test would not lead us very far. Whereas under static conditions the only variable considered is the efficient allocation of resources at a given point of time, in a dynamic world we have to consider more variables than mere static efficiency; next to it, the dynamic efficiency of the system, the growth rate, consumer satisfaction, and the distribution of income are those of basic importance.[21]

18. *Manuel d'économie politique* (Paris, 1909), chap. 6.
19. For a good exposition of the necessary marginal conditions for an optimum see K. E. Boulding's "Welfare Economics," in *Survey of Contemporary Economics* (2 vols. Homewood, Illinois, Irwin, 1948–52), Vol. 2 (ed. B. F. Haley, 1952), 14–23. See also below, Appendix A.
20. Lump-sum redistribution means a system of taxes and subsidies which, not being anticipated, do not affect the individual's effort and risk-taking.
21. These concepts will be defined and examined in the next section.

Considering these variables as success indicators, the evaluation of different economic systems requires the following:

1. *Success Indicators.* We have to extend the meaning of "efficiency test," since efficiency (static and dynamic) does not exhaust the list of variables on the basis of which a conclusion with regard to different economic systems should be reached. We can assume that different values [22] of our success indicators can be achieved under conditions postulated in various economic systems. Some of the variables are partly cumulative, in the sense that an increase in A leads to an increase in B (for example, an improvement in dynamic efficiency leads to an increase of the growth rate); some are competitive in the sense that an increase in the value of C leads to a reduction in the value of D (for example, an equal distribution of income is likely to lead to less efficient resource allocation, or a higher growth rate requires restriction of present consumption). Naturally, even for partly cumulative variables there must be at least one other variable which serves as a restraint, that is, the reduction of which is needed for a further increase of the former variable. In technical terms, for any economic system there is a maximum value of any one variable attainable, given the values of the other variables. The maximum values of the success indicators obtained in this way show the performance of the system. For example, an economic system may achieve a higher degree of static efficiency and more equitable income distribution than another system with a higher degree of dynamic efficiency and a higher growth rate.

2. *Scale of Preferences.* There is only one case where there is no difficulty in choosing between two economic systems. That is when in system Z a higher value of all five success indicators can be achieved than in system W. If some of the success indicators show a higher value in one, some in another system, we need additional criteria in order to choose between the systems. One has to decide which success indicators are of greater importance, which have higher priority; in other words, a scale of preferences

---

22. By values we mean higher or lower levels of any success indicator, some of which are quantitatively measurable (for example, growth by the percentage rate of increase of national income). Some of these, on the other hand, are not measurable quantitatively (for example, static or dynamic efficiency); for them only ordinal ranking can be used.

is needed. The choice between different economic systems should be made on the basis of their proficiency in the various fields enumerated above, given a certain scale of preferences with regard to the success indicators.

We face two questions here: Can we determine theoretically the workings of different economic systems with regard to our success indicators, and can we construct some kind of preference scale on the basis of which the importance of different values of the success indicators can be evaluated? Only if we are able to answer both questions in the affirmative is it possible to present the economist's case with regard to the choice between different systems. But even if this decision can be made, we face the further problem whether these systems can be realized in the real world in their theoretical purity.[23]

THE SUCCESS INDICATORS

Static Efficiency in the Allocation of Resources

Static efficiency may be defined as production conforming to the preferences of the community [24] when there is no possibility of increasing the production of one commodity without reducing the production of another. It has been pointed out in the last section that static efficiency can be achieved in an economic system organized according to the rules of competition. Consequently, with regard to static efficiency, the real difference is not between a free enterprise and a socialist system but between, on the one hand, free enterprise and the socialist market solution, and on the other, centralized physical planning.

From the analytical point of view the workings of a purely

23. In technical terms we have to devise a possibility function for the various economic systems, indicating the maximum achievable value of any success indicator given the values of the other variables. Furthermore, a social welfare function is needed to indicate the society's preferences for the various success indicators. That system would be judged to be superior the possibility function of which is tangent to the highest social welfare function.

24. "The preferences of the community" may mean either individual preferences or the authoritative decision of the Planning Board with regard to the final bill of goods (goods destined for ultimate consumption or investment). Efficiency as here defined corresponds to the concept of productive efficiency used by T. C. Koopmans, *Three Essays on the State of Economic Science* (New York, McGraw-Hill, 1957), p. 84.

competitive system and of the market solution for socialism, and the results they lead to, are essentially the same. Nevertheless, some analytical differences have already been noted; in addition, two more factors should be considered.

Socialist writers neglect the importance of the cost of information in the socialist market solution. Whereas in pure competition the information needed to reach equilibrium is possessed by the decision-making units, here it must be collected by the Planning Board, and its collection is time-consuming and costly. Although this disadvantage of the socialist market solution is not relevant in its Yugoslav form, the problem of incentives does arise there also. It can be argued that in a static world the profit motive as incentive leads to a more efficient allocation of resources in a free enterprise system than is possible in the competition of socialist firms.[25]

Centralized planning based on the physical allocation of resources dispenses with the price mechanism in resource allocation. Prices do not express relative scarcities in this system but serve only accounting purposes. Consequently, as will be seen in Chapter 3, efficient allocation of resources cannot be achieved. On the other hand, the use of pricing in resource allocation would make centralized planning similar to the socialist market solution.[26]

With regard to static efficiency pure competition appears to be superior to centralized planning on the physical level. Nevertheless, there are two types of "market failure"[27] which impair the efficiency of a competitive system: those existing in a static world with perfect information and foresight, and those connected with imperfect information and uncertain expectations.

The first type contains the following factors:

1. Under conditions of increasing returns competition will break down, partly because monopolies will be formed, partly because an optimum position may be reached only if enterprises

---

25. For some further problems concerning the operation of the socialist market solution see F. A. Hayek, "Socialist Calculation: The Competitive Solution," *Economica*, new ser. 7 (1940), 125–49.

26. See below, p. 46.

27. To use the convenient expression coined by F. M. Bator in "The Anatomy of Market Failure," *Quarterly Journal of Economics*, 72 (1958), 351–88. It should be noted that Bator subsumes all factors belonging to the first type of market failure under the heading "externalities."

producing under increasing returns minimize rather than maximize profit.[28]

2. Direct interaction between producers, between consumers, or between producers and consumers which is unaccounted for in market valuations, also impairs the efficiency of the system. A standard example for these external effects between producers is the apple-grower whose orchard blossoms provide food free of charge for the bees of the nearby beekeeper. Although the social productivity of apple-growing is therefore higher than its private productivity, the farmer's production decisions are based on the latter only; hence apple-growing stops short of the social optimum. A classic example of diseconomies in production is smoke nuisance.

3. Market valuation is no better guide in the case of collective goods either. Roads, education, and defense may be mentioned as examples. Proposed solutions are voting or decision by elected authoritative bodies.[29]

The second type of market failure comprises uncertainty and inconsistency of expectations, inertia and resistance to change, and imperfect information. These phenomena have dynamic implications, hence they will be dealt with in connection with dynamic efficiency, below. One further point needs mentioning here, however. Uncertainty and inconsistency of expectations will bring about fluctuations in the employment of resources. In other words, a purely competitive economy will work at least part of the time with less than full utilization of existing resources. Since static efficiency presupposes full resource use, this factor will result in inefficiencies. On the other hand, in a socialist system this form of unemployment may be avoided. Thus the shortcomings of a socialist system so far as static efficiency is concerned are (partly) counteracted by the full utilization of resources.

One final remark: in our discussion the hypothetical conditions of pure competition have been considered and we have disregarded monopolistic elements that impair static efficiency achievable in the blueprint of pure competition. Similarly, pos-

---

28. See P. A. Samuelson, *Foundations of Economic Analysis* (Cambridge, Harvard University Press, 1955), p. 232.

29. For a solution based on individual preferences see P. A. Samuelson, "Public Expenditure: A Diagrammatic Exposition," *Review of Economics and Statistics, 37* (1955), 350–56.

sible deviations of actual socialist systems from the theoretical blueprints have been left out of account.

Dynamic Efficiency

Static efficiency is concerned with efficient resource allocation at a given point in time; an economic system may exhibit static efficiency even if production is unchanged from year to year. Dynamic efficiency, on the other hand, is concerned with the growth possibilities of an economy. Dynamic efficiency can be indicated by the hypothetical growth rate of national income achievable in different economic systems under identical resource use [29a] and saving ratio.[30] (As with static efficiency, we do not require that production conform to individual preferences—it may as well correspond to the preferences of the planners.) The distinction between static and dynamic efficiency has been forcefully expressed in Schumpeter's classical words: "A system—any system, economic or other—that at *every* point of time fully utilizes its possibilities to the best advantage may yet in the long run be inferior to a system that does so at *no* given point of time, because the latter's failure to do so may be a condition for the level or speed of long-run performance." [31]

There is much disagreement on the question whether a free enterprise or a socialist economy is superior with regard to dynamic efficiency. According to Hayek, a higher growth rate could be secured in a free enterprise system "if we assumed that the same restriction of consumption, which has actually taken place [in Russia], had been caused by taxation, the proceeds of which had been lent to competitive industry for investment

29a. The term "identical resource use" is employed here as a shorthand expression for identical initial resources and the use of identical amounts of human labor.

30. In technical terms, whereas static efficiency means that the economy operates on its production-possibility frontier, dynamic efficiency can be represented by the movement of this frontier in northeast direction. For a rigorous treatment of dynamic efficiency under the assumption of constant returns to scale, absence of technological change, and the knowledge of current rates of price changes on the side of the producers, see R. Dorfman, P. A. Samuelson, and R. M. Solow, *Linear Programming and Economic Analysis* (New York, McGraw-Hill, 1958), chap. 12.

31. J. A. Schumpeter, *Capitalism, Socialism, and Democracy* (New York, Harper, 1942), p. 83. Italics in original.

purposes." [32] The contrary conclusion is reached by, for example, Dobb [33] and Sweezy.[34] Bergson also inclines toward the latter view: "One may imagine that in a highly dynamic economy a Centralist allocation of investment might lead to fewer and smaller errors than a Competitive allocation." [35] Although his remarks were addressed to the competitive (market) solution in a socialist economy, they may apply to free enterprise as well.

Some arguments of primary importance with regard to dynamic efficiency in a free enterprise system and in socialism are the following:

1. No conclusive argument can be offered as far as technical progress is concerned. It is widely held that a free enterprise system is more conducive to technical progress than a socialist economy, since both the endeavor to survive and the profit motive greatly contribute to the introduction of new production methods. On the other hand, it has been argued that under conditions of pure competition productive units are too small and the risk of introducing innovations of considerable importance is too great to permit revolutionary changes in technical methods.[36] If so, monopolistic market structures in a free enterprise economy or centralized direction of investments in a socialist system may achieve a higher rate of technical progress. However, a free enterprise economy with competing large production units could combine the advantages of the profit motive with possession of considerable means to finance innovating activity. Yet Schumpeter emphasizes that in large production units technological progress becomes automatic, "innovation itself being reduced to routine." [37] If this is true, the frequently used objection against the socialist system, that salaried employees are not interested in technical progress, loses much of its force.

32. *Collectivist Economic Planning*, p. 205.
33. *On Economic Theory and Socialism*, pp. 41–54.
34. *Socialism*, pp. 234–36.
35. Bergson, p. 443.
36. It should be added here that, according to William Fellner, in the absence of uncertainty and incomplete foresight and under the assumption of perfect rationality, technological progress would proceed in the same way under both pure competition and monopoly: "The Influence of Market Structure on Technological Progress," in *Readings in Industrial Organization and Public Policy* (Homewood, Illinois, Irwin, 1958), p. 294.
37. *Capitalism, Socialism, and Democracy*, p. 132.

Although technological change may come about sooner in a free enterprise economy than under socialism, technological progress can be smoother in a planned economy. Under free enterprise, when innovations are made by individual concerns, other firms may offer resistance; or secrecy, patents, etc. may delay the spreading of new production methods.

2. Primarily in underdeveloped countries a dynamic form of external effects is relevant. Investments in transportation facilities or public utilities are frequently unprofitable for the private producer although "profitable" from the viewpoint of social productivity. Investments of this sort, the so-called social overhead, facilitates the establishment of industrial enterprises. Here centralized decision-making has clear advantages. Nevertheless, one could object that central planning should be restricted to the provision for social overhead only and let private initiative do the rest.

3. Uncertainty and inconsistency of expectations in a free enterprise framework is frequently mentioned as a serious drag on dynamic efficiency.[38] Under competition, decisions to increase capacity are made separately by each firm, and these plans are coordinated *ex post facto* only, through the market mechanism. The lack of information on investment decisions of other entrepreneurs and the uncertainty of expectations may lead to a slowing down of investment activity because of excessive cautiousness. Furthermore, decisions with regard to the future are likely to clash, resulting in too much or too little investment in a particular field. It seems that the greater the dynamism of a free enterprise system, the higher the possible waste. On the other hand, the Planning Board (or the monopolist) has more information about investment decisions made, and can thereby avoid overlapping. Also, the planning authority may organize and coordinate investment activity well in advance. Nevertheless, this argument is not so conclusive as it seems. Thinking in terms of waste, people are liable to forget that waste may be a necessary corollary to progress. The path of growth may be smoother in a socialist economy, but a dynamic free enterprise system may achieve a higher rate of growth even at the expense of greater fluctuations. This is possible if the endeavor to survive and the profit motive overcompensate for the uncertainty and inconsist-

38. Tibor Scitovsky, *Welfare and Competition* (Chicago, Irwin, 1951), pp. 233–41.

ency of expectations. Moreover, the expectation that innovations will be made by others may act as a compelling rather than a restricting force.

These arguments and counterarguments suggest that the economist cannot make a conclusive judgment on the dynamic efficiency of the blueprints of different economic systems. It should be added that psychological and sociological factors and differences between the blueprint and its actual realization can also be of decisive importance.

Growth Rate of National Income

Distinction should be made between dynamic efficiency and the actual growth rate of national income.[39] It will be recalled that dynamic efficiency was defined as the hypothetical growth rate of national income achievable in different economic systems under identical resource use and saving ratio. The actual growth rate is affected not only by the dynamic efficiency of the system but also by the central authority's action overruling individual preferences in regard to saving versus spending and work versus leisure. Despite dynamic inefficiencies, an economic system may achieve a higher growth rate through an increase in the saving ratio [40] or through an involuntary increase in the amount of labor.

Recently more and more emphasis has been placed on the

39. Two difficulties should be mentioned here in regard to the estimation of the growth rate, although no attempt will be made to evaluate them. First, there is a conceptual problem: the definition of national income. Our results will be different depending on whether we use, for example, the Soviet concept of national income, which is equivalent to the value of material production, or a Western concept, which includes services. Second, there is the problem of measurement: no unequivocal measure of the growth rate can be found. Changes in the proportion of goods with decreasing costs, structural changes in production, new commodities, and quality changes—all make the measurement of the growth rate and the comparison of growth rates in different countries to a considerable degree inconclusive. For an extensive treatment of the problem of measurement see F. W. Nutter, "On Measuring Economic Growth," *Journal of Political Economy, 65* (1957), 51–63. Also, "Comment" by H. S. Levine, "Reply" by Nutter, and "Rejoinder" by Levine, in the same journal, *66* (1958), 352–63.

40. The objection that the saving ratio does not affect the equilibrium growth rate under conditions of constant returns to scale and in the absence of technical progress has more theoretical than practical importance. See T. W. Swan, "Economic Growth and Capital Accumulation," *Economic Record, 32* (1956), 334–42; and R. M. Solow, "A Contribution to the Theory of Economic Growth," *Quarterly Journal of Economics, 71* (1956), 65–94.

growth rate. One has the impression that in the eyes of many people the rate of growth is the *sole* success indicator. Much of the recent writing on economic growth as well as a host of political speeches convey the same impression. The dissenting voices —like that of J. K. Galbraith, who contends that "our concern for production is traditional and irrational" [41]—are comparatively few. It is not our concern here to appraise the importance of the growth rate as a success indicator. We shall rather restrict our discussion to the examination of various factors which affect the rate of growth.

In a free enterprise economy, saving is determined by the preferences of the individuals and by corporate saving. In a socialist economy, the central authorities decide what part of national income will be used for investment purposes. The possibility of enforcement of a higher saving ratio in a socialist state makes a higher rate of growth feasible. To quote Fellner: "A totalitarian government, if it could establish itself in a country such as the United States, might not find it difficult to operate the economy at a level of consumption 20 to 25 per cent lower than our present consumption level, and then let consumption rise slowly with the rise of aggregate output. By such a policy, the present American net capital formation could be *more than doubled,* and it is quite likely that the annual economic growth rate of the United States could be *almost* doubled." [42]

The disadvantage of a free enterprise system with regard to the proportion of national income invested can be offset by taxation, the proceeds of which could be lent to individuals for investment purposes, as envisaged by Hayek.[43] But would Hayek really advocate such a policy; would he plead for encroachment upon the individual's freedom to consume or save at will? In view of his doctrine implying the undesirability of forced saving,[44] this is not very likely. But we should not forget that many representatives of "bourgeois" economics have regarded forced saving, brought about by having wage increases lag behind price rises, as a necessary condition for capitalist development.[45]

41. *The Affluent Society* (Boston, Houghton Mifflin, 1958), p. 132.
42. *Trends and Cycles in Economic Activity* (New York, Holt, 1956), p. 73. Italics in original.
43. See above, p. 10.
44. See his *Prices and Production,* London, Routledge and Kegan Paul, 1931.
45. For example, J. M. Keynes, *A Treatise on Money* (2 vols. New York, 1930), 2, 152–63.

We should deal here also with a frequent misunderstanding according to which an enforced increase in saving constitutes a sacrifice on the part of the present generation, the beneficiaries of which will be our descendants only. This is not necessarily true. It can be shown that under certain assumptions the centrally determined increase in saving will lead to an increase in the well-being of the present generation not accounted for in the individual saver's decision. Savings, if invested, may have a "complementarity effect" on wages that is not foreseen by the individual saver. Let us assume that there is sufficient technological change to counteract the fall of the interest rate that would result from an increase in the stock of capital under unchanged technology. Such being the case, the wage rate will rise (because of the increase in capital stock) with interest rate unchanged. Consequently, as soon as the addition to the capital stock has been completed, the savers will enjoy an additional—and at the time of saving unexpected—benefit in the form of wage increases. This complementarity effect appears as an argument for interference with the amount of saving based on individual preferences.

It is another question if we assume that the amounts invested will be used less productively in a centrally planned economy. Such a situation might arise from bureaucratic mismanagement or from the absence of a sufficient guide—in the form of the interest rate—for the comparison of investment alternatives. But even if this assumption is made, our problems would still not be solved. Let us assume the following hypothetical situation: in a socialist economy the saving ratio is 20 per cent, one-fourth of investment is "wasted" (because of the above-mentioned factors), and the growth rate is 6 per cent. Now in a free enterprise economy let us postulate a saving ratio of 10 per cent, no waste in investment, and a 4 per cent growth rate. How are we to decide the merits and demerits of these two hypothetical economies? We need some kind of "preference scale" to evaluate them, and Hayek's preference scale will surely differ from Dobb's.

The central authority may also overrule individual preferences in regard to work and leisure. It can enforce an increase in the amount of work performed: by forced labor, by an enforced extension of labor-hours, or by indirect pressure through the reduction of real wages to raise the number of workers per family. Such practices will lead to a higher growth rate at the expense of leisure.

Consumer Satisfaction

In discussing the three success indicators examined above, we have postulated that production should correspond to the preferences of the community, which may mean individual preferences as well as those of the planners. In other words, in evaluating these indicators no distinction has been made between a system based on consumer sovereignty and one based on autocratic decisions. We have disregarded the problem of *who* decides the goals of the economy and considered only *how* and *whether* these goals are attained. It can be said that the first three indicators are free from value judgments. Advancing consumer satisfaction as the fourth indicator, we introduce the possibility of making value judgments in evaluating the performance of various economic systems. It should be noted, however, that the above duality of the success indicators (individuals' or planners' preferences) can be further retained: although consumer satisfaction may serve as an indicator, the planners will assign zero value to it if they decide to disregard it completely. On the other hand, this indicator makes it possible to differentiate between the performance of economic systems based on consumer sovereignty and those based on autocratic decisions. If two economic systems achieve the same degree of static and dynamic efficiency and the same growth rate, the one based on consumer sovereignty will be judged as more desirable if consumer satisfaction is regarded as an objective. Three factors can be said to contribute to consumer satisfaction: (1) correspondence of production targets to individual preferences, (2) correspondence of the actual saving ratio to the saving ratio desired by individuals, and (3) correspondence of actual work performed to individuals' preferences for work versus leisure.[46]

Consumer satisfaction in its last-mentioned two forms does not affect static and dynamic efficiency but can be regarded as a constraint to the growth rate. We have seen that, given the dynamic efficiency of an economy, the rate of growth can be increased only by overruling individual preferences with regard to saving versus spending and work versus leisure. Such a decision entails a diminution of consumer satisfaction. In other words,

46. For qualifications, see below, pp. 19 ff.

given dynamic efficiency, an increase in the growth rate of national income requires loss of satisfaction on the part of the individuals. In the von Neumann model maximization of the growth rate presupposes that the population is being held on the subsistence level: the portion of national income above the amount necessary for subsistence is re-invested.[47] In this study we consider the direct or indirect pressure on the part of the central authority to increase the work performed as a further factor that increases the growth rate and reduces consumer satisfaction.

The level of consumer satisfaction reached can be indicated by the living standards of the population. In appraising this we have to take into account whether the goods produced are those desired by individuals, and also have to consider leisure. For a longer period, the temporal change in living standards should be considered. In this connection it should be noted that over a period sufficiently long to enable the population to enjoy the results of investment activity, a high growth rate may raise future consumption.[48] Yet this is not necessarily so: if, for example, the planners regard the increase of military capacity as their primary objective, a high growth rate will be accompanied by a permanent restriction in consumption.

Distribution of Income

In the works of economists following Pareto, income distribution has been said not to affect efficiency. It is assumed that once an efficient allocation of resources has been reached, income distribution can be changed at will, without impairing efficiency, by the use of lump-sum redistribution.[49] But this is far from being true. Lump-sum redistribution is not only impractical; in a dynamic economy even lump-sum measures will affect efficiency. Lump-sum taxes and subsidies altering income distribution in one period will affect the amount of work supplied and risk-taking in the succeeding periods, which, in turn, will affect the dynamic efficiency of the economy.

Consequently, income distribution in its impact on effort and risk-taking has considerable effect on the other success indicators

47. See Dorfman et al., *Linear Programming and Economic Analysis*, p. 296.
48. See p. 15.
49. See above, p. 5.

and primarily on the efficiency of the system. It can rightly be assumed that if risk-taking and superior performance are not properly rewarded, the efficiency of the economic system will suffer. On the other hand, income distribution is not only one of the factors affecting other success indicators but a success indicator in itself. The distinguishing characteristic of this indicator is that we need a value judgment in determining what kind of income distribution is desirable and how different distributions are valued. *A* may prefer an equal distribution of income, *B* may give priority to distribution on the basis of productivity, the problem of unearned incomes enters the picture, natural scarcities complicate the issue, etc.[50] The economist can hardly do more than state the fact that income distribution is one of the success indicators which influence the other variables in the economic system, when evaluation of the desirability of different income distributions cannot be made without invoking value judgments.

WHOSE PREFERENCES?

We have now examined the five success indicators which would provide a way to measure the performance of different economic systems. Let us assume for the moment that the values and relationships of these variables for various economic systems are known. As has been seen, we then face the problem of devising some kind of preference scale on the basis of which the values of the success indicators can be rated. The question arises, whose preferences should be relied upon? Two extreme cases may be mentioned: we may say that the decisions of individuals should be considered, or we may rely on a paternalistic authority whose decisions overrule consumers' preferences.

The Case for and against Consumer Sovereignty

Consumer sovereignty may mean two things: (a) Consumers are free to choose among the commodities available, or (b) Consumers are able to guide production decisions via their demand for consumer goods. The first alternative must be rejected, since it is

50. For conflicting interpretations of the concept "just distribution" cf. T. J. B. Hoff, *Economic Calculation in the Socialist Society* (London, Hedge, 1949), pp. 34 ff

compatible with central determination of quantities produced
of various consumer goods; here the consumer market is only a
rationing device to distribute the given amount of goods among
consumers. On the other hand, the second alternative means that
consumer decisions should regulate the allocation of resources
among alternative uses.

If we unconditionally accept consumer sovereignty as the guiding rule, there is no problem of evaluating the various success
indicators, since a free enterprise economy with no government
intervention would result in such values of these variables that
correspond to the individuals' wishes. But are consumers' preferences a reliable guide? Consumer sovereignty has been exalted by
many exponents of free enterprise as a measure of freedom. Nevertheless, free consumers' choice can be ensured in a socialist economy as well; the proponents of the market solution also favor
consumer sovereignty and reject the authoritative decision-making
of the Planning Board with regard to consumer goods.[51]

The doctrine of consumer sovereignty is based on two assumptions. First, it is maintained that it is morally right that the consumer decide what should be produced and what proportion of
national income should be saved, and the consumer's decision is
realized on the market by "voting," where money serves as a
"ballot"; second, it is assumed that there is no interaction in consumption and consumer demand is determined by factors independent of production. The following qualifications are intended
to show the inadequacies in these assumptions and the limitations
of the doctrine of consumer sovereignty.[52]

1. It has been pointed out by many that the existing distribution of wealth and income cannot be regarded as desirable. The
"ballots" in the possession of the individuals are only partly the
result of one's own productive activity. In Knut Wicksell's words:
"There is one inequality from which we can never abstract, without making a serious mistake, namely social differences and the
unequal distribution of property."[53] If this is so, state interven-

51. Cf. Lerner, "Economic Theory and Socialist Economy," pp. 53–54; Lange, "On
the Economic Theory of Socialism," pp. 93–95. Note that these authors do not
accept consumer sovereignty with regard to saving decisions.

52. Market imperfections on the production side have already been dealt with
(pp. 8–9).

53. *Lectures on Political Economy* (2 vols. London, Routledge and Kegan Paul,
1934), *I*, 77.

tion is needed to change the quantity of "ballots" in the hands of some individuals.

2. Against the assumption that consumer wants are independent of production, the social determination of individual tastes and wants has been argued. To quote Samuelson: "Individual tastes and wants are socially conditioned by advertising and custom so that they can hardly be said to belong to him in any ultimate sense." [54] Galbraith uses the analogy of the squirrel wheel: the squirrel (production) moves upward but the wheel turns—that is, individuals, acquiring new tastes, consume the newly produced goods.[55]

Consumption being, in part, socially determined (either by advertising or by the consumption of others), it cannot be said that consumer demand is an independent factor; one can even argue that state intervention may be needed to correct socially conditioned consumer wants.

3. Collective consumption presents similar problems. It has been noted before that a considerable part of national income is spent on goods which are consumed not individually but by the society. Education, road construction, defense, and internal security are the most conspicuous examples. The market mechanism cannot be used to determine the quantity of goods collectively consumed. Galbraith remarks that there is a tendency in the present-day United States to belittle the importance of collective consumption, which is partly due to the conditioning of demand for private goods by advertising.[56] The need for a proper balance between private and collective goods has been emphasized by James Tobin: "Government dollars spent for such things as fire and police protection, education, postal service, highways, parks, hospitals, libraries, sanitation and flood control, need have no inferiority complex with respect to private dollars spent for steaks, television, freezers, alcohol, horse racing, gasoline, comic books, and golf." [57] The need for collective consumption arises from indivisibilities; another form of interpersonal relations appears in the

54. *Foundations of Economic Analysis,* p. 224.
55. *The Affluent Society,* p. 156.
56. Ibid., chap. 18.
57. "The Eisenhower Economy and National Security: Two Views. I. Defense, Dollars and Doctrine," *Yale Review,* 47 (1958), 329.

external effects of consumption. One person's consumption may increase the satisfaction of another person (an increase in the telephone network is a good example), or may reduce someone else's well-being (for example, boisterous behavior caused by excessive drinking).

4. Another qualification is connected with the problem of time horizon. Forming their plans, individuals consider time periods of differing lengths for which plans are made. The implications of the clash of individual decisions on time horizon and on investments have been explored by Jan Graaf, who maintains that "these are not decisions which households, acting separately, are equipped to make . . . Politics—or paternalism—is involved." [58]

5. A. C. Pigou contends that preference for present goods does not imply that the utility of present consumption is greater than the utility of future consumption. In his opinion mankind's "telescopic faculty" is perverted in the sense that, apart from the fact that we do not attach sufficient importance to the welfare of future generations, we are unable to size up our future satisfactions from future goods. In Pigou's words: "the aggregate amount of economic satisfaction which people in fact enjoy is much less than it would be if their telescopic faculty were not perverted, but equal (certain) satisfactions were desired with equal intensity whatever the period at which they are destined to emerge." [59] Consequently Pigou advocates state intervention in saving, since "economic welfare could be increased by some rightly chosen degree of differentiation *in favour* of saving." [60] The idea of man's telescopic faculty crops up also in the writings of some socialist authors, for example in the works of Dobb.[61] Reference should also be made to the previously mentioned complementarity effect, which is independent of man's telescopic faculty.

6. Another argument is that we are inconsiderately using up coal and other scarce natural resources, hence state intervention is needed to preserve such resources. This argument certainly has importance, for example in the case of forests. In other cases it appears to be somewhat overrated: Jevons' fears about the exhaus-

58. *Theoretical Welfare Economics* (Cambridge University Press, 1957), chap. 6.
59. *The Economics of Welfare* (London, Macmillan, 1932), p. 26.
60. Ibid., p. 29. Italics in original.
61. *Political Economy and Capitalism*, p. 309.

tion of coal reserves have not been realized, because of the substitution of other sources of energy for coal.

On the basis of all these arguments one comes to the conclusion that consumer sovereignty in its pure form cannot serve as a guiding rule in evaluating different economic systems. We turn now to its very opposite: the paternalistic solution.

The Paternalistic Solution

The unconditional acceptance of consumer sovereignty lurks behind advocacy of complete freedom from state intervention. At the other extreme, it is asserted that the planning authority knows the individuals' and the community's needs better than the individuals themselves. The central authority appears, according to this view, to be omniscient and omnipotent. A typical expression of this view can be found in the *History of the Communist Party of the Soviet Union:* "The power of the Marxist-Leninist theory lies in the fact that it enables the party to find the orientation in any situation, to understand the inner connection of current events, to foresee their course and to perceive not only how and in what direction they are developing in the present, but how and in what direction they are bound to develop in the future." [62]

If this is so, why do we need individual preferences? Can't we leave everything to be determined by the infallible authority—the Party? Some Western socialists adhering to the centralist solution put the manner more mildly, calling authoritarian decision-making "a diet prescribed by a doctor to a patient." [63] On the other hand, for those who rightly reject totalitarian schemes and the idea of the infallible central authority assistance is furnished by proponents of the socialist market solution. Lange writes, on the abrogation of consumer sovereignty: "Mr. Lerner has sufficiently shown the undemocratic character of such a system and its incompatibility with the ideals of the socialist movement. Such a system would scarcely be tolerated by any civilized people." [64]

---

62. New York, International Publishers (1939), p. 355. This book was officially ascribed to Stalin and until recently was regarded as one of the holy books in the Communist orbit.

63. Dobb, *Political Economy and Capitalism*, pp. 307–14.

64. "On the Economic Theory of Socialism," p. 95. Cf. Lerner, "Economic Theory and Socialist Economy," pp: 51–61.

A Compromise?

We have attempted to find criteria on the basis of which the relative importance of our success indicators could be evaluated and the merits and demerits of different economic systems judged. We have seen that this evaluation can be made either by unconditionally accepting consumer sovereignty or by letting a central authority decide the issues. In the first case the market would automatically supply the answer; in the second case a central authority would make the decision. But these extreme cases do not stand up to searching criticism. It may be suggested that in some form or other we should rank and weigh individual preferences in regard to the success indicators. A may think that the efficient allocation of resources is the measure of success for an economic system, B may give priority to the growth rate, C may favor an equal distribution of income; but is it possible to strike an average of supposedly widely differing opinions? Can we construct a preference scale for the whole community based on individual preferences? The answer is in the negative. It would require a "superman" to compare and rank the preferences of individuals, hence the community's preference scale in regard to the success indicators cannot be devised.

CONCLUSION

We can conclude, then, that economic arguments are not sufficient to make a choice between economic systems—in the present case between the blueprints of a free enterprise and of a socialist system. Two reasons have been established: we cannot determine the performance of the various blueprints with regard to the five success indicators, and we are unable to construct a scale of preferences which would give the ranking of different values of the success criteria. Moreover, even if the relative merits and demerits of the blueprints of various economic systems could be judged, their actual realization shows substantial deviations from the theoretical construction. Also as a result of sociological and psychological factors, a free enterprise blueprint may work better in one and worse in another country. Similar considerations are relevant with regard to a socialist blueprint.

Not only do noneconomic factors influence the workings of an economic system, but noneconomic objectives may also modify any results reached by the use of our success indicators. The planners may set targets that are in no way connected with the economic performance of a system. A dictator may be interested exclusively in increasing his power and may disregard economic considerations. Political objectives may exclude the use of efficiency prices if the central authorities do not want to disseminate information on the relative valuation of military and consumer goods. Furthermore, the objective of centralization in decision-making for fear of sabotage on lower levels may hinder the decentralization of production decisions. In all these cases, non-economic "success indicators" would appear on the scene. Nevertheless, we do not include these indicators in our model, since they are not amenable to evaluation by economic tools and would bring a considerable degree of vagueness into the discussion.

Although our success indicators do not give much help in evaluating the blueprints of various economic systems, they can be useful in appraising the performance of real-world economies. In the examination of any economy two questions can be raised: How does the actual working of the economy differ from the blueprint? How does the economy under consideration "score" in terms of our success indicators? The present study will deal with these questions in examining the experience of a Soviet-type economy, that of Hungary. We will try to show how the model of centralized physical planning has been realized in the Hungarian economy and will evaluate the performance of Hungarian planning on the basis of our success indicators.

2. Background: Hungarian Economic Policies during the Postwar Period

The Reconstruction Period, 1945–1947

PRIOR TO 1945 Hungary was an agricultural country in the process of industrialization.[1] According to the data of the 1941 Census, 48 per cent of the working population was engaged in agriculture, 25 per cent in mining and industry, 9 per cent in trade and transportation, and 18 per cent in other occupations. The national income figures on current prices show that in the year 1936–37 the share of agriculture amounted to 35.9 per cent of national income, whereas mining and industry produced 34.8 per cent. If one compares these figures with the corresponding percentages for 1924–25 (agriculture, 46.7; mining and industry, 30.4), the process of industrialization is noticeable. It is true that even in 1938 almost half of those engaged in industry were employed in the handicraft trades, but manufacturing showed a steady development: in 1925 the number of workers employed in factories was only 199,000; it increased to 289,000 by 1938 and reached 392,000 in 1943. The considerable increase between 1938 and 1943 was due to the investment plan launched in 1938, and to armament.

Hungarian agriculture was characterized by extreme polarization of holdings. The data of the 1935 Agricultural Census show that 0.8 per cent of the landholders owned 46.4 per cent of the agricultural land, whereas 76.1 per cent owned 12.0 per cent. Extensive cultivation methods were predominant.

In per capita national income Hungary was far behind the lead-

1. The data on the period prior to 1945 have been taken from successive issues of the *Hungarian Statistical Yearbook;* M. Matolcsy and S. Varga, *The National Income of Hungary, 1924/25–1936/37*, London, P. S. King, 1938; and the U. N. Economic Commission for Europe, *Economic Survey of Europe in 1948* (Geneva, 1949), p. 235.

ing industrial countries in Europe: according to U.N. statistics, in the middle thirties it was only $112, in comparison with $378 in the United Kingdom and $367 in Sweden; but among the countries presently belonging to the Soviet orbit, only Czecho-slovakia had a higher per capita income ($176); Poland's was $104 and Bulgaria's $68.

World War II inflicted heavy damage on the Hungarian econ-omy. In the manufacturing industry, among the 4,863 factories existing at the end of 1944, 651 were destroyed and 3,864 dam-aged.[2] Loss of capacity in all factories amounted to about one-third. If the comparison is made with the 1938 rather than the 1944 figures, the reduction in capacity is considerably less, since there were only 3,990 factories in 1938. The official Hungarian statistics compare the achievements of the post-1945 period with the 1938 data. But we have to keep in mind that capacity and employment in manufacturing expanded considerably during World War II.

The work of reconstruction was begun immediately at the end of the war. A flexible economic policy was applied, and state intervention was not stronger than in wartime. It seemed then that no structural changes were being contemplated in the Hun-garian industry. Entrepreneurs and workers embarked alike on rebuilding the economy. This was helped by the first phase of inflation, when wages lagged badly behind prices and the forced saving was reinvested in factories. Inflation, however, became an obstacle to economic activity as it accelerated, reaching astronomi-cal figures before the stabilization of August 1, 1946.

This stabilization, which introduced the new monetary unit, the *forint* instead of the defunct *pengö*, was adroitly planned and skillfully carried out. Although the supply of money expanded considerably during the following years, the wholesale price index reached only 123.9 in May 1949, when the last official price indices were published.

The year following the stabilization brought about further increases in production, even though in 1946–47 national income was still less than 70 per cent of the prewar level. Despite the great strides made, agriculture and industry lagged equally behind prewar production. Yet productive capacity in mid-1947 was greater than the national income data suggested. The decisive

2. *SSz*, Nos. 1–6 (1946), 22–27.

part of reconstruction was accomplished and increased production depended mainly on the elimination of existing bottlenecks in the supply of various raw materials and on the increase in industrial employment coupled with improved work discipline.

In 1945 profound social changes were made in agriculture. About one-third of the agricultural land was expropriated and distributed among the landless and among holders of dwarf and small farms. Changes in the ownership of industry were effected mainly in the second part of the period. Before the war the following enterprises were owned by the state: the post office, shipping on the Danube, railways, and such state monopolies as those in tobacco, industrial alcohol, and salt. About 10 per cent of the workers employed in mining, manufacturing, and transportation worked in state undertakings. On January 1, 1946, the coal mines were taken into state management, and on June 26, 1946, their nationalization was completed, thus increasing the percentage of workers in state-owned industry to 22 per cent. Subsequently, on September 14, 1946, the most important electricity plants and, two months later, the iron and steel industry were taken over by the state; now the percentage of workers in the state sector had reached 43 per cent. On June 21, 1947, the four largest banks and the industrial firms owned by these banks were nationalized. As a result, the nationalized sectors were employing 50 per cent of the working force in mining, manufacturing, and transportation. This was the situation on August 1, 1947, when the Three Year Plan was launched.

The Three Year Plan, 1947–1949

The Three Year Plan was originally envisaged to extend over the period of August 1, 1947, to July 31, 1950. It provided for the continuation of reconstruction and endeavored to outstrip the production records of 1938. National income was to increase 74.4 per cent in comparison with 1946/47 and to exceed the national income of 1938 by 14.2 per cent at the end of the period; the standard of living was to increase 72.4 per cent compared to 1946/47 and to surpass the living standards of 1938 by 3.4 per cent. The Plan did not contemplate any major structural change in the economy; it aimed at a balanced development of industry and agriculture. The greatest change in comparison with the prewar period was to be a doubling of the proportion of national income allotted for investment purposes.[3]

The work of planning required some organizational changes in the economy. The Supreme Economic Council assumed the task of deciding on matters of high-level economic policy, and the newly created Planning Office functioned as an interministerial coordinating body. Increased in number, the ministries were charged with supervision of large sectors of the national economy. The Supreme Economic Council allocated investment credits on the recommendation of an interdepartmental Committee for Credit Allocation, in which the Planning Office played a predominant role. The Investment Bank was in control of investment activities in major industry, and the National Credit Institute of Cooperative Societies had similar control of investment in agriculture and small-scale industry. Nationalization of banks was followed by a reshaping of the banking system, and the National Bank assumed control over receipts and expenditures of enterprises by way of the so-called single-account system. Nevertheless, during the period of the Three Year Plan these controls were to a considerable extent formal, and tighter controls were not imposed till the next period.

Nor was there much rigidity in planning itself. In fact, the Three Year Plan at its inception resembled more the plans of Western Laborite governments in the period immediately following World War II than the Soviet plans or the subsequent Hungarian Five Year Plan. It outlined only general developments in production and some investment projects of outstanding importance. The plans submitted by the enterprises were based on the order books of the firms; the production plans were not dictated from above by the Planning Office but were drawn up much as a capitalist enterprise makes its projections according to existing and expected orders. It is to be emphasized that at the outset the factories under state management employed less than 40 per cent of the labor force; almost complete nationalization was achieved only in mining and to a somewhat lesser degree in transportation. On the other hand, wholesale and retail trade was almost entirely in private hands. It is true that a considerable

3. Data on the Three Year Plan are given in *The Hungarian Three Year Plan* (in English), Budapest, 1947.

part of the production programs was based on state orders, not only for iron and steel but to a smaller degree for textiles; yet this was the situation during the war also.

As the production program of the first year was drawn up, the enterprises had orders for almost three-quarters of a year. A considerable flexibility in the plans was retained; even in the second part of the period enterprises did not have to submit detailed plans, and modifications were easily made. The plan was in the nature of a forecast, and wide rates of variation in its fulfillment for commodity groups (ranging sometimes from 50 to 280 per cent) show its flexibility. A certain resilience was ensured also by the fact that wholesale and retail traders were not bound by plans, a situation that did not change considerably even in 1949, when the wholesale trade organizations were nationalized. Nevertheless, the increased rigidity introduced in 1949 foreshadowed the comprehensiveness of the Five Year Plan.

The Three Year Plan started out with a sizable private sector in manufacturing which almost disappeared by the end of the period. On March 26, 1948, all industrial firms employing over 100 workers (with the exception of foreign enterprise) were nationalized. A provision that other businesses might also be nationalized if such an action was required by public interest led to further nationalization measures. As a result of this decree the proportion of workers employed in the state sector increased to 84 per cent in mining, manufacturing, and transportation. The decree of December 28, 1949, nationalizing every establishment with ten or more employees—as well as mills, automobile repairs shops and garages, barges, and ships above a certain capacity limit —increased this percentage to 99 per cent. At this time foreign enterprises also were taken over by the state, the only exception being factories owned by the Soviet Union. Yet up to 1949 nationalization did not have much effect on planning methods; the enterprises' plans were still based mostly on their own forecasts rather than on a breakdown of plans from above.

Instead of the projected three years, the Plan was carried out in two years and five months. The increase in national income and especially in industrial production is impressive by any standard, although official data seem to overestimate the achievements of the period. The statistical blackout in the middle of

1949 hampers critical analysis of the official figures; nevertheless, attempts to scrutinize the data have been made by A. Eckstein,[4] G. Kemény,[5] and L. D. Schweng.[6]

The official report on the execution of the Plan claims a 97 per cent increase in national income in comparison with 1946–47, and the surpassing of the 1938 level by 24 per cent.[7] The results were somewhat exaggerated by not allowing enough for replacement and by making rather favorable assumptions concerning the ratio of input to gross output. According to Eckstein's computations, national income in 1949 exceeded that of 1938 by 16 per cent,[8] whereas Schweng arrives at an increase of 18 per cent.[9]

According to official data, agricultural production reached 84 per cent of the prewar level. Production in manufacturing was claimed to have exceeded prewar production by 53 per cent in 1949. This last figure seems to be rather exaggerated; a shift from handicraft to manufacturing distorts the results, the allowance for depreciation is not sufficient and the method of gross indices employed shows higher figures, due to an increase in verticality. Kemény arrives at a 35 per cent increase, on the 1938 basis.[10] According to this estimation the increase in manufacturing production if compared to the prewar level is attributed almost entirely to the growth of the labor force employed in manufacturing. In 1938, 289,000 workers were employed in manufacturing, whereas in 1949 this number reached 382,000, an increase of 32 per cent. Labor productivity seems to have surpassed the prewar level by 2 per cent only. Nevertheless, the labor force employed in manufacturing was in 1949 still slightly less than in 1943. Investment amounted to 10,300 million forints (less than $1 billion)

4. "Postwar Planning in Hungary," *Economic Development and Cultural Change*, 2 (1954), 380–96.

5. *Economic Planning in Hungary, 1947–49*, London, Royal Institute for International Affairs, 1952.

6. *Economic Planning in Hungary since 1938*, New York, Mid-European Studies Center, 1951.

7. Data on the fulfillment of the Plan are presented in Z. Vas, "The Execution of the Three Year Plan—A Victory For Our People," *TSz*, No. 3 (1950), 131–51.

8. "Postwar Planning," p. 382. A considerably lower estimate, using different price weights, is given in another paper by him: "National Income and Capital Formation in Hungary, 1900–50," *International Association for Research in Income and Wealth* (London, Bowes, 1955), Ser. 5, p. 222.

9. *Economic Planning in Hungary since 1938*, p. 16.

10. *Economic Planning in Hungary, 1947–49*, p. 63. Eckstein, p. 386, calculates with a one-third increase of industrial production.

surpassing the planned figure by more than 50 per cent. Actually, the real value of investment was somewhat less, partly because price increases were not accounted for, partly because of inadequate allowance for replacement. The increase in investment activity in comparison to the originally planned figures indicates a preference for industry, especially heavy industry (engineering and power generation in particular) over agriculture, although agricultural investments were also higher than planned.

The official claim that real wages in manufacturing in 1949 surpassed the 1938 level by 40 per cent appears to be unfounded. The report did not present detailed computations, but according to my estimate based on official data disclosed in 1957, real wages in 1949 reached only 98 per cent of the prewar level.[11] Similar results were reached by Schweng, according to whom the standard of living was "slightly below prewar" (p. 40), and by Eckstein, who estimates the standard of living, as personal consumption per capita in 1949, at 96 per cent of the prewar level (p. 387).

The Period of Accelerated Industrialization, 1950–1953

The Three Year Plan envisaged a balanced development of the Hungarian economy. The Five Year Plan, launched in 1950, was designed to accelerate the country's industrialization, with primary emphasis on the growth of heavy industry.[12] The change in policy can well be seen from the planned allocation of investment funds. Whereas the Three Year Plan prescribed that 25 per cent of the investment funds should be used for the purposes of industry and 31 per cent in agriculture, the Five Year Plan in its original version allocated 42 per cent of the investment funds to industry and 16 per cent to agriculture. At the same time 86 per cent of investment in industry was to serve for development of heavy industry. Net investment was to reach about 25 per cent of national income. In this figure, inventory change was not taken into account, although the low level of stocks made an increase in inventories inescapable. The plan set high targets for the economy: national income was to increase by 63 per cent, in-

11. Cf. below, p. 226.

12. Data on the original version of the plan are given in *The Five Year Plan of the Hungarian People's Republic* (in English), Budapest, 1950.

dustrial production by 86, production of heavy industry by 104, agricultural output by 42 per cent. It was predicted that the standard of living would rise by 35 per cent.

Allegedly, the increase in production in the first year of the Five Year Plan was greater than planned, and at the Second Congress of the Hungarian Working People's Party (February 25, 1951) augmented targets were disclosed.[13] The revision of the plan was motivated by an effort to further accelerate industrialization and, above all, speed up the development of heavy industry. The amount of investment was raised from 51 billion forints to 85 billion. The share of investment was to reach 30 per cent of national income. Investments for the purposes of industry were to increase by 87 per cent in comparison with the original version of the plan. The share of industrial investments was to be raised to 47 per cent, and the share of agricultural investments was to be reduced to 15 per cent. In the words of Ernö Gerö, who with Mathias Rákosi was primarily responsible for policy decisions, Hungary was to be "transformed into a country of steel and iron"—a rather pretentious claim if we take into consideration that she has to import 80 per cent of her iron ore and more than 90 per cent of her coking coal. The augmented plan projected a 280–90 per cent increase in the production of heavy industry, a 120–40 per cent increase in national income, and a 50–55 per cent rise in the standard of living, in comparison with 1949.

It soon became obvious (according to Zoltán Vas, former president of the Planning Office, by the end of 1951 [14]) that the augmented Five Year Plan was unrealistic. But almost two more years elapsed before Rákosi, the chief propounder of the augmented version of the plan (for years both general secretary of the Party and prime minister) admitted that "we committed a fault first of all by changing over to an excessively fast development of our heavy and producer goods industries and by often neglecting in our planning the material resources and realistic possibilities of our country. But the most important of our faults was committed when, in February 1951, the industrial targets of our plans were raised by us to much too high levels." [15]

13. Data on the revised version are given in E. Gerö, *The Results of the First Year of the Five Year Plan and Our Future Tasks in Building a Socialist Economy*, London, 1951.

14. *SzN*, October 27, 1954.

15. Ibid., July 12, 1953.

Criticism of the augmented plan concentrated on the unbalanced development of the economy: the excessive growth of heavy industry coupled with the neglect of light industry, handicrafts, and agriculture when the material basis for heavy industry was largely lacking. As it was put by Vas in his October 27 article, "Our present difficulties are in part the bills for the Great Power policy of the 'country of iron and steel.' . . . As a consequence of excessive industrialization and the neglect of agriculture, our national economy has lost its natural balance, which it is now no small task to restore."

Imre Nagy, the new prime minister, noted in 1953 [16] that the development of heavy industry "became an end in itself," that the augmented targets were "exceeding our resources" and "too heavily taxing our capacity." The one-sided development of heavy industry can be seen from the official figures on plan fulfillment in 1952. Heavy industry was said to have increased its production by 21.5 per cent, whereas for industry as a whole an 8.2 per cent increase was claimed. The two figures indicate a decrease in the production of light industry. During the first three years of the plan less than 3 per cent of the investment funds were allocated to light and food industries [17] and this amount, together with the meager funds for replacement, was not sufficient to cover even the wear and tear of equipment.

High taxes and a deliberate endeavor to cut off most of the supply of material led to a decline of the handicraft trades. From 1948 to 1953 the number of gainfully occupied persons in the handicraft industry decreased from 273,000 to 42,000.[18] As an editorial of the *Közgazdasági Szemle* puts it, "We were witnesses to a deliberate corruption of the world famous Hungarian small-scale industry in 1949–53." [19] It was not only the export possibilities of the handicraft trades that declined—so too did their services for domestic use. According to Árpád Kiss, the minister of light industry, by the middle of 1953 2,000 villages out of 3,500 were without cartwrights, blacksmiths, shoemakers, barbers, and tailors.[20]

Another area suffering the policy of accelerated industrialization was agriculture. On the basis of official pronouncements by

16. In a speech before the National Assembly: ibid., July 4, 1953.
17. *SE*, p. 46.
18. Ibid., pp. 128–29.
19. Nos. 11–12 (1956), 1289.
20. *Economic Bulletin for Europe*, No. 2 (1954), 31.

Nagy [21] and Rákosi,[22] the main errors committed in agricultural policy can be listed as follows:

1. the stepped-up pace of collectivization and the violation of the principle of voluntary joining of collectives
2. the high targets and the frequent changes in compulsory delivery
3. the use of force in signing production contracts
4. the policy of liquidation of kulaks (peasants possessing more than 13–14 hectares of land)
5. the insufficiency of investments for agricultural purposes

As a result of these measures "a considerable section of our working peasants was in a state of uncertainty: they frequently abandoned their land." [23] The area left fallow almost tripled at a time when there were shortages in many agricultural products.[24]

Another criticism was of developments in living standards. The original version of the Five Year Plan promised a 35 per cent— the revised plan a 50–55 per cent—increase in the standard of living. The reports on plan fulfillment seemed to indicate that the standard of living was raised as planned or even more. According to Gerö, "the living standard of our people increased faster in the first year of the Five Year Plan than prescribed." [25] On December 2, 1951, he claimed again that "the living standard of the working people . . . rose and a general abundance of industrial products was created." [26] But the workers were very much aware of the actual deterioration of the standard of living, and in the middle of 1953 Nagy had to admit this openly.[27] Recently published official data show an 18 per cent reduction in real wages of workers and other employees from 1949 till 1952.[28]

Another characteristic of this period was the striving for autarky, a kind of paradox in the face of the lack of raw materials. The policy of excessive industrialization aimed at self-sufficiency in every branch of heavy industry built on imported materials. Experiments to produce materials (for example, cotton) under unfavorable conditions, or materials (for example,

21. *SzN*, July 4, 1953.
22. *For a Lasting Peace, for a People's Democracy*, July 24, 1953.
23. Ibid.
24. See below, p. 252, Table 17.
25. *Results of the First Year*, p. 7.
26. *The Position of the Hungarian Economy and the Tasks of Its Development* (in English, Budapest, 1953), p. 4.
27. *SzN*, July 4, 1953.
28. *SE*, p. 296.

coking coal in Komló) which later proved to be inadequate for the desired purposes, caused considerable unnecessary costs to the economy.

It can be concluded that the period of accelerated industrialization has considerably increased industrial capacity, but it led to a lopsided development of the Hungarian economy. Nagy in his inaugural speech before the National Assembly aptly characterized the main deficiencies of this economic policy: "there is no reason whatsoever for an excessive industrialization or any efforts to achieve industrial autarky, especially if the necessary sources of basic materials are wanting." [29]

THE NEW COURSE, 1953–1954

Announcement of the New Course was a political as well as economic decision. After Stalin's death the ferment of destalinization soon reached Hungary. Rigid imitation of Soviet economic policy, excessive development of heavy industry keyed to military production, isolation from the West—all of which were required "virtues" in the period of accelerated industrialization—seemed to become increasingly grotesque in the light of halting liberalization. The Soviet Union herself, having decided on a more liberal course, was receptive to changes in the satellite countries. The new Russian masters, especially Malenkov, looked for more flexible satellite leaders. It should be emphasized that the political change for more liberalization and the new economic policy were largely reflections of the happenings in the Soviet Union. In his "dissertation," as he calls his writing in defense of the New Course, Nagy is quite explicit about the circumstances of his nomination: "For the sake of truth, it must be stated that it was not Mathias Rákosi, but the Soviet comrades—Comrades Malenkov, Molotov, and Khrushchev—who recommended what Comrade Rákosi and all members of the Hungarian delegation [in Moscow] accepted with approbation. Thus Rákosi . . . bears no responsibility for my nomination." [30]

The New Course aimed at a balanced development of the Hungarian economy, as frequently emphasized by Nagy and

29. *SzN*, July 4, 1953.

30. *Imre Nagy on Communism. In Defense of the New Course* (New York, Praeger, 1957), p. 252.

other leaders. It called for a better proportioned industrial structure in conformity with the economy's resources, a serious development program in agriculture, participation in the international division of labor, and a significant increase in the standard of living.

These changes in economic policy can best be seen in the light of the modification of investment plans. Investments were cut in the second half of 1953 and a further reduction was planned for 1954. Considerable changes were introduced in allocation of investment funds as well. Comparing 1954 with 1953, investments in heavy industry were reduced by 41.1 per cent, while the increase in investments in light and food industries was 11.9 and in agriculture 20.2 per cent.[31]

The reorganization in industry, which required suspension of work on several large projects and a slowing-down on others, was announced by Béla Szalai, president of the Planning Office. The new directives for industrial policy were well expressed in 1954 by Zoltán Vas' October 27th article in *Szabad Nép:* "Industrialization shall not mean one-sided development at any price of the metallurgical and the engineering industries, but a program aimed at the well-timed and well-proportioned development of the entire industry—above all, the chemical industry, light industry, food industry, and local industries."

Even factories in heavy industry were required to produce consumer goods. The October 31, 1953, Resolution of the Central Committee of the Hungarian Working People's Party called for the production of consumer goods in the enterprises of heavy industry. This goal was further stressed in 1954 when J. Csergö, minister of metallurgy and engineering, stated that the ministry would double the production of consumer goods.[32]

Another measure aimed at bettering the supply of consumer goods was that to encourage handicraft trades. From February 1, 1953, to December 31, 1954, the number of gainfully employed persons in the handicraft industry more than doubled.[33] This was achieved by more liberal issuance of licenses to small craftsmen and by an improvement in their supply of materials.

31. *SE,* pp. 39, 46. In Hungarian statistics "investments" denotes gross fixed investments, where renewal, allowance for depreciation, and inventory changes are not accounted for.
32. *SzN,* November 6, 28, 1954.
33. *SE,* pp. 128–29.

One of the main goals of the New Course was the development of agriculture. As the October 31, 1953, Resolution of the Party declared: "The main issue on which our whole future development depends . . . on which we must concentrate all our efforts, is the further development of agriculture. . . . This is our most important task now and in the coming two or three years." [34]

Various measures were introduced to serve this purpose:

1. The principle of voluntary joining of the collectives was restored; provisions were made for the possibility of exodus from collective farms, and their dissolution was permitted if the majority of members so wished; as a result, membership in the collectives decreased between May and December 1953 from 457,000 to 250,000.[35]
2. Private household plots of collective farmers were increased from ½–¾ acre to 1–1½ acres.
3. Compulsory delivery quotas were reduced, and prices paid for state delivery were raised.
4. Tax arrears were waived for individual farmers and collectives alike.
5. A more lenient policy toward the kulak was introduced.
6. Free lease and tenure of land was permitted.
7. State investments for agricultural purposes were considerably increased.

The encouragement of production on individual farms resulted in an increase in private investments in agriculture and in a significant reduction in the area left fallow.[36] Increase in the purchase of agricultural tools amounted to 73 per cent, that of small agricultural machines to 220 per cent.[37]

Last but not least was the endeavor of the new economic policy to raise the standard of living—labeled by Imre Nagy as the basic principle of the new economic policy.[38] Two price reductions in 1953 and 1954, the increasing abundance of consumer goods; the new directives for agriculture, and light and food industries, and the stepping-up of investments for social and cultural purposes— all equally served this goal. According to official data the real wages of workers and employees rose by 6 per cent in 1953 and 18 per cent in 1954. The increase in real income of the peasants during the same period is said to have been even greater.[39]

34. *SzN*, November 6, 1953.
35. Ibid., May 16; *SE*, p. 197.
36. See below, p. 222, Table 7.
37. F. Vági, "The Purchasing Power and the Commodity Supply of the Population," in *Yearbook*, p. 293.
38. *SzN*, July 4, 1953.
39. *SE*, p. 296.

Implementation of the new economic policy ran into resistance at many places. Rákosi and his followers began to countermine the New Course as early as July 1953. His speech given one week after Nagy's pronouncements attempted to tone down somewhat both the criticism of the previous economic policy and the changes to be effected.[40] Subsequently the die-hard Stalinists, with Rákosi's help, tried to forestall execution of the new program. For a time Nagy had the upper hand. The October 31, 1953, Resolution of the Party's Central Committee stated:

> The Central Committee has established the fact that, despite the attained results, the extent to which the resolution adopted at the June meeting has been carried out is unsatisfactory. Reasons for the failure are the lack of willingness to understand the resolution on the part of some economic and Party functionaries, an attitude of clinging to the old and customary practice, in fact in several instances a resistance against the correct policy adopted by the Party and the government.[41]

But the resistance to the New Course did not decrease; actually, it increased in 1954. A member of the Party's Central Committee, I. Kovács, said in October 1954: "Resistance has further increased against the new program, and the general directives of reorganization have still not been worked out." [42]

Not much more time elapsed before resistance to the New Course killed it completely.

The New Industrialization Period, 1955–1956

Malenkov's downfall at the beginning of 1955 soon had important repercussions on Hungarian economic policy. Khrushchev's January 25, 1955, speech, reaffirming the primary importance attached to heavy industry and repudiating the view that main attention should be given to light and food industries, was quickly followed up in Hungary. The *Szabad Nép* on February 20, 1955 published a long theoretical defense of the central importance

40. *SzN*, July 12, 1953.
41. Ibid., November 6, 1953.
42. Ibid., October 14, 1954.

of heavy industry in building socialism. The Cominform journal, *For a Lasting Peace, for a People's Democracy,* chided the *Szabad Nép* for having "failed to explain to its readers that the priority of the development of heavy industry has been and remains the Party's chief task." [43] The *Szabad Nép* meekly acknowledged its errors and promised henceforth to serve faithfully the cause of heavy industry.

The change in Soviet policy permitted the forces which disapproved Nagy's policy to re-establish themselves. Probably with the approval of the Soviet rulers, a vigorous campaign was started against the "right-wing deviationists." The March Resolution of the Party's Central Committee indicted the economic policy of the previous one and a half years in sharp terms: "The causes of the serious difficulties which have become manifest in the situation of our national economy can be found primarily in the fact that since June 1953 rightist, anti-Marxist, anti-Party, and opportunist views have gained currency." [44]

A personal attack on Nagy, who virtually personified the New Course, followed. He was accused of having led and directed the deviationist economic policy. The April Resolution of the Party's Central Committee alleged that "Comrade Nagy tried to throttle the motor of socialist building, socialist industrialization, and especially the development of heavy industry and in the provinces the movement of the agricultural cooperatives." [45] The main charges against Nagy's economic policy were neglect of industrialization; encouragement of laxity and lack of discipline in productive work, resulting in a decrease of national income; hindering socialist transformation in agriculture; and unduly raising the standard of living.

An editorial in the *Társadalmi Szemle,* the ideological review of the Party, stated that "the rightist deviationists raised their voice against socialist industrialization and particulary against the policy of development in heavy industry; actually, they aimed at the retrogression of our heavy industry." [46] An unsigned article in the *Szabad Nép* [47] charged Nagy with having wanted to stop investment projects which were allegedly based on domestic

43. February 25, 1955.
44. *SzN,* March 9, 1955.
45. Quoted in *Imre Nagy on Communism,* p. xliii.
46. No. 5 (1955), 16.
47. June 12, 1955.

materials. The same newspaper pointed out that while the production of light industry increased by 9.5 per cent in 1954, production in heavy industry dropped by 3.1 per cent.[48]

It was alleged that encouragement of laxity had resulted in a decrease of national income.[49] To find the true reasons for this decrease is not easy. It seems that political liberalization actually resulted in a laxer work discipline, and this, coupled with the loosening of norms in many places, led to a decline in productivity. It can be contended that any totalitarian system that engages in some liberalization is likely to face such difficulties. The endeavor to reorganize the economy met with serious obstacles, because of the inflexibilities in planning, and was aggravated by resistance to the New Course by many functionaries. Moreover, there were great faults in the way the new program was carried out. Economic aspects were often neglected, as previously in the period of accelerated industrialization. Work on certain projects was abruptly discontinued; as a result, construction of some buildings was stopped at a time when only the roof remained to be placed. Furthermore, agricultural projects were begun without sufficient preparation; in some cases construction of farm buildings was started before roads to the farm were built. Although lack of systematic policy obviously caused many losses to the economy, it is difficult to decide who should be blamed for the unfavorable developments.

Other charges against the "rightist deviationists" were that they thwarted the policy of collectivization, made undue concessions to the kulaks, reduced compulsory delivery and praised and assisted individual production in agriculture. If one regards collectivization as an end in itself, the critics of the New Course may be right. But if the increase of agricultural production is our measuring rod, the years of the New Course show a good record. A sensitive indicator of the effect of agricultural policy on the productive fervor of the peasantry is the change in the area left fallow. Whereas between 1953 and 1954 this area on individual farms was reduced by 46 per cent, in 1955 it increased by 55 per cent.[50] Furthermore, because of increasing uncertainty,

48. January 30, 1955.
49. According to *SE*, p. 39, national income decreased 4 per cent in 1954.
50. See below, p. 252, Table 17.

purchases of agricultural tools and machines decreased by 15 to 20 per cent in 1955.[51]

It was also alleged that "the higher living standards of our working people . . . do not rest on the solid foundation of steadily rising production." [52] The Cominform journal in the previously quoted article criticized the assertion that the policy of the New Course "turned toward the working people," and asked the rhetorical question: "Did not the Party's economic policy . . . turn 'toward the working people' prior to June 1953?" [53]

The accusation that the rise in the standard of living outstripped the increase in production does not stand up in the light of the official data for the period of the Five Year Plan as a whole. And only this can be the standard of comparison, since the policy of the New Course intended to remedy the reduction of the standard of living in the face of an increase in national income. Official pronouncements allege that national income increased by 53 per cent in the Five Year Period, whereas consumption grew by 31 per cent.[54] If the upward bias of the two series should be of similar magnitude, it can be deduced that the rise in living standards actually fell behind the growth of national income.

The repudiation of the New Course was followed by a return to the policy of 1950–52, but in a somewhat milder form. It was officially maintained that the (never published) 1953 June Resolutions of the Hungarian Working People's Party had been basically sound, but they had been distorted from the beginning by Imre Nagy and his followers—dating from the presentation of Nagy's program in the National Assembly on July 4, 1953.

The plan for 1955, prepared in March, partly still reflected the policy of the New Course. Investment planned for this year was the lowest figure during the whole Five Year Plan.[55] The substantial difficulties connected with the new policy reversal at a time when repercussions of the previous reversal of policy in 1953 had not yet been fully absorbed by the economy certainly

51. Vági, *Yearbook,* p. 293.
52. *SzN,* March 11, 1955.
53. *For a Lasting Peace, for a People's Democracy,* February 25, 1955.
54. *SE,* p. 39. For a critical examination of the data see below, pp. 208 ff.
55. Nine billion forints, 23 per cent less than the actual figure for 1954: *SzN* March 9, 1955; *SE,* p. 46.

impeded productive work. This fact explains the setting of less bold targets. The policy of renewed industrialization became more conspicuous during the execution of the 1955 plan. Investment targets were raised and actual investment figures show a 24 per cent increase in comparison to the original targets.[56] Further strides were made toward the development of heavy industry in the plan for 1956. Investments were raised by 35 per cent, in comparison with the targets for 1955, and the share of heavy industry in investment was raised to 39 per cent. Production in heavy industry was planned to exceed the 1955 level by 10.1 per cent, whereas for industry as a whole a 6 per cent increase was projected, implying almost no change in the production of light and food industries.[57] At the same time, collectivization measures in agriculture were stepped up.

ECONOMIC POLICY ON THE EVE OF THE REVOLUTION, 1956

By the middle of 1956 the policy of accelerated industrialization seemed to be in full swing again. Yet at the same time a liberal shift in politics became noticeable. There was a contradiction between the emphasis on heavy industry and on collectivization (which was looked upon as a relic of the Stalinist period) and the feeble attempts to liberalize. Voices were raised to reinstate Imre Nagy, and the government had to retreat somewhat in its economic policy. On July 24, 1956, András Hegedüs, chairman of the Council of Ministers, announced that the original draft of the Second Five Year Plan (1956–60), published only three months previously, should be modified. Hegedüs stated that reduction was needed in planned investments and in the planned increase of industrial production, especially in heavy industry.[58]

The extent of these modifications did not become manifest, because of the Revolution of that year. The general opinion of the populace on the policy pursued in 1956 and prior to 1956 seemed to be identical with the conclusion reached in an article written in the periodical of the Hungarian economists after the Revolution had been crushed by the Soviet troops: "there are

56. Ibid.

57. Figures for the 1956 plan were given in a speech by A. Berei, president of the Planning Office: *SzN*, November 17, 1956.

58. Ibid., July 24, 1956.

organic defects in the structure of the national economy, the removal of which requires a change in economic policy." [59]

The rapid turns in economic policy during the years preceding the Revolution can be characterized as being based largely on political deliberations, while economic considerations were greatly neglected in the drawing up of new policies and in the process of carrying them out as well. Even in designing basically sound measures, as in 1953, economic examination of the issues was rather inadequate. One is bound to agree with the conclusion of a 1957 article in the *Közgazdasági Szemle*: "Since 1953 we have stated on the occasion of every political change and of every change in economic policy the absolute necessity for a coherent and scientific examination of the errors committed. Since this has never been done, it is impossible to establish whether fundamental progress has been made in the correction of these errors." [60]

59. S. Ausch and M. Gerö, "On the Danger of Inflation," *KSz*, Nos. 11–12 (1956), 1321.

60. A. Mód, "Overcoming Inflation—Our Reserves and Prospects," *KSz*, No. 6 (1957), 606.

3. Planning Methods

BLUEPRINTS OF CENTRALIZED PLANNING

IN COMPARING BLUEPRINTS of economic systems in Chapter 1, only one form of centralized planning was considered: the physical allocation of resources among alternative uses by a central authority. Yet reference has been made to the possibility that central planning may be carried out also by the use of pricing in the allocation process. Here we shall give a brief exposition of different types of central planning.

Centralized Market Solution with Consumer Sovereignty

It is pointed out in Appendix A that the working of the market mechanism in a free enterprise economy can be visualized as the automatic solving of equations representing the demand functions of consumers, the supply functions of resource holders, and the production (transformation) functions of producers. Within certain simplifying assumptions, in pure competition the price mechanism and the profit motive ensure the efficient allocation of resources among alternative uses. Long ago Barone emphasized that—theoretically—the same result could be achieved if a central authority possesses all the relevant information on consumers' demand functions, resource holders' supply functions, and producers' transformation functions. In this case, instead of an automatic solution on the market, this equation system (which in this case is expressed in mathematical form) is solved by the Planning Board. On the basis of this solution, the Planning Board allocates resources among firms and industries and makes the production and price decisions. It should be noted, however, that in this case only the prices of consumer goods and of productive factors are market prices in the usual sense (assuming free market for consumer goods and for at least some resources, like labor). Prices of intermediate goods are solely "shadow prices,"

44

used in the allocation process but not appearing on any real market.

Based on consumer sovereignty and making use of scarcity prices, this form of central planning would—theoretically—allocate resources efficiently, like a purely competitive system. Nevertheless, because of certain characteristics of the centralized market solution, it is likely that the amount of resources used for the production of a given final bill of goods would differ.

1. There are certain economies of information in pure competition.[1] An individual entrepreneur needs to know only the prices of factors he uses and of commodities he produces, the market supplying the required information free of charge. On the other hand, a central authority needs the information available to all producers, consumers, and resource holders; and it needs to know also the preferences of consumers and resource holders. Collection and processing of data is costly in terms of resources, since factors of production—for example, labor and machines—are withdrawn from productive uses. This cost can be regarded as a reduction from the quantity of final commodities made available.

2. The time problem is also an important consideration. Consumers' preferences, technological coefficients in production, and resource holders' decisions to supply their resources are changing continuously. In a competitive system the market is assumed to be sufficiently sensitive to take care of these shifts. In centralized decision-making the collection and processing of information takes time, and any solution, no matter how fast the electronic computers may work, will tend to lag behind the actual situation. Furthermore, all such changes, which require recalculation of the equilibrium solution, impose additional costs on the economy.

3. In describing the workings of pure competition, we emphasized that the operation of the price system and the profit motive leads to an optimum (efficient) solution. A central authority, mechanically equating marginal cost to price in every production unit, may not achieve cost reductions attainable in a competitive system.

4. There are, however, certain deficiencies of a competitive

1. See F. A. Hayek, "Economics and Knowledge," *Economica, 4* (1937), 33–54; Koopmans, *Three Essays on the State of Economic Science,* pp. 22–23.

system, the so-called market failures,[2] which could be avoided in a centralized solution.

The described model assumes that every commodity can be produced in a great number of ways with small changes in factor combinations as relative prices change, and it presupposes the measurability of marginal costs. The mathematical complexity of the problem can be substantially simplified if a linear-programming model is used. Here it is not assumed that marginal costs are necessarily known quantitatively. Substitution between factors, products, or factor-product combinations is carried out through shifts from one alternative process to another, where the number of processes is limited. A deficiency of this method is that it assumes constant returns to scale for each alternative process. Nevertheless, its better manageability makes the linear-programming model far superior to the Barone model.

Exploring the applicability of the linear-programming method to planning, T. C. Koopmans has arrived at the conclusion that decentralization in the making of production decisions will simplify the task of directing the economy.[3] Under the decentralization of production decisions, as suggested by Koopmans, prices are calculated by the Planning Board and firm managers have the task of expanding productive processes yielding a profit and contracting those leading to a deficit, thereby bidding up or lowering the prices of factors. If the planners decided to decentralize the process of decision-making in production, the mathematically derived prices would be theoretically the same as the trial and error prices of the socialist market solution.[4]

Centralized Market Solution without Consumer Sovereignty

In the model of centralized planning just described we postulated the use of pricing and the retention of consumer sovereignty. It should be remembered that consumer sovereignty, as defined, means that consumers' tastes direct the allocation of resources in the production of various commodities. The use of pricing for the efficient allocation of resources is also conceivable

2. See above, pp. 8–9.
3. "Efficient Allocation of Resources," *Econometrica, 19* (1951), 455–65.
4. See above, p. 3.

if consumer sovereignty is dispensed with. In this case the Planning Board decides the final bill of goods and allocates the commodities produced among consumers by rationing or by using appropriate consumer prices that will clear the market of each consumer good.

In the present case, the quantities to be produced being determined by the Planning Board, producer prices for the final goods are fixed at the point where the quantity supplied at that particular price equals the quantity decided upon by the Planning Board. Determination of the quantities of final commodities produced may be dependent on relative costs; in such a case we can visualize the planners' demand functions as price elastic. For some commodities the determination of quantities to be produced may be made with no regard to costs; the demand functions of the planners can then be termed price inelastic. To give an example: the decision on the quantities of shirts and shoes produced may be dependent on the planners' preferences and on the relative costs of shirts and shoes, whereas the quantity of intercontinental ballistic missiles may be determined without regard to production costs. In all these cases the prices of final commodities, of intermediate goods, and of resources are scarcity prices; they reflect scarcities of resources in regard to the final bill of goods determined by the decision of the planning authority. Consequently, efficient resource allocation will be reached to the same degree as by using the centralized market solution with consumer sovereignty.

Apart from outright rationing, the planning authorities may distribute the predetermined quantity of consumer goods by devising appropriate consumer prices to equate the fixed supply of consumer goods with the consumers' demand for them. In this case we speak about the rationing function of consumer prices. From the viewpoint of consumer satisfaction, the second alternative is superior to the first, since in outright rationing the quantities of commodities allotted to each individual are centrally determined. Nevertheless, on the same basis, the second alternative is also inferior to consumer sovereignty because of the restriction imposed on consumers' choices by the fact that the quantities of various commodities produced is determined by the planning authority.

It can be seen that if the centralized market solution without

consumer sovereignty is used, we have two price systems: scarcity
prices, for calculation in production; and consumer prices, to
allocate the given final bill of goods among consumers. Since
both forms of centralized market solution avail themselves of
pricing for the sake of efficient resource allocation, in the following we shall refer to the centralized market solution as "price
planning."

Centralized Physical Planning without Consumer Sovereignty

This solution is characterized by the physical allocation of
resources among the final bill of goods determined by the central
authority. Scarcity prices are not used in the allocation process.
Production requirements are estimated on the assumption of
constant technological coefficients. If we assume that resource
needs are calculated from above: starting with a given final bill
of goods and estimating resource requirements on the basis of
constant coefficients in production, surpluses and shortages will
ensue in various resources and intermediate goods. Consequently,
the hypothetical bill of final goods and/or the production methods
considered by the planners have to be adjusted to avoid these
discrepancies.

In adjusting targets, the planners use the method of "successive approximation"; the feasibility of the targets is checked by
so-called economic balances.[5] In this equilibrating process the
adjustments can be made in successive rounds (iterations), each
round bringing the planners closer to equilibrating every balance.
In the planning process there is a ranking of objectives corresponding to the planners' preferences, with high-priority targets
decided upon first and the selection of low-priority targets limited
by the resources that are left. For example, if military objectives
have the highest priority, the amount of common yarn allotted
to manufacture civilian clothes may be residual after the needs of
army clothing have been satisfied.

Shortages and surpluses in various resources may also induce
changes in production methods. If, for instance, there is a shortage

5. "Physical balances," confronting the availabilities of and requirements for
particular factors and products in quantity terms; and "synthetic balances," comparing aggregates (for example, the production and use of national income) in
value terms.

in lumber, the use of lumber may be prohibited or restricted for certain types of construction activity. Nevertheless, changes in the production coefficients serve only as imperfect substitutes for scarcity prices, since it is impossible to consider all possible alternatives of resource-use in physical terms. For example, the repercussions of the partial substitution of concrete for lumber on the scarcities of resources cannot be traced through the sectors without the use of scarcity prices.

Another deficiency of physical planning is that in the absence of scarcity prices the planners cannot satisfactorily compare the cost of the different products in terms of resource scarcities. If we postulate that in determining the quantities of final commodities relative costs should be given consideration, then the rationality of choice among alternative final products is impaired.

Since the planning authorities determine the quantities of consumer goods produced, a set of consumer prices must be devised to clear the market for every consumer good. For this purpose —as in price planning without consumer sovereignty—outright rationing or appropriate consumer prices are made use of.

In the following we shall refer to centralized planning without consumer sovereignty as "physical planning" or "planning on the basis of physical allocation."

Centralized Physical Planning with Consumer Sovereignty

Theoretically it is possible to devise a system in which the physical allocation of resources is used to produce a final bill of goods planned on the basis of estimated consumer demand.[6] Analytically, the working of this system would be identical with physical planning without consumer sovereignty, the only difference being that the final bill of goods would be determined by the consumers' rather than the planners' preferences.

EQUILIBRIUM UNDER CONDITIONS OF PRICE-PLANNING AND PHYSICAL PLANNING

Let us start with the assumption that the goals to be achieved by both types of central planning are given. By goals we mean

6. Nevertheless, the absence of scarcity prices interferes with rational choice among alternative final products (see above).

the final bill of goods, including both consumer and investment goods. It is assumed throughout the rest of this chapter that the proportion of national income to be invested, the allocation of investment funds among industries, and the production of various investment and consumer goods have been determined *prior* to the allocation process. (Problems connected with investment activity will be considered separately in Chapter 6; therefore the question of dynamic efficiency does not concern us here Decision-making on the production of consumer goods will be dealt with in the next chapter.)

The final bill of goods being given, our purpose is to compare the performance of price-planning and physical planning in achieving these targets. For this purpose we introduce two concepts of equilibria: [7] (a) partial equilibrium on individual markets [8] is reached if supply and demand for particular factors and products are balanced; (b) general equilibrium for the economy as a whole is achieved if resources are allocated in an optimum way among given ends.[9]

Partial Equilibrium

Equilibrium on individual markets can be achieved in both price planning and physical planning. In the case of price planning, particular equilibria with regard to factors and product will be reached at a price that equates supply and demand. Yet partial equilibria are not affected merely by the supply of and demand for the product or factor in question; partial equilibrium in any factor and product market is part of general equilibrium.[10] The equilibrium price and quantity of any factor or product depends ultimately on the final bill of goods, on the transformation functions in production, and on resource endowments.

In the case of physical planning, partial equilibria are reached by the method of balances: the production possibilities of one

7. Analysis along similar lines is given in H. Hirsch, *Mengenplanung und Preisplanung in der Sowjetunion* (Basel, Kyklos Verlag, 1957), pp. 86–91.

8. The concept of the market is being used here in a broad sense to include dealings between socialist firms based on the decrees of the planning authority.

9. See above, p. 5.

10. For example, the demand for butter is affected by the supply and the price of margarine, whereas the supply of butter is affected by the possibilities of alternative use of resources in the production of milk, cheese, and cream, etc.

commodity or the availabilities of one factor are compared with their use in manufacturing other commodities or in final consumption. Prices are not considered in the equilibrating process.

General Equilibrium

It has been shown in the previous section that price planning satisfies the formal conditions of general equilibrium (optimum). Under conditions of price planning, general equilibrium is reached because the determination of scarcity prices makes a rational choice among alternative production methods possible. With regard to given ends, we have only one such equilibrium position in price planning.[11]

In contradistinction, an infinite number of "general equilibria" are possible in physical planning. But these are not general equilibria in the sense that they correspond to optimal resource allocation; they are merely statistical equilibria—that is, all the physical balances and synthetic balances are in equilibrium (there are no shortages or surpluses in any field). Statistical equilibrium is a necessary but not a sufficient condition for general equilibrium. There is an infinite number of possible statistical equilibria, but only one is a position of general equilibrium, an optimum situation. Physical planning offers no guiding rule for achieving general equilibrium. In the absence of scarcity prices that make a rational choice among alternative production methods possible, no rule exists that would, for example, increase the employment of a factor in producing a commodity if the additional value of the product attributed to the factor exceeds the scarcity price of the factor, or decrease its employment if the opposite were true. In physical planning all factors and products can be put into use but it cannot be ensured that resources will be used efficiently.

Price planning and physical planning give the same results only when there is but one possible way to produce intermediate products and final goods and the determination of the final bill of goods is made with no regard to relative costs. Here—the technological coefficients being constant and the final goods determined disregarding relative costs—we have only to calculate the quantity of intermediate products and resources needed to produce the desired commodities (and to modify the desired

11. Here we neglect the possibility of multiple equilibria.

final bill of goods if resource availabilities are not sufficient to produce the originally planned goods). Assuming there are no substitution possibilities between factors of production and between intermediate products, the calculation of the resource and intermediate goods requirement follows as a matter of course. But substitution possibilities are not to be neglected, particularly if we consider different kinds of labor and machines as different factors. For example, one gallon of beer or, say, an airplane may be produced by using a larger or smaller quantity of skilled or unskilled labor, with a greater or smaller number of machines of different types, etc. Furthermore, although costs may be disregarded in the production of some commodities (ballistic missiles in our earlier example), rational choice among commodities requires consideration of relative costs in most cases (our former shirts-shoes example is a case in point). Since various needs can be served by several goods, in determining the output of these products relative costs cannot be left out of account. And the ranking of needs in their varying degrees of satisfaction may also be made dependent on relative costs. Consequently even if constant technological coefficients are assumed, price planning is superior to physical planning, since in the latter the absence of scarcity prices interferes with rational choice among alternative end products. (It should be noted that at the last point we revoked our former assumption that the final bill of goods is determined prior to the allocation process, since here we considered the decision-making on end products and on resource allocation among these products as a simultaneous process).

To establish statistical equilibrium we need to use an input-output system, first devised by W. Leontief for the economy of the United States.[12] In this system the physical balances are

12. This system can be briefly described: the entries on the input-output table are arranged in a checkerboard fashion, each row and the corresponding column of figures bearing the name of a separate industry—steel production, grain milling, etc. The entries along any one row show the distribution of total output of the particular industry among all the other sectors of the economy (transportation, households, and government are separate sectors). The last entry in each row shows the total output of the industry. If read by columns, the same figures indicate the quantities of the various kinds of inputs absorbed by each individual industry. The input-output table shows interindustry relationships in production. Any change in production of one commodity will change both the quantity of this commodity used up in other sectors and the input requirements for the production of the commodity. These changes result in chain reactions, and equilibrium is restored only after the necessary adjustments have been made.

expressed in value terms and are consolidated in a balance sheet demonstrating the interdependence of the various sectors in the economy. With the help of such a system it can be shown how changes in one sector affect other sectors. But the input-output system reveals only whether a solution is possible; it does not show whether it is efficient. This is a consequence of the assumption of constant technological coefficients; in other words, it is assumed that only one process can be used in the production of any commodity.[13] But just as there are infinite numbers of statistical equilibria, there are infinite numbers of possible input-output systems,[14] since any input-output table represents a statistical equilibrium.

It can be objected that physical planning has an advantage over price planning, since less information is needed for the former than for the latter. Physical planning operates with constant technological coefficients, hence there is no need for information on alternative production methods. On the other hand, even if a linear-programming method is used in price planning, information is needed for some alternative processes in production, and the cost of information is therefore higher in the latter case. It seems, however, that if all the information needed for physical planning has been collected and processed, the cost of additional information on alternative production methods is overcompensated by the savings realized, because an efficient solution is reached instead of an inefficient one. Moreover, on this point price planning has an advantage over physical planning. As has been argued above, if production decisions are decentralized the cost of information can be reduced in price planning without impairing efficiency. On the other hand, if physical planning is decentralized, although the heavy load of bureaucracy can be alleviated up to a certain point, the allocation of resources will become even less rational, for the number of independent decision-makers will be increased and the compatibility of production targets cannot thereby be ensured. As P. Wiles contends,

13. Mathematically, the input-output system cannot handle more than one scarce resource, hence only one production process can be relevant in the production of any particular commodity. See R. Dorfman, P. A. Samuelson, and R. N. Solow, *Linear Programming and Economic Analysis* (New York, McGraw-Hill, 1958), chap. 10.

14. To be precise, we can devise as many input-output tables as we have scarce resources in the economy. In the short run, since existing plant equipment is also considered as a scarce resource, the number of scarce resources is very large.

"under this, local bodies . . . would proceed by direct allocation within their areas and make treaties with other bodies almost as if they were independent states." [15]

It can be argued that further improvement can be achieved in price-planning if the formation of prices for a considerable number of goods is left to the market consisting of socialist firms, but evaluation of this form of decentralized planning (it has been called the Yugoslav solution) lies outside the scope of the present study.

The Process of Planning in Soviet-Type Economies

In the first two sections of this chapter a comparison has been made between theoretical blueprints of centralized planning. In the following we shall endeavor to show how a system of physical planning actually works.

Although our model presupposes centralized decision-making for every detail of the production and allocation process, the absolute realization of such a system is hardly achievable in practice. In the experience of Soviet-type economies, while the main decisions on production and allocation are made by the planning authorities, enterprises have a certain latitude in determining the output and input mix and/or modifying output and input figures prescribed by the central authorities. This activity of the enterprise can be carried out by the use of legal, semilegal, or illegal methods. Legal methods are used if the prescribed targets are not completely detailed and the enterprise is entitled to specify them (for example, if the production of a type of woollen fabric is prescribed but the enterprise has a choice among fabrics). Semilegal methods are used if the enterprise modifies the dictated targets with the connivance of supervising agencies. Illegal methods are employed mostly to procure materials by means of personal connections and even of bribes, to circumvent the bureaucratic system of material allocation. Notwithstanding these qualifications, planning in Soviet-type economies can be characterized as physical planning, since decisions of the planning authorities

15. "Changing Economic Thought in Poland," *Oxford Economic Papers,* 9 (1957), 196.

regulate the process of production and allocation in physical terms in considerable details.

The planners have two basic problems to face: (a) to establish priorities with regard to needs in temporal terms (that is, for different periods), and (b) to establish priorities with regard to needs in quantitative terms (that is, for a given period). In the process of planning the planners have first to determine the basic goals of the economy. Maximization of the growth rate, increase of military potential, or maximum satisfaction of consumer needs are examples of possible basic objectives. The first two objectives seem to be relevant to Soviet-type economies. The second step is the establishment of the "leading links"—that is, determination of targets, such as development of the iron and steel industry or improvement of the transportation system. These leading links are considered to be of decisive importance in a given period in pursuance of the primary objectives of the economic policy.

On the basis of these decisions, in drawing up the plan for a particular period further decisions must be made concerning the share of investment and consumption in national income, allocation of investment funds among industries and the bill of investment goods to be produced, the bill of consumer goods, and allocation of resources among the investment and consumer goods to be produced.

In this chapter we are concerned with the last decision. We should not forget, however, that the determination of the final bill of goods and the allocation of resources in the production of these goods cannot be made separately in a system of physical planning, for the simple reason that existing resources may not permit the production of a preconceived bill of goods. As has been mentioned, a method of successive approximation is applied whereby targets (especially those of low priority) are modified in the face of resource availabilities. It should also be noted that some commodities (iron, steel, bricks, etc.) which are considered as final goods in the plan of a particular period may be intermediate goods from the point of view of the whole production process, embracing more than one planning period.

In the examination of the actual operation of physical planning in Soviet-type economies, the following problems should be considered:

1. the organization of planning
2. the system of economic balances
3. the practical use of economic balances in material allocation
4. the bargaining process among the participants of economic planning
5. the problem of information and centralized decision-making
6. the employment of efficiency considerations in the practice of physical planning

In the subsequent sections of this chapter these problems will be explored in the framework of the Hungarian economy.

THE ORGANIZATION OF PLANNING IN HUNGARY

The Process of Planning

In Soviet-type economies the initiator of the planning process is the Central Committee of the Communist party.[16] It is held that the Party, relying on the ideology of Marxism-Leninism, "recognizes and applies the economic laws of socialism" in deciding the targets of the plan.[17] A similar view is expressed in a Hungarian textbook: "the directives of the plan are determined by the Party. The Party, able to apply the science of Marxism-Leninism, decides the tasks to be accomplished in the forthcoming period. In this way it ensures that the plan will not lose touch with the objectives of the Party. The decisive part of the Party's policy is realized through the plan." [18] It is emphasized that "the plans are worked out by state organizations on the basis of the directives given by the Party." [19]

The directive role of the Party frequently extends down to fairly small details. As it was expressed in the Resolution of the Central Committee of the Hungarian Working People's Party during the period of the New Course: "The fault is that the Party has excessively dominated the state and economic leadership of the country . . . We can assert that the government was in reality

16. In Hungary from 1948 to 1956 the Communist party was called the Hungarian Working People's party; after 1956 its name was changed to the Socialist Worker party.

17. *Politikai gazdaságtan. Tankönyv (The Soviet Textbook of Political Economy)* (Budapest, 1956), p. 462.

18. *Anyagellátási ismeretek (The System of Material Allocation)* (Budapest, 1954), p. 15 (cited as *Material Allocation*).

19. Ibid., p. 16. *Tervgazdasági ismeretek (The System of Planning)*, Budapest, 1952 (cited as *Planning*).

a shadow government, which approved Party resolutions that
had already been passed and that the authority and the responsibility of the ministries was also greatly curtailed." [20] This self-
criticism proved to be short-lived, since after the repudiation of
the New Course the Party's authority was as great as ever.

Whereas the main objectives are decided by the Communist
party and communicated to the public, usually jointly with the
Council of Ministers, the preparation of the national economic
plans is the task of the Planning Office. In Hungary during the
first years of planning a separate body served as intermediary between the Council of Ministers and the Planning Office (in
1947–49 the Supreme Economic Council and in 1949–52 the
People's Economic Council). In 1952 this supervising agency
was dissolved. Since that time the following organizations have
taken part in planning:

Planning Office, general departments
|
Planning Office, industrial departments
|
Ministries, general departments
|
Ministries, directorates
|
Trusts
|
Enterprises
|
Plants

The general departments of the Planning Office (economic,
financial, labor, technical development, material-allocation, and
investment) draw up the plans for the entire economy. The subordinated industrial departments are concerned with plans for
particular sectors of the economy, such as agriculture, construction, light industry, etc., and are in close contact with the general
departments of the corresponding ministries. The organization
of the general departments in the ministries corresponds to those
of the Planning Office. The directorates in the ministries, besides

20. The resolution was passed in June 1953. Quoted in *Imre Nagy on Communism,*
pp. 249–50.

their function in planning, are responsible for the direction of productive activity in particular branches of industry. They direct and supervise the work of the trusts and of those enterprises which do not belong to any trust. In general, four to six enterprises form a trust. The plans of enterprises are subdivided among plants.

The preparation of the yearly plans consists of three stages: [21]

1. *Preliminary draft.* On the basis of directives from the Party the Planning Office, in cooperation with the ministries, prepares the first version of the plan, using statistical data on previous periods, average coefficients indicating input requirements for various types of industrial activity, and economic balances. The preliminary plan includes only the main targets for the planning period, and not more than a small number of economic balances are prepared.

2. *Final plan.* On the basis of the preliminary draft approved by the Council of Ministers, in the second stage the final plan is prepared. Here the method of "parallel planning" is used: the Planning Office and the various ministries draw up the plan separately, and the Planning Office then coordinates the two plans. Statistical data in greater breakdown, coefficients on material, labor, and machine needs of certain commodity groups and of industrial activities, and economic balances are employed in the second stage.[22]

3. *Detailed plan.* After the final plan has been approved by the Council of Ministers, the plans of the particular ministries are fixed and their breakdown follows among the enterprises (and within the enterprises among plants and workshops).[23] It is emphasized that "the enterprises do not prepare their plans according to their own ideas but . . . receive plan orders." [24] After the planned targets have been communicated to the enterprises by the directorates, each enterprise prepares its counterplan. In this the firm usually attempts to modify its targets downward, in order

21. This description of the planning process is largely based on *Material Allocation*, pp. 27 ff., and *Planning*, pp. 105 ff. It covers the preparation of the yearly plan. The drawing up of long-term plans corresponds roughly to the first two stages and the quarterly plan to the last two stages described below.

22. For the yearly plans 400–500 balances were worked out: S. Ausch, "Some Major Problems in the System of National Economic Balances," *KSz*, No. 6 (1958), 564.

23. "After approval [by the Council of Ministers] the plans assume the force of law . . . the planning targets are divided among the enterprises, which on this basis prepare their detailed plans" (*Planning*, p. 108).

24. Ibid., p. 106.

to achieve a higher degree of plan fulfillment. The enterprises are also required to specify the dictated targets in greater detail. The counterplans are then revised by the ministry. Although it is possible to modify the targets prescribed for an enterprise, such modifications are chiefly made within the framework of the ministry's plan. Modification of the latter is possible only in special cases and after a long, bureaucratic process, since it requires approval by the Council of Ministers.[25]

That the process of planning is protracted is self-evident when one considers that the breakdown of the final plan approved by the Council of Ministers proceeds through six stages before it reaches the enterprise level. The counterplan prepared by the enterprise travels along the same route (if modification of the ministry's plan has also been made necessary); and as a last step the newly approved version of the plan descends by the same stages back to the enterprise. As an example of the time needed, the second version of the 1954 plan for the Ministry of Heavy Industry was transmitted to the ministry from the Planning Office on October 9, 1953, and the plans of the enterprises were approved in March and April of 1954.[26] Although attempts have been made to alleviate paperwork by parallel planning, five to six months appear to be the average duration of the planning process in the case of yearly plans. Not only the process of planning but also the frequent modifications of plans require a great deal of time. These modifications often start before the original plan has run its course.

The Temporal Structure of Planning

In the process of planning, distinction should be made between long-term plans, yearly plans, and quarterly and monthly plans.

Long-term plans, such as the first Hungarian Five Year Plan, contain the general objectives to be achieved by the economy. In addition, the first Five Year Plan also prescribed detailed targets for many activities. For example, it stated how many work clothes, motorcycles, and motion pictures should be produced during the five-year period, and also determined the quantities of certain commodities (for example, shoes) to be produced in yearly

25. *Material Allocation,* p. 108.
26. "Some Problems of Material Planning," *SSz,* No. 4 (1955), 351.

breakdown.[27] Yet the importance of a long-term plan is in its projection of the rate of development in various industries, its directives for investment activity, and its investment planning in the narrower sense. Production decisions are usually made over a year or a period even shorter, but the planning of investments should embrace a longer period.

Actually, not only were the specific targets of the first Five Year Plan forsaken, but because of its numerous and extensive modifications it did not provide much of a basis for the yearly plans either. It has been held by many that the original Five Year Plan and its modifications were inadequately prepared and that the investment plans were merely "forint-plans" whose real content was not specified until the preparation of plans for much shorter periods, or even not until the investment projects were already in process of being carried out.[28] Hungarian economists complain that the lack of long-term plans and directives has caused considerable loss to the national economy in many fields.[29]

During the period of the first Five Year Plan the enterprises did not prepare long-term plans. In 1956, for the first time, 200 large firms were instructed to draw up five-year plans, but lack of information about future production requirements denied any semblance of seriousness to these plans. The managers of each enterprise regarded the task as a required exercise, without any practical importance.

For the national economy as a whole, the *yearly plans* are the guides for economic activity, and the main decisions on production and allocation are made within their framework. Yet these yearly plans are of less importance in the eyes of the firms' managers, for the following reasons:

1. The yearly plans of the firms are usually not completed before March or April of the year in question, and often the actual figures for the first quarter are inserted in the quarterly breakdown of the plan.

2. The yearly plans are frequently modified, for various reasons such as changes in general political directives, fluctuations

27. *Planning*, p. 52.

28. Cf. F. Deák, D. Sóky, and G. Szende, "The Efficiency and Planning of Investments," *SSz*, Nos. 1–2 (1957), 61. M. Turánszky, "Some Problems in Investment Planning," *SSz*, No. 12 (1957), 1026–27. F. Deák, "The Preparation and Economic-Technical Planning of Investments," *SSz*, No. 4 (1956), 298–99.

29. Turánszky, p. 1026; Deák, p. 298.

in agricultural production, uncertainty of export demand and the supply of imported materials,[30] and lack of information on actual needs during preparation of the plan.

3. In many cases the yearly plans give only general directives. For example, for a woollen cloth factory the yearly plan prescribes the value of planned production in forints and the production of certain commodity groups in quantity terms. More detailed specifications are made only in the quarterly plans.

4. Bonuses to management are not paid on the basis of the yearly plans; consequently enterprise managers have no incentive to follow the directives of these plans. Furthermore, they know that if the sum of the figures in the quarterly plans add up to the figures of the yearly plan, it is by sheer chance. During 1952–55, for example, in most sectors of light industry the original yearly production plans of the various sectors were in the majority of cases not fulfilled.[31] Deviations are even larger if individual enterprises instead of sectors are considered. As a result, often not until the end of the year does the ministry decide on what to regard as the yearly plan, and frequently actual production results of the first two quarters are taken into account in determining the final version. The case of six Hungarian construction trusts that received their yearly plans for 1954 on January 21, 1955 is not exceptional.

Because of these circumstances the yearly plan does not enjoy high prestige among the enterprises or even the ministries. It is contended that its value, apart from a degree of political importance, lies mostly in its informative figures rather than as a plan *per se*.[32] It is beyond doubt that in physical planning there is need for yearly plans on the national economy level to provide guidance for productive activity and to establish interconnections in the production and allocation process. Yet planning would not suffer if the breakdown of these plans was worked out for shorter periods only.

The managers of enterprises therefore base their activity on the *quarterly plans*. But these also frequently undergo modifica-

30. The cotton fabrics industry is an example. In this the foreign trade organizations give the specifications of the export commodities only forty-five days in advance. At the same time the import of raw cotton is frequently delayed, causing stoppages in production. See Kornai, pp. 19, 142.

31. Ibid., p. 13.

32. Ibid., p. 15.

tions. Although the Council of Ministers in March 1955 prohibited this, the regulation has never been enforced, and in fact it was altered in the same year to permit one modification in the course of each quarter.

In addition to the quarterly plans, *monthly plans* are prepared in some industries, although by 1955 they had been mostly discontinued.

Structure of the Plans

The structure of the plans—identical for the entire national economy, ministries as well as enterprises—is as follows: [33]

1. the production plan (production in value terms on constant prices and on current prices, production in quantity terms for selected commodities and commodity groups, and assortment plan)
2. the technical development plan (capacity norms, mechanization, and input-output ratios)
3. the material supply plan (material requirements for production, inventories at the beginning of the planning period [actual] and at the end of the period [planned], and procurement)
4. the labor plan (labor requirements for production, labor productivity, labor supply, and wages)
5. the cost plan (planned costs for selected commodities and commodity groups, and costs and value of production for the whole enterprise)
6. the investment plan (investments to be made during the planning period)
7. the renewal plan (replacements and major repairs)
8. the financial plan (balance of receipts and payments, and credits)

The question arises: What incentives do enterprises have for fulfilling targets set by these plans? It has been pointed out that they are concerned with fulfilling quarterly plans only. But in these the ministries prescribe about 100 to 150 indicators for most industries, and it would be foolish to assume that the enterprises attempt to fulfill so many targets. In practice the activity of the

33. *Material Allocation,* p. 28.

enterprise is aimed at fulfilling those which are related to its material interest (usually the production plan and the profit plan), the other indicators being neglected. One can observe a maximization process in the enterprise, which will be described in Chapter 5.

THE SYSTEM OF ECONOMIC BALANCES

In Soviet-type economies the system of economic balances is designed to check the compatibility of planning decisions and to allocate materials and products among alternative uses.[34] The balances employed in planning can be classified into two groups: physical balances, to compare the production possibilities or availabilities of one factor or product with the requirements for the factor or product in physical terms; and synthetic balances, to compare availabilities and the use of aggregates in value terms.

In the following a description and evaluation of the system of balances in use in the Hungarian economy will be given.

Physical Balances

1. Material balances are drawn up for basic materials, subsidiary materials, fuels, construction materials, tools, prefabricated parts, agricultural products, and consumer goods.[35]

During the preparation of the yearly plans, material balances are drawn up for 400–500 materials and products (mostly in groups), called funded commodities. They comprise about 50 per cent of the national product.[36] For commodities produced and used by enterprises belonging to the same ministry, balances are prepared by the ministry. The relative weight of these latter goods in the national product is insignificant.[37]

We have pointed out that detailed balances are prepared in the second stage of planning. The balances are drawn up on the basis of statistical data for previous periods or by using average coefficients indicating input requirements for the production of

---

34. For a detailed presentation see J. Marczewski, "Le Rôle des comptes nationaux dans les économies planifiées de type Sovietique," *Income and Wealth*, Ser. 4, pp. 167–241.
35. *Planning*, p. 68.
36. Ausch, *KSz*, No. 6 (1958), 564.
37. *Material Allocation*, p. 46.

various commodity groups or for industrial activities. It should be emphasized that in Hungary material balances are not based on plans of the enterprises, but, on the contrary, the enterprises' plans are based on the balances prepared by the Planning Office and the ministries. It follows that in preparing material balances the planning authorities have to rely primarily upon statistical averages on input-output relations. Input requirements can be estimated on the basis of technological norms only for the commodities that can be considered homogeneous, such as pig iron or oil. It has been pointed out that the use of technological norms in planning is rather infrequent.[38]

The scheme of the material balances is as follows: [39]

Total Supply	Total Requirements
Inventory at the beginning of the period	Use for further production
	Use for investment
Production	Use for consumption
Agricultural procurements	Use for state purposes
Import	State reserves
	Export
	Inventory at the end of the period

Both requirements and availabilities appear on the material balances in the ministry breakdown.

2. Machine balances indicate the supply of and requirements for different types of machines. These balances were discontinued in 1954 and resumed in 1958.[40]

3. Transportation balances express the capacity of transportation equipment and transportation needs in quantitative terms.[41]

4. Labor balances compare labor requirements and availabilities. Separate balances are prepared for the following purposes: the balance of youth, the balance of labor requirements and availabilities for different sectors of the economy, distribution of laborers among sectors in occupational breakdown, and consolidated labor balance.[42]

38. "The Economical Use of Materials," SSz, No. 12 (1955), 1055.
39. Planning, p. 70.
40. A. Máriás, "Some Problems in the Allocation of the Means of Production," KSz, No. 4 (1958), 383.
41. Planning, p. 70.
42. G. Pogány and G. Bán, "Some Problems of the Labor Balance System," KSz, Nos. 8–9 (1958), 949–52.

Synthetic Balances [43]

Synthetic balances are designed to avoid disproportionality in aggregate relations (to ensure, for example, that the planned personal income of the population does not exceed the value of commodities available for consumption), and to allocate value aggregates among alternative uses (for example, to allocate investment funds among various sectors). The synthetic balances used in Hungarian planning are:

1. the balance of national income (production and use of national income)
2. the balance of personal income (personal income of the population and its uses)
3. the monetary balance of the population (money receipts and payments of the population)
4. the balance of the state budget (receipts and payments of the state)
5. the consolidated financial balance of state enterprises (a summation of receipts and payments of state firms)
6. the balance of investments (allocation of investment funds among the sectors of the economy)
7. the balance of payments (receipts and payments of the state in its relations with other countries)

Evaluation of the System of Balances

In evaluating the system of balances we have two problems to consider, one theoretical—whether the balances in use in the Hungarian economy are adequate tools to ensure the compatibility of planning decisions—and one practical—whether, in the process of preparation of the balances, the production requirements of the economy are rightly reflected, and whether actual allocation and production conforms to the planned balances so as to ensure that surpluses and shortages will not arise. In this section we shall be concerned with the first problem.

It has been shown above that to establish statistical equilibrium

43. M. Ács, "The Role of the National Economic Balance System in Planning," *KSz*, No. 5 (1956), 235-44.

in physical planning—in other words, to demonstrate interrelationships in the national economy—an input-output system should be drawn up. The preparation of such a system ensures the compatibility of planning decisions. The question arises whether the system of balances used in the Hungarian economy is adequate for this purpose.

We contend that the Hungarian system of economic balances, although certainly useful in indicating broad proportions in the economy and in checking gross errors, is an inadequate tool for establishing statistical equilibrium and leaves open the possibility for discrepancies in the allocation process.

First, it is necessary to connect the physical balances with the synthetic balances; otherwise it cannot be known whether the two systems of balances square, and targets planned in value terms may be different from those in physical terms. In Hungarian planning no connection has been established between physical and synthetic balances because physical balances have not been expressed in forints.[44]

Secondly, in drawing up the physical balances, not only the direct but also the indirect uses of materials and products should be considered. A change in the production of one commodity will affect the production possibilities of other commodities through its material, fuel, and energy needs. In estimating these interrelationships we need to know both the direct and the indirect inputs; and if any modification is needed in one balance, the repercussions of the change should be traced through the entire system of balances. In this connection the physical balances are deficient in Hungary, since "in the balances only direct uses are taken into account; at present indirect uses are estimated only very roughly in regard to some basic commodities but not for the whole national product."[45] Consequently, compatibility of the physical balances is not ensured either.

Thirdly, the method of physical balances in Hungarian planning actually corresponds to partial equilibrium analysis. The balances presently prepared comprise about 50 per cent of

44. It is asserted that the connection could not be established; since the physical balances are gross balances, they depend on verticality, and there are differences in the methods of estimating the degree of completion: Ausch, p. 564.

45. Ibid., p. 565.

the national product and can be regarded as the individual parts of an as yet not interconnected input-output table. Ausch observes that the existing huge gaps could be theoretically filled out by preparing new partial balances. This is partly accomplished from time to time. "But all this is not a substitute for a unified input-output table, because the place and the magnitude of the gaps are actually not known to anybody, since the detailed calculations are worked out in many different places—in ministries, directorates, etc." [46]

Articles in Hungarian economic journals emphasize the need for an input-output system,[47] pointing out that the presently used "system of balances is not quite suitable for recognizing the existence or lack of equilibrium." [48]

In 1956 Hungarian economists and statisticians began to explore the possibility of constructing an input-output table on the Hungarian economy. In the fall of that year the Hungarian Academy of Science set up a committee (of which I was to be a member) to conduct research on the application of the input-output technique designed by Leontief. It was reported that existing methods of collecting statistical information are unsuitable for the preparation of a detailed input-output table.[49] The main deficiencies of the statistical methods are described by Bródy as follows:

1. There exist no data on the allocation of a considerable number of commodities . . . Consequently one is unable to find out what happens to more than half of production in heavy industry.

2. Where we do have data, classification is deficient. Material balances have been prepared exclusively in corre-

46. Ibid., p. 568.

47. Ács, pp. 235–44; A. Bródy, "Changes in some Quantitative Indicators of Heavy Industry," *Yearbook*, pp. 134–55.

48. Ausch, p. 562. In the same article he notes that "on the basis of research hitherto conducted on the system of economic balances, it can be established that our system of balances is not quite suitable for concluding with satisfactory accuracy whether the production of the following year or even of the current year will correspond to needs (assuming that needs are properly estimated)" (p. 563).

49. Bródy, p. 13; Ausch, p. 566. It is interesting to note that in Bródy's opinion the only possible exceptions are the years 1948 and 1949 (just before large-scale planning became dominant), when the breakdown of the data was suitable for the preparation of such a table (though it was not prepared).

spondence with the groupings of the organization of industry supervision, hence according to the prevailing organization of the ministries; therefore (because of organizational
changes) it is impossible to form time series or to compare [the balances] with the production statistics [of the
Central Statistical Bureau]. In general the nomenclature
of the Central Statistical Bureau changes from one department to another . . . Moreover, since the classification
schemes used have not been put in writing in the various
departments themselves, we can rightly say that each
"room" has its own procedure.

3. In 1949 . . . the number of industries was reduced from
200 to 84 in the Hungarian classification scheme.[50]

In the absence of a detailed input-output scheme, tables in
nine sector breakdowns (industry, agriculture, construction, foreign trade, consumption, investment, transportation, crop collection, domestic trade) were prepared for planning purposes by
the Planning Office in 1954 and 1955, while statistical balances
were worked out by the Central Statistical Bureau for 1951, 1952,
and 1953. Both balances proved to be highly unreliable. To give
an example, according to the Central Statistical Bureau, transportation services for industry amounted to 1,412 million forints
in 1953, whereas the Planning Office planned the same services
to the value of 2,814 million forints for 1954.[51] Since no price or
structural changes occurred in the meantime, the difference is
likely to be due to errors in estimation. The unreliability of the
estimates led the Statistical Bureau to drop the project in 1954,
and the Planning Office discontinued it in 1956.

A Hungarian statistical periodical has said that an input-output
table was to be prepared on the basis of statistical data for 1957
in a fifty-five-sector breakdown.[52]

50. Bródy, pp. 139, 152. By comparison, the U. S. classification scheme for 1947
consists of 450, the English scheme of 300, entries (ibid., p. 151).

51. Ausch, p. 567.

52. SSz, Nos. 1–2 (1958), p. 140. It can be pointed out that the lack of input-
output schemes is not a special characteristic of Hungarian planning. According
to the report of a delegation of Hungarian planners visiting the Soviet Union, input-
output tables were not used there in 1956. The Congress of Soviet statisticians found
the input-output table wanting in 1957 also. Ausch, pp. 568, 570.

Economic Balances and Material Allocation [53]

In the last section we dealt with some theoretical and statistical problems which arise in conjunction with the evaluation of the system of economic balances in Hungary. The present section will be devoted to an examination of the practical application of these balances, and will attempt to answer two questions: Are the actual production requirements of the economy rightly reflected in the physical balances, and does the physical allocation process ensure the equilibration of markets of the individual commodities? In other words, whereas the last section was concerned with consistency in the system of economic balances, now we will deal with consistency between, on the one hand, physical balances and, on the other, enterprises' plans and actual material needs.

Expression of Production Requirements in the Physical Balances

The physical balances used in the material allocation process in Hungary are not based on the enterprises' plans.[54] As indicated above, the Planning Office and the ministries make use primarily of statistical averages on input-output relations in drawing up these balances. The input-output coefficients calculated from the actual data of previous periods are to a considerable degree aggregated, which is indicated by the fact that the 400–500 balances prepared comprise about 50 per cent of the national product. It has been rightly noted that "the production plan consisting of a few consolidated value or quantity indicators . . . does not give sufficient basis for determining material needs." [55] The use of statistical aggregates in the planning of material allocation gives rise to certain discrepancies and disproportions in the process of material allocation. The main deficiencies of this procedure can be stated as follows:

53. It should be noted that although we speak about material allocation, we understand the allocation of materials, intermediate products, and machinery. The planning of consumer goods will not be considered until p. 110, below.

54. F. Sovány, "Theoretical Problems in Simplifying Our Material Allocation System," *KSz*, No. 9 (1956), 1043.

55. Ibid.

First, by using input coefficients for groups of commodities based on data of previous periods, there is an implicit assumption that the composition of output within the group has remained unchanged. Actually, the assortment of products is continually changing; hence input needs will be distorted in the material allocation plans.

Secondly, changes in technology are also not taken care of by the use of statistical averages for previous periods.

Thirdly, even if the group balances are equilibrated correctly, shortages and surpluses may arise in the allocation of individual commodities. For example, notwithstanding the equilibration of the balance for steel, there may be surpluses and shortages in various types of steel differing in diameter, quality, etc.

The deficiences in the use of statistical aggregates coupled with errors and inadequacies in statistical data have resulted in a certain dichotomy between production planning and material supply planning: the dictated production targets and the material supply plans to a considerable degree lack consistency.[56] In other words, because of the lack of links between the physical balances and the enterprises' plans, and because of the use of aggregated coefficients in the process of planning, production requirements of the economy are not satisfactorily reflected in the physical balances, discrepancies arise between production targets and material allocation, and the described deficiencies lead to imbalances as the plans are actually carried out.[57]

Equilibration in the Physical Allocation Process

We have made the first step toward evaluating the practical application of the system of material balances by exploring the relationship between physical balances and the enterprise's plan. The second step is to examine how the physical allocation process works on the enterprise level.

Difficulties and deficiencies in the preparation of the enterprise's material supply plan. As we have seen, material allocation

56. Sovány mentions this as "a well-known fact" (ibid., p. 1045).

57. Similar conclusions have been reached by the prominent Hungarian economist (university professor, and president of the Central Statistical Bureau) G. Péter: "Planning from above . . . has meant that detailed plan regulations have lost touch with requirements in regard to the production and material allocation plans as well" Péter, p. 60).

plans are rigidly binding at the ministry level. Now, the rigidity of the enterprise's material supply plan depends on whether the ministry carries out flexible rearrangements among the enterprises. The ministry may accept modifications on the basis of the enterprise's counterplans, or may effect the breakdown of the material allocation plan in advance and narrow considerably or rule out completely the possibility of modification.[58] However flexible the rearrangement of material allocation plans may be in the ministry, its own material plans are in any case binding, thereby imposing a restraint on reapportionment of materials. Furthermore, the ministries are aware of deficiencies in the preparation of the enterprise's material supply plan and realize that enterprises frequently present inflated requirements (anticipating cuts in the actually allotted quantities); hence they are reluctant to effect extensive modifications. The ministries therefore often have more faith in the material plans prepared by themselves, on the basis of past experience, than in the enterprise's plans. As a consequence, the enterprise's material plan is constrained by the breakdown of plans from above.

Besides the constraints imposed on the enterprise's plan by the breakdown of the ministry's plan, the preparation of the enterprise's material supply plan is also hindered by lack of sufficient knowledge of production targets at the time when the plan is worked out. Not only are export possibilities frequently unspecified, but government orders, and to an even greater degree requirements of other firms, are largely unknown at that time. Production targets prescribe in most cases the quantities of certain commodity groups or forint figures and will be made more specific only in the plans simultaneously prepared by the user firms.[59] The implications of the lack of sufficient knowledge on the breakdown of production targets have been aptly described by Sovány:

> Only a production program based on actual orders could serve this purpose [that is, of preparing the material plan], but this is not available at the time the plan is drawn up. The practice of preparing the material plan on the basis of

58. Sovány, p. 1043.
59. Lack of a breakdown of production plans is most conspicuous in the construction and transportation industries: "Some Problems of Material Planning," p. 351.

the *envisaged breakdown* of the production plan down to individual products—with the incidental use of material norms,
but mostly *without the knowledge of future needs*—does not,
in general, improve the accuracy of planning.[60]

Even if we assume that production targets are fully specified,
we encounter a further deficiency of material planning in the
form of the unreliability of input coefficients (material norms)
used in planning. The main deficiencies of these norms are:

1. Most of them are purely statistical norms, or statistical norms
corrected by technological calculations. With the exception of
the machine industry, there are technological norms in use at a
few places only. Even if technological norms are used, they are
frequently averages for a whole industry, which do not take into
consideration the differences in equipment and technology of
particular plants.[61]

2. A considerable part of the norms being based on commodity
groups, changes in the composition of production will bring about
modifications in input requirements that are not reflected in the
norms.[62]

3. In the absence of norms for a considerable number of commodities, for some commodity groups the material requirements
are estimated on the basis of the average input coefficients for
production in the value of one million forints.[63]

4. Because of changes in technology, equipment, and quality,
a significant proportion of the norms is outdated.[64] The official
newspaper of the Communist party complained that in 1955 most
of the norms were lax, having been worked out in 1952.[65]

Other deficiencies in the preparation of the enterprise's material supply plan are the neglect of the time lag between the
purchase and the actual use of materials, and disregard of material requirements arising from a change in the stock of unfinished production.[66]

60. Sovány, p. 1043. Italics in original.

61. *SSz*, No. 12 (1955), 1055. Statistical norms are statistically determined average
input coefficients for a previous period; technological norms are theoretical input
requirements based on existing technology.

62. *SSz*, No. 4 (1955), 351.

63. Ibid., p. 351.

64. *SSz*, No. 12 (1955), 1055.

65. *SzN*, February 25, 1955.

66. Sovány, pp. 1043–44.

In the face of these difficulties and deficiencies in the preparation of the enterprise's material supply plan, statements that "the material plans are not realistic" [67] do not seem to be entirely unfounded. It has been established that in the process of carrying out the plan, deviations from the material plans often amount to between 40 and 50 per cent.[68] Thus the considerable time and energy spent on preparation of the material supply plan seem to be rather unproductive.[69]

The role of procurement contracts. The actual exchange of materials among state enterprises takes place on the basis of procurement contracts. These are of two types: contracts on the ministry level concluded between the supplier and the buyer ministry, based on the plans of the two ministries and the specifications made by the enterprises; and contracts between the enterprises concerned.[70] This latter type will be examined here.

The procurement contracts are based on the breakdown of the national material supply plan; the enterprise can order only quantities corresponding to its material plan. If the breakdown of the plan has not been finished by the time the orders are to be sent out, the enterprise bases the orders on its own estimates. These orders (provisional contracts) will be modified after the breakdown of the plan has been completed and the ministry has checked to see whether the material orders of the enterprises under its authority conform to its own allocations. Both methods of ordering materials have the common disadvantage that they presuppose a knowledge of material needs many months in advance and conformity of the enterprise's needs with the ministry's material allocation plan—preconditions which are generally lacking.[71]

Not only the funded materials (that is, those planned centrally) but also the nonfunded materials (those for which material balances are not worked out) are procured on the basis of supply contracts. Procurement contracts are concluded simultaneously by all enterprises in every quarter. This simultaneity leads to con-

67. *SSz*, No. 4 (1955), 351.

68. Ibid., p. 355.

69. To give an example: in the Mávag, a Hungarian machine factory, the preparation of the material plan for 1954 required 2,500 hours of work, and the perfected plan, on paper, weighed 40 pounds (ibid., p. 351).

70. *Material Allocation*, pp. 142–43.

71. See Sovány, p. 1044, and the preceding part of this section.

siderable difficulty in the allocation process. Since every enterprise, whether it is a supplier or a user, has to enter into a contract at the same time, no enterprise is able to draw up a material plan in conformity with the material requirements of the products ordered from him. Sovány observes: "The system of procurement contracts concluded simultaneously by every enterprise leads to the procurement of materials independent of, and frequently contradictory to, the actual needs of production, and restricts into narrow bounds the volume and composition of the supply of materials." [72]

For the fulfillment of its production plan every enterprise has to procure materials in time before the production process starts. But many materials should be ordered ninety days before delivery, and imported materials and metallurgical products three to six months, ironwork, locks, and hardware nine months before delivery.[73] It frequently happens that the enterprise does not know its production plan but has to order materials anyway. In addition, the firm as producer has different interests than as user. As producer and supplier it endeavors to obtain the orders of other enterprises as soon as possible, for the sake of establishing its production program. On the other hand, as purchaser and user it tries to postpone the placing of orders until its production plan is known, unless regulations on material allocation force it to do so much sooner, often five to nine months before actual use.[74]

This system of material allocation results in considerable disproportions: there is a cleavage between the actual material requirement of production and the material contingents allotted on the basis of procurement contracts. As a result, production will often be based not on the material requirements of other enterprises but on the actual material allocation of the producer.

Problems connected with carrying out the enterprise's plan. In carrying out the material allocation plan of the enterprise, in addition to the errors committed in drawing up the plan, the following factors may result in deviations from the original plan:

1. Over- or underfulfillment of the plan will modify material requirements in the enterprise, and over- or underfulfillment of

72. Ibid., p. 1045.
73. M. Krémer, *A szállítási szerződések és a népgazdasági tervezés* (*The Procurement Contracts and National Economic Planning*) (Budapest, 1955), p. 105; Sovány, p. 1045.
74. Ibid.

the plans in different industries affect other branches of the economy.

2. Technological changes may ensue during the planning period, and these can be of varying magnitudes in the production of different commodities.

3. Modifications of plans are frequent, because of errors in measuring needs on the part of the government, changes in political objectives, crop conditions in agriculture, and modifications in export or import plans. The importance of this last factor should be stressed, since foreign trade has an important role in the Hungarian economy. In 1955 foreign trade amounted to 41 per cent of national income and accounted for about 50 per cent of the materials for heavy industry; [75] and 80 per cent of the materials for light industry were imported.[76]

All these changes have a chain effect on the entire economy, since deviations from the plan of one enterprise require modifications in the production and material supply plan of other enterprises, and may create further discrepancies in the allocation process.

The inventory problem. The system of material allocation employed in Hungary imposes strains on the individual enterprise and leads to frequent shortages and surpluses in different fields. The disruptive effect of these discrepancies is aggravated by a lack of free capacity to fulfill new orders and by a lack of sufficient inventories.[77]

The plans are based on the full use of capacity and are generally strained to achieve the goals of economic policy. Consequently, "the rapid fulfillment of needs not anticipated and coming up unexpectedly is almost impossible." [78] The suppliers have no interest in obtaining new orders; their objective is to fulfill the plan, and they will often not comply with changed material requirements of other firms even if it is possible to do so.

In the above discussion we have neglected the role of the trading organizations. These so-called stockpiling companies serve as intermediaries in many fields between the supplier and the user. They do not trade in the sense the word is used in a free

75. T. Kiss, "The Interrelations of National Income and Foreign Trade in Hungary," *KSz*, No. 6 (1957), 645, 655.
76. Kornai, p. 18.
77. Sovány, p. 1048.
78. Ibid.

enterprise economy. They are administrative organizations which automatically take the products from the enterprises and are no interested in the assortment and quality of the products.[79] The do not possess significant stocks, and even these are allocated in advance. At the same time the stockpiling companies (the name sounds paradoxical) cannot accept orders from users unless the producers have already undertaken to manufacture the products.[80]

In the face of this lack of excess capacity in the producing enter prises and of sufficient inventories in the stockpiling companies enterprises endeavor to build up inventories of their own, since this is a requisite for the fulfillment of their production plans "The entire mechanism of our material allocation (planning and distribution) induces the enterprises to overinsure themselves, a a sort of self-defense, by stockpiling materials—at the expense of other enterprises."[81] It is self-evident that this process leads to decentralized inventories, to stockpiling of materials which partly prove to be unneeded later, and to shortages of materials for enterprises which neglected to stockpile. Because of dispersion of the stocks at the enterprises, inventories are considered unsatis factory on the national level.[82]

The question arises: Could not the discrepancies arising from the deficiencies of the material allocation process be overcome by sufficient inventories? On the theoretical level we can say that two types of costs are to be compared: the cost of holding inven tories and the cost of disturbances in production resulting from shortages in materials. The centralized system of material alloca tion results in additional costs for the economy; the question is only the form these will take.[83]

In Hungary the authorities have chosen the alternative of

---

79. Péter, p. 94.

80. Sovány, pp. 1045–46. He emphasizes that "our system of material allocation endeavors to eliminate to a great extent the inventories of the stockpiling companies.'

81. Ibid., p. 1048.

82. "We do not possess satisfactory reserves either in domestic or in imported materials; in some materials even the quantities necessary for continuous production are not available at the proper time" (ibid., pp. 1041–42). See also Péter, p. 115; Kornai, p. 146.

83. It is interesting to note that in the Soviet Union—although shortages in ma terials have frequently been observed—the inventory-output ratios seem to be higher than in the United States. See R. W. Campbell, "A Comparison of Soviet and American Inventory-Output Ratios," American Economic Review, 48 (1958), 549–65.

listurbances in production in preference to higher cost of inventories. The reasons for this choice are overstrained plans, lack of sufficient foreign currency reserves, and the fear that high inventories would slow down the growth rate.

Péter contends that the loss due to the lack of sufficient stocks s much greater than the cost of inventories, since in the absence of stockpiling, discrepancies in production and allocation are transmitted to other sectors of the national economy in the form of chain reactions.[84] A similar opinion is expressed by Kornai, who emphasizes that "we pay a high price for the saving in fixed and circulating funds due to the lack of inventories and lack of capacity reserves. The price: various disturbances in production, waste in the use of materials, lack of improvement or even deterioration of quality, drabness of assortment of commodities, sluggish development of technology." [85]

One can summarize the main consequences of the lack of sufficient reserves as follows:

1. Frequent shutting down of factories (in the construction industry, for example, there were stoppages on many projects because of lack of bricks, steel, cement, or even gravel every year. Similar phenomena were observed in factories working with imported materials, as in the textile industry).[86]

2. Frequent retooling of machines (in the largest Hungarian cotton mill, retooling of machines because of changes in the quality of material supplied was in 1955 equivalent to five complete resettings of the entire factory).[87]

3. Cross-hauling of materials (construction enterprises working in different parts of the country were often forced by the shortage of materials to transport them from one building site to another across the country. The cost of cross-transportation frequently reached 5 per cent of the entire material cost).

4. Waste of material (in 1953 the woollen industry had about 4.5 million forints of excess cost, because of the use of higher quality material when the prescribed material was not available).[88]

84. Péter, p. 115.
85. Kornai, p. 162. "Funds" corresponds to the concept of capital in Western economics.
86. Ibid., p. 143.
87. Ibid.
88. Ibid., p. 145.

5. Deterioration of quality (if the necessary material was not available, not only more expensive but also poorer material was used).

Conclusion. Having examined the main problems connected with the allocation process in Hungary, we are in a position to answer our question in regard to the equilibrating function of the system of physical allocation. It has been stated [89] that theoretically the material balances for individual commodities can be equilibrated in physical planning. Yet an examination of the actual workings of the allocation process in Hungary has revealed some practical obstacles which impede the realization of this goal. These obstacles, as they appear in Hungarian planning, can be summarized as: (1) lack of links between physical balances and the enterprise's plans, (2) lack of sufficient knowledge of production targets at the time of preparation of the enterprise's material supply plan, (3) lack of compatibility between plans of different enterprises, (4) changes and modifications put into effect during the planning period, and (5) lack of sufficient reserves.

These deficiencies have resulted in a situation characterized as "the system of shortage of goods" [90] and have led Hungarian economists to believe that "the equilibrium of supply and demand for every product . . . cannot be ensured in planning." [91]

It may be objected that some of these deficiencies can be avoided by introducing improvements in the process of planning. This is certainly true, but it should be emphasized that we have to pay a price in the form of alternative expenses for any modification in the system of allocation if physical planning is retained. For example, if physical balances are to be based on the enterprises' plans, an additional cost of information will arise and the time lag in planning will considerably increase, partly defeating our purpose by rendering the plans obsolete at the time of their execution. Similarly, as has been mentioned, the cost of inventories also appears as an alternative form of cost if the waste due to the absence of satisfactory reserves is to be avoided. In introduc-

---

89. Above, pp. 50–5.

90. Péter, p. 127. It should be noted here that the deficiencies of the material allocation system *per se* would lead to shortages as well as surpluses. In fact, shortages have been much more significant than surpluses, because of a lack of incentive to cater to the user's needs (see below, p. 129) and because of overstrained plans: Máriás, *KSz*, No. 4 (1958), 388.

91. Ibid., pp. 129–30.

ing reforms in the framework of physical planning, the alternative costs of possible modifications should be weighed.

On the basis of the evidence given above, it can be concluded that in the actual realization of physical planning, disequilibria on particular markets—that is, on the markets of individual commodities—will arise. In the absence of the equilibrating function of prices, supply of and demand for factors and products are not balanced.[92] The existing disequilibria on particular markets have led some Hungarian economists to the conclusion that price changes are needed to restore the equilibrium of supply and demand.[93] But introducing prices as an equilibrating factor would mean a step from physical planning toward a form of price planning.

PLANNING AND BARGAINING

W. Eucken states that in the absence of scarcity prices the allocation of resources will be greatly influenced by the bargaining force of the participants in planning.[94] The Hungarian economy is a good example for establishing the validity of Eucken's theorem. Bargaining plays an important role on two levels, among ministries and among enterprises. There are two main incentives for bargaining: the urge for power and the desire for higher earnings.

In view of the great importance attributed to political and military objectives and because of the absence of satisfactory productivity measurements, the range of bargaining has been considerably large, and it has been relatively easy for ministries

92. A similar observation is made in somewhat stronger form by the prominent Yugoslav economist R. Bicanic: "The balancing of supply and demand in a centrally planned economy occurs in offices where a few people unaware of the real effects of their authoritarian plan become the supreme judges of the destinies of all producers and consumers through their bureaucratic machine. From this source of authority, plans lead further down to smaller bodies, splitting unrealistic averages into still smaller averages, according to norms born in offices which, when they reach the enterprise level, have little resemblance to the conditions of actual life": "Economic Growth under Centralized and Decentralized Planning: Yugoslavia. A Case Study," *Economic Development and Cultural Change*, 7 (1957), 66.

93. Péter, p. 135. Also: "the equilibrium of supply and demand in our economy is not an absolute characteristic intrinsically ensured by central plans; the equilibrium, in many cases, could be brought about by the appropriate fixing of prices only" (ibid., p. 133).

94. W. Eucken, *Grundsätze der Wirtschaftspolitik* (Tübingen and Bern, 1952), p. 79.

to underline their demands with vague arguments. G. Csatár describes this bargaining process in the following way:

> Frequently real bargaining is going on about the determination of some [planned] figures. They [the ministries] defend their standpoint neither on the basis of technically established norms nor with reference to economic relationships, but on the basis that "I'll yield, so you should also yield." They ask originally for more investment funds than needed, more material, more labor for production—expecting (and knowing) that "if we have to yield somewhat, then we had better yield from a higher amount." [95]

The ministries endeavor to increase their power and prestige; consequently every minister attempts to increase his ministry's allocation of materials, labor, and investment funds. The Planning Office has had the task of coordinating the ministries and judging their claims from the viewpoint of the whole national economy. The Hungarian situation shows the weakness of the Planning Office.

The bargaining power of the ministries and the authority of the Planning Office has largely been determined by the ability and political influence of those who have directed them. In the first years of planning, while Zoltán Vas was its president, the authority of the Planning Office was undiminished; he personally was able to wield the necessary power over the ministries. In 1952 Vas was removed from the Planning Office, and his successors have been too weak to maintain their authority. In many important questions not the opinion of the Planning Office but the will of the strong ministries has been decisive, where good connections with the Central Committee of the Party were often more important than economic arguments. It has been observed that "the ministries . . . have carried out only those decrees which were in harmony with their interests. The decrees in which the interests of the ministry were opposed to those of the national economy have not been carried out, or if they were, then only formally." [96] It has been maintained that in addition to the chauvinism of the ministries, vacillation and indolence in the Planning Office have contributed to the defeat of its own orders. "As the

95. "On Ministry Chauvinism," SzN, February 12, 1956.
96. Turánszky, SSz, No. 12 (1957), 1036.

hauvinism of the ministry manifests itself in the fact that in
ase of a conflict between the interests of the national economy and
hose of the ministries the former falls into the background, the
hauvinism of the central planning authorities shows itself in
avoring the interest of the office over that of the national econ-
my." [97] Some actual cases of this bargaining process will now be
presented.

There was a long-standing dispute between the ministries over
whether only the Ministry for Construction or other ministries
s well should have construction enterprises under their jurisdic-
ion. The Minister for Construction argued that economical con-
truction work requires the subordination of every construction
irm to his ministry. Other ministers asserted that they needed
heir own building enterprises to undertake the execution of some
maller projects in the framework of the ministry and to ensure
hat if they have any urgent construction project it should not be
efused by the Ministry for Construction because of lack of
apacity. The dispute lasted for years, and the Planning Office
vas unable to settle the issue. Finally, in 1955, the Council of
Ministers resolved the problem by deciding that construction
nterprises should be operated solely by the Ministry for Con-
truction and (for the purpose of road and railroad construction)
by the Ministry for Transportation. But the other ministries did
not give up their building firms for many months, and after they
had been called upon again finally established enterprises under
alse names (for example, enterprise for building repair) in order
o continue construction activity.

Another example is supplied by the discussion about the completion date of the rolling works at Sztálinváros. The Ministry
or Heavy Industry desired that the works to be finished by 1959,
while the Ministry for Construction denied the possibility of such
an early date, basing its arguments on a thorough examination of
he available plans. In spite of the well-reasoned arguments of
he Ministry for Construction, the question was decided in 1956
n favor of the Ministry for Heavy Industry, on the basis of the
assertion that "the needs of heavy industry should be satisfied."

The bargaining process has served not only the prestige and
power of the ministries but in some cases their material interest
as well. It has been said that hidden personal interest has played

97. Ibid., p. 1037.

a role in investment decisions. The employees of investment directorates have endeavored to grab large investment funds for the
purpose of obtaining jobs as managers in the new enterprises at
a considerably higher salary than that enjoyed at the directorate.
Consequently they have favored the establishment of new factories instead of the reconstruction of old ones, and have tried to
locate the enterprises in Budapest, where they lived.[98]

Turánszky concludes, in connection with the role of hidden
personal interests in investment planning, that it "has created
such an atmosphere in many ministries that the procurement of
investment credits is regarded as the primary task of the investment directorates, when the interests of the national economy are
not carried through even to a minimal degree." [99] It is also emphasized that bargaining for investment funds, materials, labor, etc.,
"is not only a question of sporadic examples but a general phenomenon." [100]

Bargaining has played an important part in the affairs of the
enterprises as well. The difference between bargaining of the
ministries and bargaining of the enterprises has been primarily
in their power relations. Whereas some ministries have been
powerful enough to overrule decisions made by the Planning
Office, the ministries have enjoyed uncontested authority over
the enterprises. Consequently, a significant factor in the ministries' decisions has proved to be the personal relationship of the
firms' directors with the leading personnel of the supervising
directorate. Enterprises have bargained to reduce their output
targets, to ensure the procurement of more materials and more
labor, and to get better contracts, new investment funds, etc. The
twin motives, power and earnings, appear here. Power can be
augmented through new investments, amalgamation of enterprises, increase of the working force, etc. Earning possibilities
increase if plan-targets are reduced and prices and material allotments are increased, since in this way the chances to get higher
bonuses are better. The drive for greater power is also partly
conditioned by striving for higher earnings, since enterprises are
categorized according to the value of their productive capacity,
and higher capacity entails higher salary for the managers.

98. Ibid., p. 1042.
99. Ibid.
100. Csatár, SzN, February 12, 1956.

It is small wonder that the enterprises try to achieve these bjectives also by concealing facts that might hinder them in ob- aining better terms. The following table shows the profit rates lanned by the enterprise, the rates approved by the ministry, and he realized profit rates in the leather and shoe industry for the rst quarter of 1956.

Name of Firm	Profit Rate (percentage)		
	PLANNED		REALIZED
	Proposed by the Firm	Accepted by the Ministry	
Duna	4.4	5.1	8.3
Tisza	8.5	10.9	12.8
Bortex	−0.3	5.3	11.5
Ifjusági	−0.9	4.0	5.3
Kecskeméti	3.2	3.9	3.9
Hajdusági	−22.9	6.2	6.2

Source: Kornai, p. 118.

The figures indicate that the enterprises tried to obtain very avorable targets from the ministry, but they overfulfilled the tricter targets as well.

By way of conclusion we can state that the apparently quite onsiderable role of bargaining is not likely to be an efficient vay of choosing between investment alternatives or other targets; nd the cost imposed on the economy by the inefficiencies due to he bargaining process may be significant, although it cannot be stimated.

The Problem of Information and Centralized Decision-Making

The economies of information in free competition have been xamined in connection with price-planning.[101] The problem of nformation arises in physical planning as well. The core of the nformation problem was stated first by Hayek:

> Clearly there is here a problem of the *Division of Knowledge* which is quite analogous to . . . the problem of the division of labor . . . The problem which we pretend to solve is how the spontaneous interaction of a number of people, each possessing only bits of knowledge, brings about a state of

101. Above, p. 45.

affairs in which prices correspond to costs etc., and which could be brought about by deliberate direction only by somebody who possessed the combined knowledge of all those individuals.[102]

Although some socialist theoreticians try to belittle the need for bureaucracy in centralized planning,[103] it can be established that the problem of information is of utmost importance in physical planning. The administrative organizations have two interrelated tasks here: to collect information on available resources, production capacities, input-output coefficients, and consumer demand; and to make decisions on production and allocation.

The collection of information itself imposes a considerable burden on the economy, since it requires a significant amount of time. The cost of information consists largely of the expenses of statistical bureaus and the statistical apparatus of ministries and enterprises. The Hungarian experience suggests that the expenses of centralized decision-making are likely to be considerably higher than the cost of collecting statistical data. The cost of decision-making includes the expenses of the planning apparatus and of the various organizations—Planning Office, ministries (including directorates), and trusts—directing the production and allocation process.

It should be emphasized that this cost does not consist solely of expenses of the administrative apparatus partaking in the making of decisions; there is also the factor of delayed action, attributed to time lags in decision-making. Three forms of time lag can be mentioned: the lag between the need for action and the recognition of this need; the lag between the recognition of the need for action and the taking of action; and the lag between the action and its effects.[104] The magnitude of these costs cannot be estimated, but they are not likely to be negligible. Additional costs may arise from lack of personal interest on the part of a bureaucratic apparatus, which may result in mismanagement of resources.

Turning back to the Hungarian economy, the reasons for the

102. Hayek, *Economica*, *4* (1937), 49. Italics in original.
103. Dobb, *Political Economy and Capitalism*, pp. 303–4.
104. See Milton Friedman, "A Monetary and Fiscal Framework for Stability," *Readings in Monetary Theory* (New York, Blakiston, 1956), p. 382.

existence of a large apparatus are threefold: (1) the collection of information and centralized decision-making, (2) the need for control, and (3) the test of political reliability.

1. There is little to be added to what has been said on the need for an apparatus to perform the tasks of collecting and processing information and centralized decision-making. The existence of a large apparatus for this purpose cannot be avoided in any country operating on a system of physical planning.

2. It is self-evident that in a centralized planning system there is need for control over the execution of the decisions. But the striving for control has gone rather to extremes in Hungary; Kornai emphasized that "the repression of democracy in 1949–53 created an atmosphere of mistrust . . . which is one of the sources of excessive centralization. The less the manager trusts the subordinate employees, the more he tries to decide in their stead." [105] This atmosphere had led to a situation in which the ministries tried to regulate and control the work of the trusts and enterprises down to the smallest details. The quantity of regulations and the number of instructions and controls have increased to large proportions. To give some examples: a county received 1,328 regulations and decrees from the Ministry for Agriculture in the first four months of 1954, while another county received 3,400 regulations and directives from the Ministry of Domestic and Foreign Trade in 1953.[106] Not counting plans, financial regulations, collection of statistical data, etc., 102 written instructions arrived solely in connection with production activity at the Ujpest leather factory during the period of September 1 to December 31, 1955.[107] Examples of controls: the Conveyor factory in Budapest was audited and inspected 1,500 times in the course of a year; in the Mirelite deep-freezer factory several controllers investigated tramway tickets for three days to see whether those marked for official use had been used on Sundays.[108]

3. The regime lays great stress on the necessity of political reliability of state employees. This consideration frequently comes into conflict with economical production. There has been a tendency to spurn the "bourgeois" experts in the Planning Office

105. Kornai, p. 181.
106. Péter, p. 26.
107. Kornai, p. 64.
108. G. Csatár, "The Record of Bureaucracy," *SzN*, June 3, 1956.

and the ministries. Competence has been taken into consideration increasingly as we approach the enterprise level, since errors can be more easily detected here and the relationship between the work of the manager and the actual results in production is closer than in the work of the planners. Political considerations have been of correspondingly less importance in the lower echelons. Nevertheless, managers often complained that they had to employ incompetent Party members who were superfluous to the enterprise. The personnel departments had their own cadre-development plans, which aimed to improve the social composition of the employees by weeding out bourgeois elements and increasing the contribution from the working and peasant classes. The frequent fights of the director and the personnel departments over persons with good knowledge and experience but less desirable social background indicated that fulfillment of the cadre-development plan frequently ran counter to fulfillment of the production plan.

The above-mentioned three causes, then, have jointly contributed to the creation of a huge bureaucratic apparatus in Hungary.[109]

In what follows we shall present some data showing the growth of bureaucracy. With regard to manufacturing, the changes in the ratio of employees other than workers to productive workers is of importance: [110]

	(1) Productive Workers	(2) Employees Other than Workers	(3) Total Employees	(4) (2) as a Percentage of (1)
		IN THOUSANDS		
1938	289	58	347	20.1
1947	323	78	401	24.7
1955	686	218	904	31.7

An increase of similar magnitude was observed in public administration. Whereas in 1930, 127,000 people were employed in state administration, in 1956 their number more than doubled, reaching 264,000.[111] The process of bureaucratization has been

109. Kornai remarks: "It is an iron law that excessive centralization results in the growth of the bureaucracy" (p. 178).

110. Data for 1938 are taken from *ASH*, p. 136. For 1947: *GT*, No. 8 (1948), 448–49. For 1955: *SE*, p. 88.

111. Data for 1930 are taken from L. Lengyel, "Changes in Employment in Hungary, 1949–57," *SSz*, Nos. 8–9 (1958), 752. For 1956: *SSz*, No. 7 (1957), 648.

especially strong in the construction industry. Here in 1940 the number of employees other than workers amounted to only 4 per cent of that of the productive workers; in 1949 this percentage reached 10–12, and in 1955 it grew to 37.[112] Similar development can be recognized in domestic trade. At the beginning of 1949, 212,000 people were employed; after nationalization, their number reached 275,000.[113] This increase has been due largely to the extensive growth of administration and control apparatus in domestic trade. The contribution of domestic trade to national income was said to have increased by only 4 per cent in the same period.

During the New Course attempts were made to cut down on bureaucracy, which, it was maintained, impeded further progress. The Resolution of the Third Congress of the Hungarian Working People's Party (1954) stated that "the development of the Party and also the growth of the people's democracy is impeded by bureaucracy, by excessive centralization." The so-called "rationalization" was carried out by reducing the number of nonproductive employees and by lessening administrative work. Results were far from impressive. In light industry, for example, the official figures show a decrease of the ratio of "employees other than workers" to "productive workers" of only 2 per cent—from 27 to 25 per cent—between 1954 and 1955.[114] But even this modest reduction of the administrative apparatus was partly fictitious, for the discharged nonproductive employees were mostly re-employed as "productive workers," and they continued their previous work—a process called "hiding." It has been revealed that in 1954 hiding amounted to 6.5 per cent in the Ministry for Metallurgy and Engineering and to 6.8 per cent in the Ministry for Heavy Industry.[115] Yet these figures show only the hiding discovered, and the true percentage may be much higher. For example, instead of the official 3.9 per cent in the construction industry, experience suggests that it may have amounted to 6 per cent or more. Rationalization has brought no greater results in lessening administrative work. Kornai cites the

---

112. Data for 1940 and 1949 are from J. Tar, "Some Problems of the Development and Organization of the Hungarian Construction Industry," *SSz*, No. 4 (1955), 36. For 1955: *SE*, p. 60.

113. *SE*, pp. 39, 57.

114. Kornai, p. 188.

115. G. Bács, "Staff-Concealment in Industrial Enterprises," *SSz*, No. 8 (1954), 610.

case of the leather industry, where the number of plan indicators prescribed by the ministry increased from 117 to 139 between 1955 and 1956.[116] Similar cases can be found in other fields.

In view of these developments, a statement from the Party's official paper fits the situation rather well: "although tens of thousands of people have been affected by changes, and strict regulations defined the terms of dismissals, bureaucracy has not decreased. Therefore, the real cause of the trouble must be looked for elsewhere. Today many people admit that bureaucracy is connected with the exaggerated centralization of economic management." [117]

Efficiency in Resource Allocation in Hungarian Planning

In Chapter 1 we defined efficiency in resource allocation (static efficiency) by the requirement that there should be no possibility of increasing the production of one commodity without reducing the production of another, under the assumption that the final bill of goods corresponds to the community's preferences. Alternatively expressed, static efficiency denotes the choice of least-cost production methods in producing the commodities desired by the community. In the case of physical planning, the preferences of the community are taken to be equivalent to those of the planners.

Up to recent times planners in Soviet-type economies did not seem to care much about efficient resource allocation. Orthodox Soviet authors chided those who had proposed the use of "the unhistorical idea, long unmasked in Marxist literature of 'maximum effect for minimum outlay.' " [118] The situation in Hungary was similar, as can be seen from the testimony of I. Tatár: "We have to break with the narrow-minded point of view whose representatives during the last years have actually branded the views of those emphasizing the importance of economical production as hostile." [119]

It was emphasized that production should be economical from

116. Kornai, p. 190.

117. *SzN*, October 14, 1954.

118. Mstislavsky's criticism of Khachaturov in the Soviet monthly journal *Voprosy Ekonomiki* (1948), p. 132, quoted in P. Wiles, "Scarcity, Marxism and Gosplan," *Oxford Economic Papers*, 5 (1953), 304.

119. "Actual Problems of Our Foreign Trade," *KSz*, No. 2 (1957), 189.

the long-run point of view, but this rule has not been adhered to in practice. As T. Liszka observes:

> The discussion of economical production has been unfruit-ful in coping with the principal question: basing the national economic plan on productivity calculations and analyses. The result is only a generally accepted rule, which empha-sizes the importance of economical production and states that it should be analyzed from the viewpoint of the long-run development of the entire economy, subordinated to the economic laws of socialism. These statements have one defect only [!], that in this general form they do not give any help to economic planning, to practical work.[120]

The neglect of efficiency considerations has been attributed principally to the quantitative point of view, which emphasized the achievement of quantitative increases in various industries and left out of consideration the efficient use of the produced quantities. An excellent criticism of this idea is given by F. Jánossy, vice president of the National Office for Building Af-fairs: [121]

> If in national planning we study only the produced quantities and neglect the examination of efficiency in production, we are exposed to the danger that, because of deterioration of efficiency, the national income will not rise sufficiently side by side with the quantitative increase in production, or it will even stop increasing. This is not merely a theoretical question, as can be seen from the results of the first Five Year Plan . . . it can be stated that during the first Five Year Plan the quantities produced of a significant part of industrial products, like coal and steel, or cement and ma-chines, have increased by 50 or 100 per cent, or even more, but this has not resulted in a proportionate increase of na-tional income . . . the one-sided "quantitative point of view" has in fact resulted in a deterioration of efficiency.[122]

---

120. "Experimental Calculations on the Efficiency of Investments and of Our Participation in the International Division of Labor," *KSz*, No. 5 (1956), 18. A similar opinion was expressed by Turánszky: "We do not have any methods for the evaluation of the requirements of profitability as viewed from the standpoint of the national economy" (*SSz*, No. 12, 1957), 1026.

121. This office supervised construction activity in the entire economy.

122. *ME* (July 20, 1956), p. 3. Jánossy mentions that "on the occasion of the

Jánossy's contentions have been borne out by calculations of A. Bródy. Bródy prepared input-output tables for seven sectors of the Hungarian economy (coal-mining, metallurgy, electrical energy, machine industry, railway transportation, labor as input, and external production as output) for 1952, 1953, and 1954. He found that "the results of the development of our heavy industry are partly used up through deteriorating efficiency in heavy industry; heavy industry does not feed light industry, construction, and agriculture as much as it feeds *itself*." [123] The conclusions are based partly on a decrease in the share of external production (production for use outside of the five sectors of heavy industry),[124] partly on a deterioration in input-output coefficients during the period in question. Among the coefficients, 16 show considerable increase, 6 some increase, 5 some decrease, and 1 considerable decrease in input requirements per unit of output.[125] The changes are mostly continuous from 1952 to 1953 and 1953 to 1954. Calculating the 1954 external production with the coefficients of the year 1952, the following percentage increases in input requirements are revealed: coal mining, 5.5; metallurgy, 1.2; electrical energy, 5.2; machine industry, 2.7; railway transportation, 11.5; and labor, 1.4.[126]

On the basis of practical experience, Bródy extrapolates these changes for the entire period of the Five Year Plan and reaches the following conclusion: "If we say that the average deterioration of the coefficients was about 15 to 20 per cent, we are likely to underestimate it." [127]

It can be concluded that physical planning as applied in Hun-

---

preparation of the directives for the second Five Year Plan this lesson was not properly taken into consideration" (ibid.).

123. *Yearbook,* p. 148. Italics in original.

124. The proportion of external production in the industries in question is as follows (ibid., p. 148):

	1952	1953	1954
Coal mining	45.8	45.1	45.5
Metallurgy	33.1	28.9	29.5
Electrical energy	55.4	53.4	51.7
Machine industry	87.5	88.0	86.1
Railway transportation	66.4	62.3	57.8

125. Ibid., p. 144. Among the six coefficients indicating an improvement, four are said to be highly unreliable (those of the machine industry).

126. Ibid., p. 149.

127. Ibid., p. 148.

gary has been to a considerable degree inefficient in the allocation of resources, for two main reasons: (1) a system of physical planning is not conducive to efficient resource allocation even if the economic balances are equilibrated; and (2) in practical application, disequilibria arise on the markets of both factors and products. In addition, the quantitative point of view, the need for a large bureaucracy, and the existence of bargaining in the planning process also contribute to this result. These inefficiences have been partly counteracted by the virtually full utilization of resources.

It should be emphasized that inefficiency in resource allocation is not a special characteristic of Hungarian planning only. If efficiency considerations come to the foreground, physical planning lacks the mechanism on the basis of which rational choice between alternative uses of the resources can be made. In most cases, quantitative comparisons are not sufficient for this purpose. Nor will prices be much help, since they do not express resource scarcities but are determined by authoritative decision of the planners. The problem of pricing in physical planning, and particularly in Hungarian practice, will be examined in the next chapter.

4. Pricing in Theory and Practice

PRICES IN PHYSICAL PLANNING

IN THE PRECEDING CHAPTER we have already touched upon the role of prices in physical planning. This question now needs to be explored in more detail.

Under conditions of both pure competition and price planning, prices are *scarcity prices,* being determined by resource scarcities, production functions, and the desired bill of goods (where the last item may express consumers' or planners' preferences as well). Pricing has an allocative function, in the sense that the choice between alternative production methods is determined on the basis of prices. The use of scarcity prices makes it possible to allocate resources in such a way that a given final bill of goods is produced at least cost, ensuring thereby the most advantageous use of resources.

In physical planning the final bill of goods is determined by the planning authorities. The allocation of resources takes place in quantitative terms, on the basis of constant coefficients in production, where the previously described method of "successive approximation" is used. If it is assumed that all decisions in production and allocation are made centrally, that there is no foreign trade, and that the predetermined bill of consumer goods is allocated among consumers by the use of outright rationing, there would be no need for the use of prices in the allocation process.

Nevertheless, even in this form of physical planning, for purposes of accounting there is need for a common denominator in the bewildering variety of commodities. It is rather misleading to use the notion "price" in this connection, since the function of these *accounting prices* is entirely different from that of scarcity prices. Whereas scarcity prices are used in the allocation process, accounting prices are determined after allocation in physical terms has already been effected. Consequently, the planners have an extra degree of freedom in determining the accounting prices: theoretically, any set of prices is compatible with the achievement of the same physical targets. Pricing is exogenous to physical planning, and prices (both absolute and relative) can be set at will, since pricing is an accounting device only. G. D. H. Cole's words are applicable here: "In a planned socialist economy there can be no objective structure of costs. Costs can be imputed to any desired extent . . . But these imputed costs are not objective, but *fiat* costs determined by the public policy of the State." [1]

In the above described model of physical planning some restrictive assumptions have been made. If we gradually relax these assumptions but retain the basic feature of physical planning—allocation of resources in physical terms among targets determined by the planning authorities—the need for further uses of prices will become manifest.

1. Some targets defy expression in physical terms. The central authority may plan the production of wheat and rye, iron and oil, in million tons—the production of eggs and poultry, clothes and shoes, in million units. Yet physical targets for firms producing a wide variety of goods in many different qualities are cumbersome to reckon with. Planned targets for a hardware factory in terms of iron nails, screws, bolts, locks, and hinges in various sizes do not say much. There is need to make use of prices to express these targets in money terms.

2. Aggregation cannot be performed in physical terms, either. The production of the coal industry can be reckoned in terms of coal tons of a given calorie and ash content, but the production of the organic chemical industry cannot be couched in physical terms. The possibility of reckoning in physical terms decreases as aggregation proceeds. The planners need aggregate value-figures to make comparisons with former periods, to reckon the fulfillment of the national plan, to draw up synthetic balances for ensuring the compatibility of aggregate targets, etc.

3. Prices are also needed for control purposes. Even if the planning authorities prescribe the targets for every enterprise down to the smallest detail, the control of the fulfillment of these targets can be made, in most cases, in money terms only. The perform-

1. *Economic Planning* (New York, 1953), p. 184. Italics in original.

ance of a copper mine can be measured in physical terms, but we cannot add chemicals or household utensils to control the fulfillment of production targets in a chemical or hardware factory. Furthermore, the control of the economical operation of the enterprises through profit and loss statements requires pricing. Monetary terms are also used for control purposes in other fields, as for example in inventory control.

4. Limited freedom over the determination of output and input mix may be given to the enterprise, since the central determination of every detail in the production and allocation process is hardly achievable in practice. The firm's choice between output targets and alternative inputs will be affected by the prices of products and factors. It should be noted here that the use of prices by the enterprise in making its choice between outputs and inputs may create the possibility of contradiction between physical and value targets. Prices are part of the planning and control mechanism for the planner, but they become a directing force for the enterprise. As soon as production and profits are measured in value terms, the firm endeavors to maximize those variables (for example, production and/or profits) on the basis of which its performance will be judged. The physical targets will become indifferent for the firm. It will attempt to maximize the *composite* value indicators instead of the *individual* physical indicators. In doing this, the enterprise may well frustrate the original intentions of the planner.[2]

5. In making a choice among alternative technological variants of investment projects or, in some cases, in choosing between alternative production methods, prices will be employed. For example, in deciding whether lumber or concrete should be used on certain construction projects or in choosing between alternative methods of road construction, cost calculations may serve as a basis.

6. The rationing function of prices on the consumer-goods market means that instead of outright rationing the central authorities distribute a given assortment of consumer goods by devising consumer prices to equate, for every commodity, consumer demand with available supply.

7. On the labor market prices have a function similar to that

2. This problem is examined below.

on the consumer market (assuming free choice of occupation) in directing and allocating labor among various sectors of the economy.

8. The existence of foreign trade relations also necessitates the use of prices. Exports and imports should be compared in value terms in the balance of foreign trade, and prices should be used also in evaluating alternative export possibilities.

It should now be obvious that some of the above-listed uses of prices in physical planning require some rationality, the reflection of some measure of scarcity in prices, since prices are in some cases used for choosing between alternatives in investment, production, or exports, and for effecting modifications in the output-and/or input-mix of the enterprise. The need for rational prices is in conflict with our former assertion, according to which, in physical planning, any set of prices is compatible with the achievements of certain physical targets. Because of the modifications effected in our model of physical planning, it is no longer indif-- ferent how prices are determined, since now prices serve a real function: in a limited field, prices do not stand outside of the allocation process but are used in making decisions on production and allocation. Consequently, different price structures will lead to different results. We face a dilemma here which is of utmost importance in physical planning: prices cannot be set rationally unless resources have already been allocated efficiently. The processes of pricing and allocation mutually determine each other: there is no efficient allocation of resources without the use of scarcity prices, and prices do not reflect the resource scarcities of the economy if allocation is not efficient.[3] In physical planning (also in its modified form) the main decisions in the production and allocation process are made in physical terms and the equilibration of supply and demand for particular commodities is effected by employing physical balances rather than by the use of prices. As a consequence, prices are indeterminate in physical planning; they are not rational—do not express actual scarcities—but can be set arbitrarily. Because of this arbitrariness, the use of prices in a limited field of decision-making fails to give unambiguous results: an alternative costing less on existing prices may well cost more in terms of resource scarcities than another alternative.

3. The same conclusion has been reached by J. M. Montias; see his "Price Setting Problems in the Polish Economy," *Journal of Political Economy*, 65 (1957), 486–87.

PRICING IN SOVIET-TYPE ECONOMIES

It seems to me that most economists in the Soviet orbit have not understood the indeterminacy of prices in physical planning, although, occasionally they seem to have stumbled upon it inadvertently. Stalin's famous example of the "confusion that still reigns in the sphere of price-fixing policy" deserves quotation:

> Our business executives and planners submitted a proposal [which] suggested fixing the price of a ton of grain at practically the same level as a ton of cotton and, moreover, the price of a ton of grain was taken equivalent to that of a ton of baked bread. In reply to the remarks of members of the Central Committee [of the Communist Party] that the price of a ton of bread must be higher than that of a ton of grain, because of the additional expense of milling and baking, and that cotton was generally much dearer than grain, as was also borne out by their prices in the world market, the authors of the proposal could find nothing coherent to say.[4]

Stalin clearly admits here the arbitrary setting of prices, and who can be sure that, if the planners could not do it, the Central Committee of the Party will hit upon the "right" price ratios? Mises will certainly acknowledge Stalin's statement as an argument supporting his assertion on the role of world-market prices in socialist economies.

Hungarian economists also refer to price relations on the world market as an "ultimate" proof of the irrationality of the Hungarian price structure. Péter remarks that "the contradictions of domestic price relations appear most conspicuously when comparison is made with world-market prices, namely in the field of foreign trade."[5] Some, going much further, show an understanding of the role of prices in physical planning. It is maintained that "in an excessively centralized economy, prices have only a registering function"[6] and that (in Hungary) "current prices are the products of arbitrary price-formation."[7] It has also been

---

4. *Economic Problems of Socialism in the U.S.S.R.* (Moscow, Foreign Languages Publishing House, 1952), pp. 24–25.

5. Péter, p. 57.

6. E. Jávorka, "Some Problems of the Industrial Price System," *KSz*, No. 2 (1957), 122.

7. I. Tatár, "Actual Problems of our Foreign Trade," *KSz*, No. 2 (1957), 200.

pointed out that "prices have no importance whatsoever if physical allocation is carried through completely." [8] Nevertheless, these observations have remained rather isolated, and the labor theory of value has continued to serve as starting point in discussions on pricing.

Until recent years there has been much diffuse talk on the importance of the law of value in the determination of prices. It had been maintained that in the Soviet economy the law of value is not a spontaneous force any more, because "the state understands it, takes it into account, and uses it in planning the national economy." [9] It had been alleged that "it is a great advantage of the socialist state that it can limit, exploit, and systematically utilize the law of value." [10] In regard to pricing this means that "the socialist state fixes the price of the commodities in such a way that they differ in one or another direction from the value of commodities." [11] The statement implies that the value of the commodities (in the Marxist sense: the average quantity of socially necessary direct and indirect labor expended on the production of particular commodities) can be measured, and deviations of prices from value are the result of deliberate actions on the part of the planning authorities. Yet it has been established by Soviet economists, and by Western scholars as well, that actually no attempt has been made to measure the value of the commodities; hence there is no possibility for "systematic deviations" from values in the determination of prices either.

The last few years have produced renewed discussion of price determination in Soviet economic journals. This phenomenon may be due to two circumstances: since Stalin's death there has existed some possibility of reinterpreting orthodox Marxist-Leninist dogmas; and, in connection with an apparent endeavor to utilize resources more efficiently, there has been an attempt to devise rational prices which would give expression to scarcities. All this lingers between the lines, still heavy with Marxist concepts and ideas, while development toward a more rational price structure is retarded by attacks coming from the holders of orthodox views. It is characteristic that even those economists who

8. A. Máriás, "Some Problems in the Allocation of the Means of Production," ibid., No. 4 (1958), 384 n.

9. *Soviet Textbook of Political Economy*, p. 506.

10. Ibid., p. 509.

11. Ibid., p. 507.

seem to understand the scarcity problem barricade themselves behind the façade of the labor theory of value. Our purpose is not to give a critical review of the controversy but to show alternative possibilities for pricing in Soviet-type economies, in the light of views professed by participants in the discussion.[12]

In connection with any kind of price system applied in a Soviet-type economy two questions should be answered: at which stage or stages of production will accumulation be "realized,"[13] and to what degree do prices correspond to the scarcity relationships of the economy?

The Dual Price System

In this price system producer prices generally contain "socially necessary cost" augmented by a low profit margin. This concept denotes those costs that are necessary for the production of a given commodity at the present stage of development of productive forces. Since the price of materials contains only a minimal profit rate, socially necessary cost actually means average (direct and indirect) labor costs. But labor costs differ from values, because values contain not only labor costs but surplus value.

In the dual price system, producer and consumer prices have different roles. Producer prices have an accounting function in production, whereas consumer prices are used to distribute the consumer goods actually produced among consumers. In the last

12. In presenting opinions of Soviet economists use has been made of the following articles: B. Astakhov, L. Voznesensky, F. Volkov, and A. Yudkin, "Questions of Commodity Production and the Law of Value under Socialism," *Problems of Economics,* Eng. trans. of the Soviet monthly journal *Voprosy ekonomiki* (October 1958), pp. 59–67; I. Konnik, "The Formation of Prices and the Problem of Money under Socialism," ibid. (July 1958), pp. 47–51; B. Minc, "Price and Value in a Socialist Economy," ibid., pp. 42–47; T. Nagy, "Discussion of the Use of the Law of Value and the Categories of Value in the Soviet Union," *KSz,* No. 11 (1957), 1193–1209; I. Vincze, "Principles of the Current Modification of Producer Prices," ibid., No. 11 (1958), 993–1007.

13. Using Marxist terminology, national income consists of labor costs and surplus product, which latter is not paid out to the laborers. The two items constitute the "value added" of Western economics, with the difference that the Marxist concept of national income includes value added in material production only. In the following, the notion of "realization of accumulation" will denote the realization of that part of value added which has not been paid out to the laborers (surplus product). The term "value" will be used throughout this section in the Marxist sense as defined above.

stage of production a turnover tax (plus wholesale and retail trade mark-up) is added to the producer price to form the consumer price.[14] In other words, accumulation (surplus product) is realized in the consumer price. Variants of the dual price system are presently used in Soviet-type economies. Some of its proponents are S. Turetsky, L. Maizenberg, and P. Mstislavsky.

The dual price system has two deficiencies from the viewpoint of the scarcity-prices requirement:

1. Being based on average labor costs, it disregards problems connected with the time-structure of production (the longer production period imprisons resources for a longer time) and with the limited availability of natural resources (for example, oil, copper, etc.); furthermore, based on average costs, it disregards the fact that the scarcity value of the factors of production is indicated by marginal cost rather than average cost.

2. Changes in consumer demand will not influence the enterprises to produce more of the commodities for which demand has increased but—within the limits of the possibilities to determine or modify the assortment of goods produced—enterprises will be affected only by the producer price/cost of production ratio.[15]

The Price System of the Value Type

In this system price equals value. In Marxian terminology, value consists of three parts: c (value of equipment and material used up in production), v (labor costs), and m (surplus value). Whereas under the dual price system, price $= c + v$, in a price system of the value type, price $= c + v + m$. In other words, surplus value is added at every stage of production, and accumulation is realized in the producer prices of every commodity. The advocates of this price system (S. Strumilin, J. Kronrod, M. Bor, D. Kondrashev, and others) assume that the share of the surplus product in the prices of various commodities is proportionate to labor cost. Denoting aggregate labor costs by V and aggregate surplus product (accumulation) by M, m will be equal to $v \cdot M / V$ for any commodity. Consequently, the prices of every product

14. The percentage rate of turnover tax should differ for various commodities in order to equate consumer demand with available supply for the particular consumer goods.

15. Cf. Jávorka, *KSz*, No. 2 (1957), 122–23.

will contain the corresponding part of surplus product and in a new production phase only labor costs supplemented by the pro portional part of surplus product will be added. Consumer prices will be equal to the producer prices of consumer goods plus dis-tributive margins.

Prices in this system, being based on the labor theory of value, do not reflect scarcities any better than the dual price system does. Besides, it produces widely varying profit rates in industries with differing capital/labor ratios. Furthermore, it creates disturbances on the consumer goods market, since only by chance will prices based on values equate consumer demand with the supply deter-mined by the planning authority. Either production should cor-respond to consumer demand or taxes and subsidies should be applied.

The Price System of the Production Price Type

In Marxian terminology, production prices contain the cost of production supplemented by profit calculated on fixed and vari-able funds:

$$p = (c + v)\left(1 + \frac{M}{C + V}\right).$$

Consumer prices will be equal to producer prices of the last stage of production augmented by distributive margins. Accumulation will be realized in producer prices in proportion to fixed and variable funds. This price system has been recommended by J. Malishev, Z. Atlas, and N. Scherbakov. A price system of the production-price type will certainly approximate scarcity prices better than any of the aforementioned price systems, since interest is charged on the basis of the use of fixed and variable funds, and consequently the scarcity of capital funds at least partially finds its expression in prices. With regard to the equilibration of the consumer market, the same problems arise as with the price sys-tem of the value type.

A further amendment of the price system of the production-price type has been recommended by Bachurin and Kulikov, who advocate that not only interest but differential rent should be added in the case of natural resources. This is as far as Soviet authors have advanced. By charging interest and differential rent, producer prices would certainly come nearer to scarcity prices, but they would still not *be* scarcity prices. Rational prices are further approximated from the cost side if quasi-rents [16] are also added to the above-mentioned elements of cost, thereby equating prices with marginal costs.[17] Nevertheless, this is only one side of the coin. Under physical planning, the main decisions in production and allocation are taken without regard to prices. But if the allocation of resources is determined in physical terms *before* prices have been established, prices will not reflect scarcities. As we have seen, efficient allocation and rational prices are mutually determined. It is not sufficient if improvements are achieved on the supply side by the use of marginal costs; prices should also be taken into consideration on the demand side. If demand is not considered, the application of any kind of cost principle leads to circularity. As it was expressed by a Soviet economist: "there is a vicious circle: the price depends on costs and profits and the profit on costs and prices." [18] This observation was also made by a Hungarian economist: "not only do costs affect prices, but prices affect costs. Costs depend primarily on the level of wages, and wages cannot be made independent of the level of consumer prices. Hence, actually, the interrelationship is mutual: the cost of production cannot be the center of prices, since costs are determined by prices." [19]

On the other hand, if all decisions in production and allocation are based on prices (demand side), we have left the territory of physical planning and are applying methods of price-planning. The idea that demand should be taken into account in the determination of prices crops up in some Hungarian writings,[20] but is never followed to its logical conclusion: to achieve rational prices, we have to scrap physical planning.

16. "Quasi-rent" means the differential return due to cost advantages of non-marginal enterprises.

17. Cf. J. M. Montias, "Rational Prices and Marginal Costs in Soviet-type Economies," *Soviet Studies, 8* (1957), 369–79.

18. Mme. Sollertinskaya, in *Planovoie khoziaistvo,* No. 11 (1940), quoted by A. Zauberman, "Economic Thought in the Soviet Union," Part II, *Review of Economic Studies, 16* (1948–49), 105.

19. J. Wilcsek's review of B. Csikós Nagy's book *Árpolitika az átmeneti gazdaságban* (*Price Policy of the Transitional Period*), in *KSz*, Nos. 8–9 (1958), 973. Wilcsek starts off on the right track but then, faithful to Marxist orthodoxy, declares that labor values should be made the center of prices.

20. E. G. J. Bokor, O. Gadó, P. Kürthy, T. Meitner, S. Sárosi, and J. Wilcsek, "Proposal for a New Method in the Economic Management of Industry," *KSz*, No. 4 (1957), 380. See also Jávorka, *KSz*, No. 2 (1957), 129; Péter, p. 75.

DETERMINATION OF PRODUCER PRICES

In the first part of this chapter we examined problems of pricing in physical planning and pricing methods in Soviet-type economies. In the subsequent sections we shall describe and evaluate the determination of prices in the Hungarian economy (excluding agriculture and transportation).

In Hungarian planning the following categories of prices can be distinguished: producer prices (plan prices and current prices), and consumer prices (fixed prices and free market prices). First, producer prices will be examined.

Plan prices are designed to measure the plan fulfillment of a planning period in constant prices. New plan prices have been employed for every long-term plan; generally the current prices of the year preceding the period of the plan served this purpose. Prices prevailing on January 1, 1947, were used for the Three Year Plan; prices as of January 1, 1949, served as a basis for the first Five Year Plan; prices of 1954 were used in preparing the plans for 1955 and the second Five Year Plan (1956–60). (The construction industry presents the only exception; here, since 1952, the so-called "constant January 1, 1952, prices" have been used.) Theoretically, the plan prices are constant prices. In practice, various factors, which will be examined below, have led to increases in these allegedly unchanged prices.

Current prices are in use in accounting, in the exchange among state firms, and in private dealings. Every synthetic economic balance is expressed in current prices, whereas only some of these balances (for example, the national income balance) are calculated in plan prices.

A few remarks on the history of price determination in the postwar period may help an understanding of the present structure of producer prices in Hungary.

After the runaway inflation ended in 1946, the new prices in forints were fixed on the basis of the August 26, 1939, prices. Partly, index numbers were used, multiplying the 1939 pengö prices to obtain the new prices in forints; partly, calculation methods used in 1939 were applied to determine the forint prices.[21] An overhaul of producer prices was made in 1952, with no substantial modification in the price structure. Three methods

21. S. Ausch, "Currency Stabilization in 1946," *KSz*, Nos. 7–8 (1956), 908.

were used in fixing the new prices: indexed prices (to the 1946 level), calculated prices (on the basis of the calculation scheme to be presented below), and group prices (for groups of commodities).[22] Further price modifications were introduced in 1954.[23]

It has been reported that in the course of the modifications effected no significant change has been made in the structure of producer prices, and changes in the conditions of production and in world market prices have not been given consideration.[24] The adjustments actually performed, instead of taking into account changes in scarcity relationships, distorted the price ratios by fixing the prices of the means of production and of imported products below cost.[25]

After this short introduction we can turn to the system of producer prices in Hungary, the skeleton of which is given here: [26]

1. standardized products
   a. "old" products (those produced in the year preceding the period of the long-term plan)
      (1) plan prices—current prices of the basis year
      (2) current prices—identical to plan prices if there was no cost change during the planned period, or based on current costs if there were changes in costs during the planning period
   b. "new" products (those produced for the first time during the planning period)
      (1) plan prices—calculated on the basis of current costs

22. *Planning*, pp. 100–2.

23. P. Kürthy, *Útmutató az egységes termék és árjegyzék használatához (Guide to the Use of the Uniform Product and Price List)* (Budapest, 1954), p. 33. Although the use of indexed prices had been discontinued, prices fixed on a cost basis continued to reflect the indexed prices of the former period.

24. As L. Kismarty observed in 1957: "our industrial price system was formed in 1946—with some modifications—on the basis of the previous pengö prices, with the use of index numbers . . . In the meantime, partly because of the change in the industrial structure, partly because of shifts in price ratios on the world market, the price-determining factors have changed; yet meanwhile the effected price adjustments have distorted rather than improved the picture": "Some Problems of Efficiency and the Prospects of Our Metallurgy," *KSz*, No. 5 (1957), 527. Similarly, the then president of the Planning Office stated that a "considerable part of our producer prices . . . was formed many years ago, frequently without sufficient basis, and in the meantime conditions of production have changed a great deal": A. Berei, *SzN*, July 29, 1956.

25. B. Csikós Nagy, "The Reorganization of Industrial Producer Prices," *KSz*, Nos. 8–9 (1957), 818–21.

26. For the sake of brevity, the determination of current prices is presented as based on current costs. Other methods will be described later.

of the period when the commodity was produced for the first time

(2) current prices—identical to plan prices if there was no cost change after the introduction of the commodity, or based on current costs if there were changes in costs after its introduction.

2. Nonstandardized products

    a. plan prices—based on the calculation scheme valid for the planning period, with individual calculation for every product

    b. current prices—same as plan prices

The procedure of price-fixing for standardized products. Institutionally, price-fixing takes the following form. The enterprise prepares a calculation and presents it to the supervising ministry. In the case of funded commodities, the price department of the ministry gives its opinion and transmits the calculation to the Planning Office, which makes the final decision.[27] The prices of nonfunded commodities are fixed by the supervising ministry, while the prices of consumer goods are determined, on the basis of the supervising ministry's proposal, by the Ministry for Domestic Trade.

In determining the prices of standardized products, three methods of price-fixing are in use: the cost method, the identification method, and the subsidization method.

The most widely used *cost method* corresponds to the system of dual prices described in the previous section. As we have seen, interest and rent are not taken into account in calculating prices. The following scheme of price calculation is employed:

	cost of material
	$+$ labor costs
	$+$ depreciation
	$+$ other direct costs
I.	total direct costs
	$+$ indirect costs
II.	total costs
	$+$ profit
III.	price

27. In 1957 the role of the Planning Office in price-fixing was taken over by the newly established Price Office.

The indirect costs of the firm producing the commodity in question are allotted among the products in proportion to their direct costs. The profit mark-up is 2 or 3 per cent.

The price of the commodities is, theoretically, calculated on the basis of industrial average costs. Yet in Hungarian industry the majority of the standardized products are manufactured solely by one enterprise. Weighted average costs on the industry level can serve as the basis of price-fixing in the hardware industry and in some branches of light and food industries only.[28] Determination of prices based on the cost calculation of one enterprise results in considerable disproportions within the price structure, since the prices of these products depend on whether their production takes place in a firm with modern equipment or in one with backward technology.[29] Moreover, even for commodities produced in more than one enterprise, the basis of price-fixing is usually the cost observed in the firm which first began production.[30]

Disregarding some special cases, the producer prices used in the exchange among state enterprises do not contain turnover tax.[31] Turnover tax, along with wholesale and retail trade mark-up, is added only as consumer prices are formed.

The *identification method* is applied in the consumer goods industries, with the exception of the cotton, shoe, and paper industries, where the cost method is used.[32] This method consists in the identification of the price of new products with the price of similar, previously produced commodities. The identification takes place on the consumer price level. For example, if a new woollen suit model is produced, the price is to be determined in

---

28. Jávorka, *KSz*, No. 2 (1957), 128. This situation is the result of the central authorities' endeavor, apparent after the nationalizations, to increase specialization among the enterprises.

29. An example (ibid.) will show the possibility of considerable discrepancies: the production of a type of Diesel engine was redirected from the Ganz Wagon to the Györ Wagon factory; on this occasion the following differences were observed in the production requirements:

	Ganz	Györ
Weight of the engine, lbs.	2,330	6,780
Weight of the materials, lbs.	8,330	12,270
Labor time expended, hours	1,852	3,600

30. Ibid., p. 129.

31. Kürthy, *Útmutató*, p. 36.

32. R. Hoch and A. Rédei, "The Main Principles of the Determination of Consumer Prices," *Yearbook*, p. 270.

such a way that the new consumer price should "fit" between the prices of similar commodities previously produced. Producer prices are determined by deducting the percentage rate of wholesale and retail trade mark-up and the turnover tax from the newly fixed consumer prices. Thus the use of the identification method entails the calculation of the turnover tax *from above,* whereas if the cost method is used, the turnover tax is calculated *from below.*[33] Now there exist two possibilities for the enterprise: if the producer price calculated by effecting the necessary deductions from the consumer price is higher than the cost of production, the enterprise is satisfied and keeps quiet. On the other hand, if the producer price calculated from above does not cover production costs, the firm applies for an increase of the consumer price or reduction of the turnover tax. If the enterprise's proposal is not accepted, it will incur a loss in the production of the commodity in question.[34]

The *subsidization method* is used in the calculation of prices in mining and metallurgy and for some chemical products. Here the planning authority does not want to burden the successive stages of production with a high price and fixes the price of these goods below their costs. This method is used also if the manufacturing of a product is in its initial stage and cost reductions are hoped for at a later date.

The procedure of price-fixing for nonstandardized products. Plan prices and current prices are identical for these products and the price refers to a single product or a limited number of products only. Examples are construction projects, assembling and mounting, machine industry, and most of the services. Institutionally, in the case of some industrial nonstandardized products, the method of price-fixing proceeds in the same way as described in connection with standardized products; for other nonstandardized industrial products the producer enterprise forms the price with the help of the official cost-calculation scheme, or on the basis of actual costs.[35] In the construction industry, however, technical plans and calculations are mostly prepared by the design bureaus, which are subordinated to the Ministry for Construction or (in

33. Ibid.
34. Ibid., p. 265.
35. B. Csikós Nagy, *Árpolitika az átmeneti gazdaságban* (*Price Policy of the Transitional Period*) (Budapest, 1958), pp. 93–94.

the case of railroad or road construction) to the Ministry for Transportation.[36] Now the construction enterprise presents a countercalculation, which may be accepted (in its entirety or partially) or rejected by the design bureau. If the enterprise is not satisfied with the decision of the design bureau, it can turn to its supervising ministry for price modification.

Price-fixing for nonstandardized products in the machine industry, in assembling and mounting and for most of the services, is based on calculated or actual current costs. The calculated or observed direct costs are supplemented by a percentage rate of indirect costs and with profit mark-up. Consequently, prices follow changes in costs.[37] The calculation of prices in the construction industry is based on estimated direct costs, augmented by a percentage rate of indirect costs fixed for different types of construction work, a mark-up for the so-called "costs arising from the special circumstances of the working place" and, for some projects, a cost mark-up due to special conditions in construction.[38]

The next question to be considered is the upward bias in the structure of Hungarian producer prices and the ways in which price rises have come about.

The incentives for the enterprise to increase prices are twofold: an increase in plan prices will raise the fulfillment of the production plan, and a rise in current prices will improve profitability. Since overfulfillment of the production plan and (from 1954 onward) of the profit plan means higher bonuses for the management, its material interest induces the firm to hammer out price increases. Moreover, the raising of current prices has been a compelling necessity from the viewpoint of the individual enterprise, in the face of rising wages and material costs.[39] The determination of new prices can be compared to a bargaining process [40] where the material interest of the firm in price rises

36. For small projects, technical plans and calculations are made by the construction enterprises themselves.

37. Cf. Turánszky, SSz, No. 12 (1956), 1039; and O. Lukács, "The Indices of Industrial Production," SSz, Nos. 1–2 (1958), 38.

38. B. Balassa, "Cost Estimates and Calculation," in Balassa and Bakonyi, Munkahelyi tájékoztató az épitöiparban (Workshop Administration in the Construction Industry) (Sztálinváros, 1955), pp. 150–80.

39. In 1955 the index of wages in manufacturing stood at 178.3, that of purchased energy at 103.7, of materials at 119.9—all on the 1949 basis (SE, p. 26, and Prices, p. 18).

40. See above, pp. 79 ff.

is not sufficiently counterbalanced by factors that would work
against the increase in prices.

It appears that the attempts made by the Planning Office (and
later by the Price Office) have not been successful in preventing
price increases. In this endeavor officials of the Planning Office
have often been hindered rather than helped by the ministries
which have had no interest in restraining the drive for price rises
In some directorates, where the employees received bonuses for
the overfulfillment of the plan (for example, in heavy industry)
the material incentive even pointed in the direction of higher
prices. Moreover, the supervising ministries have a moral interest
in overfulfilling the production plan and achieving profit on the
ministry level. A certain live-and-let-live attitude, which appeared
not only in the ministries but frequently in the Planning Office
itself, has also been conducive to price rises. In addition, a tech
nical factor of considerable importance should be mentioned: the
quantity of price calculations presented by the enterprise to the
price-fixing authorities has been so sizable that they have often
not had sufficient time to give careful consideration to these calcu
lations. Hungarian economists have observed that "the large
quantity of incoming price calculations makes the careful con
sideration of prices impossible. Only a few minutes are all that
are available for the determination of particular prices." [41]

Another reason for the upward bias in the price structure is
that the purchasers (state enterprises and consumers as well) have
no voice in the determination of prices. They can raise no objec
tion against high prices and have to accept the decisions of the
price-fixing authority, although this is often the ministry super
vising the producer. There is no bargaining between seller and
buyer; the buyer takes the price as given. Neither does excessive
or deficient demand for particular commodities exert any influ
ence on prices. As for the question of incentives, higher input
prices have no effect on fulfilling the production plan in the buyer
enterprise, but certainly do affect profitability. The endeavor of
the firm to increase profitability in the face of rising input prices
leads to a permanent drive for higher prices.

From the point of view of evaluating production results for the

41. Hoch and Rédei, Yearbook, p. 264. Italics in original. A similar opinion is
expressed in B. Csikós Nagy, "The Role of Prices in the Socialist Economy," KSz
No. 5 (1957), 489.

entire economy, the increase of plan prices deserves special consideration. The following practices serve this purpose.

1. The plan prices of new products being determined in the majority of cases on the basis of current costs, the enterprise endeavors to produce as many new commodities as possible. As the president of the Price Office observed: "Even a rigid authoritative price system cannot hinder price rises [in the form of] disguised price increases through the introduction of new products. Since the establishment of the official price list system, the number of new commodities has immensely increased." [42] To manufacture "new" products mostly either the quantity or quality of material or the quantity of labor used in production is changed; it is also pointed out that "the firm manufactures a 'new product' from the old one with insignificant technological changes." [43] The enterprise may change the woollen content of a fabric in the textile industry or the labor requirement of a product in the telecommunications industry, and present a new price calculation. In some cases, firms manufacturing a great variety of commodities ascribe costs arising in the production of "old" products to the "new" ones.

2. Lack of sufficient differentiation in the price system entices disguised price increases.[44] For many commodities, group prices have been established. The group prices were calculated on the basis of the average cost of production of commodities belonging to each particular group. Now the enterprises endeavor to produce commodities which have the lowest production cost. Since the initial percentage distribution of the products, which was taken into consideration in fixing the group price, is no longer relevant, the result is an implicit increase in the group price.[45]

3. The pricing of nonstandardized products in the machine industry, in mounting, assembling, and construction, where current prices have served as plan prices, has led to a continuous increase of the plan prices. This question will be taken up in more detail in Chapter 6.[46]

42. Csikós Nagy, *KSz*, No. 5 (1957), 487.

43. Kornai, p. 60. Similar conclusions are reached in Csikós Nagy, *KSz*, Nos. 8–9 (1957), 829, and in E. Jávorka, "The Incentive Role of the Industrial Producer Price System," *SzN*, May 15, 1956.

44. Kornai, p. 49.

45. O. Lukács, *Iparstatisztika* (*Industrial Statistics*) (Budapest, 1953), pp. 52–53.

46. See pp. 168 ff.

Planning and Pricing of Consumer Goods

In the planning of consumer goods, the central authorities first decide the share of national income to be used for consumption purposes. But this is not the only decision the planners make with regard to consumption. In Soviet-type economies not only the share of consumption in national income but also the quantities of the various types of consumer goods to be produced are centrally planned. The ideological justification of this method is that "Big Brother knows better." [47] The practical side of the matter is that—as a result of the restrictions on imports serving consumer needs—the production of consumer goods is constrained by nonavailabilities or short supply in certain materials or imported products (tropical fruits, animal hides, cotton, rubber, etc.) [48] and by existing production possibilities (as in the case of agricultural products). Furthermore, with the use of physical balances to check the compatibility of planning decisions, not only the aggregate amount of resources designed for consumption purposes but also the amount of resources used in the production of various types of consumer goods is decided upon centrally. It is not possible, for example, to set up a wool balance without centrally planning the quantity of woollen fabrics produced. Experiences suggests that in drawing up the physical balances consumer needs are far from being classified among targets of high priority.

The quantity produced of various *types* of consumer goods being determined by the planning authorities, the question to be answered is, how the quantity to be produced of *individual* commodities is decided upon. It is argued here that three sets of preferences determine the outcome: the planners', the firms', and the consumers' preferences.

The planners' preferences affect the production of consumer goods in two ways: first by determining quantities of various commodity groups (for example, cotton fabrics, shoes) and second by deciding also the quantities of some individual commodities (for example, radios, motorcycles). The firms' preferences assert themselves in the endeavor to produce—in the framework of the plan prescribed by the higher authorities—the assortment which is

47. This argument has been referred to above, p. 22.
48. This point is emphasized in Kornai, pp. 147–48.

most favorable for the fulfillment of the plan. The consumers' preferences come into play by rejecting the commodities not desired and by expressing their wishes for the consumption of commodities which, because of strong demand for them, appear almost permanently to be in short supply. The strength of these three sets of preferences in determining the production of various individual commodities may vary under different hypothetical conditions. Here we shall indicate what influence they have had in the Hungarian economy.

It can be glimpsed from both the long-term plans and the yearly plans that the central authorities plan in quantitative terms the production of such types of consumer goods as men's outer clothing, working clothes, women's underwear, etc., and also of some individual commodities such as bicycles and radios. The breakdown of these figures takes place partly in the ministries, partly in the enterprises. But even when the ministry gives a detailed assortment plan to the enterprise, the possibility of changing the prescribed output mix is by no means excluded, since the planning authorities endeavor to ensure the observation of the assortment plan mostly with moral exhortations rather than with material incentives.

In the practice of Hungarian planning the respective roles of the producers of consumption goods, the wholesale and retail trade organizations, and the consumers can be characterized as follows: Given the directives of the planning authorities, the enterprise endeavors to produce those commodities which contribute most to the fulfillment of the (production and profit) plan. The wholesale and retail trade organizations are frequently obliged to accept commodities even if they are not demanded by the consumers. In consequence, consumers find their choice restricted to commodities brought on the market largely as a result of decisions made by the planners and the producers.[49]

49. As Kornai has observed: "In theory it was always stated: 'the duty of the trade organizations is to represent the interest of the consumers,' 'the trade organizations should not accept defective commodities from the industry,' etc. But in practice this task of the trade organizations cannot be carried through, since its material preconditions are lacking. The trade managers are glad if they are able to get any commodities, thereby fulfilling their sales plan and obtaining bonuses. For the sake of this objective they disregard the various requirements. What industry is doing with the trade organizations, it is doing with the purchaser. They tell the consumer, politely or rudely, 'If you don't like it you should not buy it, but you don't get anything better at any other place either!'" (p. 132). See also Péter,

The enterprise's endeavor to fulfill the production and profit plan affects the production of consumer goods in two ways: by changing the assortment of such goods and by causing quality to deteriorate. The assortment of consumer goods, within the limits of the plan, is influenced by two factors, labor productivity and profitability. Commodities, in the production of which higher labor productivity can be achieved, ensure overfulfillment of the production plan with a given labor force; commodities of higher profitability ensure overfulfillment of the profit plan. Because of the separate standing of producer and consumer prices, profitability in production does not correspond to the price relations on the consumer market.[50] Modifications of the assortment along these lines has led to piling up unneeded consumer goods,[51] as has been described by the director of the planning department in the Wholesale Trade Directorate:

> In accordance with the present system of planning, the wholesale and retail trade organizations accept the unneeded commodities. Thereafter these commodities are stocked in the storehouses of the trade organizations; the consumers do not accept them . . . Many enterprises fulfilled the plan and received the appropriate bonuses; then the commodities were put into storage and after a lapse of a few years their value was written off at the expense of the state budget.[52]

---

p. 84. Kornai, p. 24, says the trade organizations have more influence on production in the shoe industry. Neglect of consumer preferences is also emphasized in Csikós Nagy, *Price Policy*, p. 357.

50. "Since consumer prices have generally had no effect on supply or production, the possibility that they could be employed as economic inducement to the fulfillment of production goals of the economic plan has not been tried . . . Better quality, more attractive finishing, and superior workmanship is generally expressed in the prices of consumer goods serving identical or closely related needs, whereas in producer prices—because of the formation of prices from below (cost + average profit)—this cannot be expressed": Jávorka, *KSz*, No. 2 (1957), 123. See also Kornai, p. 50. This statement is valid primarily in regard to group prices (cf. above), where quality differences are not expressed in the producer price. It is relevant for commodity groups with uniform turnover-taxes only if producer prices are not proportional to costs.

51. Often even the ministries supervising the producer do not object to the production of unneeded commodities (G. Csatár, "Ministry Chauvinism," *SzN*, February 12, 1956).

52. Péter, p. 84.

This statement can be illustrated with data of the Clothing Directorate of the Ministry for Domestic Trade, according to which there were 450,000 meters of cotton fabrics, 298,000 meters of silk fabrics, and 690,000 pairs of shoes in the inventories of the wholesale trade organizations of the clothing industry alone on December 31, 1955 which were considered unsalable.[53]

The enterprises also used deterioration of quality as a means for higher plan fulfillment. Quality deterioration may involve reducing the working time expended on the commodity, less careful handiwork, or using material of lower quality.[54] Reduction of quality can also be achieved through disguised price increases: by devising a new product with unimportant alterations but with a higher price. With regard to consumer goods, the use of this method has been reported by the chief of the Financial and Trade Department in the Ministry for Domestic Trade: " 'new' articles have been put out with minor, insignificant alterations and, because of this 'alteration,' at a disproportionately high price." [55] There is no reliable method to calculate the magnitude of quality deterioration and disguised price increases of consumer goods. As an approximate figure we can use the estimate of the Hungarian Statistical Bureau, according to which, other things being equal, the above-mentioned factors reduced the value of consumer goods by about 10.5 per cent in the period between 1949 and 1955.[56]

We turn now to the pricing of consumer goods. In a system of physical planning two methods can be used for distributing the consumer goods produced: outright rationing, or rationing by the use of prices to equate demand for every commodity with a given supply. The latter method may be combined with informal rationing if consumer prices do not equate supply and demand and shortages and surpluses ensue.

In Hungary outright rationing was used after the second World

---

53. Ibid., p. 97. These figures do not comprise the stock of unsalable commodities stored by the retail trade organizations.

54. Kornai, p. 54; Hoch and Rédei, *Yearbook*, p. 259. According to the Party paper, "the quality of several commodities has steadily deteriorated during the last months and years but their prices have remained unchanged" (*SzN*, September 25, 1956).

55. In Péter, pp. 83–84.

56. *Prices*, p. 71.

War until 1949, and was applied once more in 1951. Outright
rationing will not be dealt with here; we are concerned with the
use of market prices only. The existence of two parallel markets
should be noted—the state market and the free market.[57] The
share of the free market in retail turnover was 20 per cent in
1952, and it decreased to 15 per cent until 1955.[58] Changes in the
price level have been widely divergent on the two markets.
Whereas, according to the official price indexes, the retail price
level on the state market increased by 66.4 per cent from 1950
to 1954, the free market prices of agricultural products, which
constituted the bulk of the commodities sold on the free market,
rose by 126.1 per cent in the same period.[59] The sharp rise on the
free market implies the nonavailability of some commodities on
the state market. In the following we shall examine consumer
prices on the state market only.

In the Hungarian economy, as in other Soviet-type economies,
a dual price system is used. As has been mentioned above, in this
system consumer demand can be equilibrated with fixed supply,
if prices are devised so as to clear the market for every commodity. This can be achieved if the following conditions are
fulfilled: (a) the planning authorities determine the quantities
produced and the enterprises have no opportunity to change the
assortment of consumer goods, (b) the planners know the elasticity
of consumer demand for every commodity, (c) in case of changes
in demand or supply, prices are modified appropriately, and (d)
the sum of personal incomes equals the value of consumer goods
and services on the market.[60]

57. The free market in agricultural products, and also sales by artisans and
private retailers.
58. F. Vági, "The Purchasing Power and the Commodity Supply of the Population," Yearbook, p. 298.
59. Ibid., p. 301.
60. The need for consumer prices to equate supply and demand in physical
planning and some of the deficiencies of price determination for consumer goods
have been voiced by Hoch and Rédei: "The price ratios have the primary task of
ensuring the structural harmony of supply and demand; this (in the case of fixed
supply) can be secured—at least in theory—solely by changes in the price ratios.
One can always find a price at which there is neither excess supply nor excess demand. There is no doubt that centrally established and officially fixed price ratios
are not adaptable to changes in the structure of demand. Consequently, the system
of fixed prices—at least its presently known system—is a permanent source of transitional disequilibria between supply and demand. And this is one of the main reasons
why the presently known systems of socialism are characterized by almost permanent

Changes in assortment have already been examined in the first part of this section. Here the remaining problems will be taken up in turn.

Since 1951 in the Hungarian economy the so-called identification method has been used to determine most consumer prices.[61] As Hungarian economists have rightly observed,[62] the use of the identification method—fixing consumer prices on the basis of an outdated price list drawn up in 1951—leads to the neglect of the equalization of supply and demand on the markets of individual consumer goods. It has also been pointed out that the consumer prices of the 1951 price list did not reflect the supply and demand conditions prevailing at that time either, since the prices were fixed at the end of the rationing period (December 1, 1951), when it was not yet known how demand would respond to the abolition of rationing and to the new prices. The absence of demand studies has contributed to the deficiencies of price determination in 1951 and in later years. After promising research on demand elasticities conducted by the Hungarian Institute for Economic Research up to the dissolution of the Institute in 1949, there was a certain reluctance to use the tools of "bourgeois" economics.[63]

Another reason for the discrepancies between supply and demand has been the reluctance to change prices. Even if consumer demand had been properly estimated when prices were fixed, changes in demand would require modifications in prices. Yet the price-fixing authorities have not even had the authority to change prices formerly fixed by themselves. Changes in existing consumer prices have been looked upon as a political process, and modifications have only rarely been effected. Consequently discrepancies have continued to increase as demand and supply conditions changed, and even errors in price-fixing have not been remedied. To quote Hoch and Rédei again:

sometimes smaller, sometimes larger) shortages in commodities" (*Yearbook*, pp. 251–52. Italics in original).

61. See above, p. 105.

62. *Yearbook*, pp. 256–66. See also Kornai, p. 50.

63. The lack of computations on demand elasticities is noted by I. Varga, "Elasticity of Demand for Consumer Goods," *KSz*, Nos. 11–12 (1956), 1369–70. Ausch, also, notes that income and price elasticities have not been estimated: "Some Major Problems in the System of National Economic Balances, *KSz*, No. 6 (1958), 564. The importance of demand studies is emphasized in Csikós Nagy's *Price Policy*, pp. 271–72.

In our present price system the subsequent recognition of the right price cannot be utilized. Our price authorities do not have the right to modify previously approved prices, which can be altered only by the Council of the Ministers. Much time is needed to obtain such a modification, it requires so much correspondence, so many conferences that one has recourse to it in very exceptional cases only . . . As the saying goes, our commodity prices are firm as a rock, with prices fixed once and for all, which cannot follow the fluctuation of supply and demand.[64]

The main reasons for the absence of price changes are said to be political. It is forbidden to make small changes. If prices are reduced, the fact should be made conspicuous and be utilizable for political propaganda.[65] Price increases, however, are not trumpeted and are partly disguised by quality deterioration and hidden price increases—in this case on the initiative of the state rather than the enterprises.[66]

When changes in consumer prices were undertaken, a great number of commodities was affected. But one should not suppose that on the occasion of these price rearrangements economic considerations prevailed:

Rearrangements of prices of this kind were not preceded by careful and extensive economic research, or by a thorough going examination of the price ratios, or by an analysis of the present state and of the anticipated changes in supply and demand . . . "Political price reductions" of this kind may have detrimental economic consequences because of the lack of economic preparation. It depends on mere chance whether they cause incorrect price ratios to deteriorate further. In the form of disguised price changes, those economic inevitabilities which were not taken into account in modifying the prices will come to the surface. The disguised price increases impair the transitional political impact of the general price reduction.[67]

64. Hoch and Rédei, *Yearbook*, pp. 267–68.
65. Ibid., p. 268.
66. Ibid., p. 261. Vági, *Yearbook*, p. 289.
67. Hoch and Rédei, pp. 268–69.

Use of these methods in the planning and pricing of consumer goods has resulted in surpluses and shortages in many commodities. As we have seen, the surpluses have caused a piling up of unsalable stocks of commodities. Sometimes discounts have been applied to get rid of the stocks. Primarily in village stores, but also in towns, tied-in sales have been used, where the purchase of one commodity was made a condition of the acquisition of another that the consumer actually intended to buy. The shortages have had informal rationing as a corollary. Up to the time of the Revolution, meat, dairy products, high quality fabrics, motorcycles, many household implements, etc. were in short supply. These commodities were allocated partly on a first come, first served basis, partly (for example, meat) by queues formed as a commodity made its appearance in the stores, partly by good "connections," which could help in the purchase of the desired commodity. Some of these commodities were resold with profit by lucky purchasers.

During the years of planning, shortages have been of considerably greater importance than surpluses. Three reasons can be given for this phenomenon: first, the purchasing power of the population exceeded the value of the available goods; secondly, the population was anxious to purchase the available goods as prices kept rising; and thirdly, the nonavailability of certain commodities induced the population to buy goods they would not have bought if they had had wider choice.

The situation of the Hungarian consumer has been well characterized by Péter:

> The domestic consumers have no possibility of implementing their demands . . . The workers—the purchasers—do not have much choice; they cannot set up requirements, since the supply of commodities is deficient in many respects in quantity as well. A part of the consumer goods are only rarely available and are difficult to procure . . . Under these circumstances, the purchaser is at the mercy of the distributive organizations and ultimately of the enterprises which produce these goods: he is forced to buy the less suitable and the more expensive commodity.[68]

68. Péter, pp. 46–47.

In view of the preceding discussion, one could add that—besides the behavior of enterprises—the shortcomings in the planning of consumer goods and the deficiencies in pricing should also be blamed for this situation.

After consideration of the micro-aspect of our problem (surplus and shortage on the markets of particular consumer goods), we turn to the macro-aspect: the relation of personal income to the value of available consumer goods. It is maintained by some people that "inflation is apparently an indispensable aspect of the working of the Soviet economic system." [69] I disagree with this opinion, and maintain that inflation can be avoided in a Soviet-type economy, and that if there *is* inflation, it is mostly due to deliberate action. Inflation ensues if there are more claims to consumption than the value of consumer goods and services available. The balance of personal income, which confronts the planned value of wages and other income of the population with the planned value of consumer goods and services, makes it possible to avoid inflation.[70] Deviations from the planned figures [71] can be remedied by budgetary measures; thus the value of money used by the population is decided upon by the planning authority. Nevertheless, deficiencies in planning can result in shortages and surpluses in various commodities.

Inflation in 1949–53 in Hungary was also "planned." According to not widely publicized official views, the disproportionality between personal income and available commodities was considered desirable.[72] The propounders of these views referred to a statement made by Stalin back in the thirties, according to which "in the Soviet Union, the purchasing power of the people is constantly growing and *exceeds* the growth of production." [73] A

69. F. J. Mladek, E. Sturc, and M. R. Wyczalkowski, "The Change in the Yugoslav Economic System," *International Monetary Fund Staff Papers* (November 1952), p. 21.

70. A similar opinion is expressed by J. Marczewski, *Planification et croissance économique des démocraties populaires* (Paris, Presses Universitaires, 1956), 2, 428, and in Csikós Nagy, *Price Policy*, pp. 348, 354.

71. Discrepancies may occur, for example, because of poor harvest, changes in personal savings, and difficulties in estimating income *in natura,* and in separating the commodities purchased by the population and by the state enterprises. Cf A. Csernok, "Personal Income Balance of the Population and Estimation of Purchasing Power," *SSz*, Nos. 8–9 (1957), 656–72. Disparities can also occur if nonplanned credit is extended to the enterprise and the credit is used to hire additional workers.

72. Kornai, p. 158; Csikós Nagy, *Price Policy*, pp. 349–50.

73. "Report to the Sixteenth Congress of the Communist Party of the Soviet Union," *Stalin's Collected Works*, in Hungarian (Budapest, 1950), p. 345. My italics

Polish economist has advised me, moreover, that Stalin in another place explicitly states the necessity for the deterioration of the value of money in the period of building socialism. The application of this method has psychological implications. The enormous investment activity requires the restriction of consumption. This goal can be achieved by the use of two methods: holding down wages, and debasing the value of money.

The implicit assumption in the use of the second method is that the first cannot be solely relied upon, and the extent of the sacrifice forced upon the people should be partly disguised. In other words, it is assumed that the wage earners are lulled by a money illusion: they watch, primarily, money wages rather than real wages.[74] It is another question whether this device really works. In my opinion people are less real-wage conscious if changes in the value of money are not continuous and/or the speed of inflation is negligible. If the inflation process is continuous and speedy, workers are very much aware of price changes and even anticipate them. The Hungarian inflation, up to the period of the New Course, was of considerable magnitude. People, having no reliable cost-of-living index to calculate with, used arbitrary indicators (the price of lard, bread, etc.). A good case can be made for the conclusion that the Hungarian people, partly because of their mistrust in the government, partly because of their "propensity to exaggerate" sacrifices, overestimated the degree of inflation and thereby the reduction in real wages.[75] This would not be the only case where totalitarian propaganda had an effect contrary to that desired.[76]

EVALUATION OF PRICING IN HUNGARY

Consumer prices have been scrutinized in the previous chapter and will not be considered here. With regard to producer prices, two questions should be answered: How do Hungarian prices reflect scarcities, and how can these prices be used to choose among alternatives in production, investment, and exports?

It can be stated that, because of the following factors, Hungar-

74. For a similar view see Zauberman, *Review of Economic Studies, 16,* 110.

75. The detrimental psychological effects of the disguised reduction of real wages have been pointed out by Hoch and Rédei, and by Vági in *Yearbook,* pp. 261, 289; and by Csikós Nagy in *Price Policy,* p. 412.

76. On this point see B. Balassa, "Zur Psychologie des Kollektivizmus," *Junge Wirtschaft, 2* (1957), 74–76.

ian producer prices fall short of the first objective and fail to re
flect the scarcities of the economy: [77]

1. It has been indicated that in physical planning the demand
side is neglected in the determination of prices.

2. Producer prices based on labor costs leave out of account
the scarcity of capital and material resources as well as differences
between average and marginal costs.

3. Since in Hungary the majority of the commodities are pro
duced in one enterprise only, the accidents of specialization
greatly influence the price ratios. Errors in specialization are re
vealed only if a product is redirected from one factory to another;
otherwise one cannot be certain whether specialization has been
rightly effected and how costs (and prices) would differ if the
commodity were manufactured in another enterprise.

4. Supply and demand relations are largely neglected in price
determination,[78] and surpluses and shortages rarely lead to modifications of producer prices.

5. Hungarian producer prices of 1957 still reflected to some
degree the price relations of the prewar period.

6. During the period under consideration the products of
heavy industry were considerably undervalued and those of light
and food industries overvalued.[79]

77. In the evaluation of producer prices we abstract from world market relations. Problems connected with international trade are introduced below, p. 172.

78. It has been stated that "in the entire framework of price determination we
do not find a single organization that would even try to weigh the supply and demand relations in fixing prices" (Hoch and Rédei, *Yearbook*, p. 265). See also Kornai,
p. 50.

79. The existence of over- and undervaluation can be seen in the following
figures, which show the magnitude of price changes required to equate the existing
prices with prices of the value type or of the production-price type:

	Prices of the Value Type	Prices of the Production-price Type
Coal	+100	+60
Electrical energy	+15	+50
Chemical products	−10	0
Metallurgical products	+95	+100
Machines, technical products	+25	+37
Construction materials (without lumber)	+15	+10
Products of light industry	−30	−44
Lumber and related products	−10	−15
Food	−12	−9

These figures show considerable deviation from actual prices, whether prices of
the value type or the production-price type are used as a standard of comparison.

The irrational character of Hungarian producer prices has resulted in the distortion of comparisons of production, investment,
and export alternatives. The irrationality of decisions based on
irrational prices has been voiced by some Hungarian economists.
The following quotation shows the pitfalls of pricing in Soviet-
type economies:

> The interests of the national economy require in our country
> that enterprises, wherever possible, should use other materi-
> als—for example, concrete—instead of lumber. The major
> part of lumber must be imported; its procurement is expen-
> sive, while concrete is cheaper. But the centrally fixed price
> of lumber is lower than that of concrete. Now, since costs
> do not appear where they emerge, nobody can make out
> which should be used. What is expensive is "cheap" and what
> is cheap is "expensive." On the one hand, we require the en-
> terprises to manufacture their products with the least possi-
> ble expense, at the lowest cost: consequently they should use
> more lumber, since it is "cheaper" and the substitution of
> concrete for lumber will show an increase in costs, hence a
> loss in the accounts. On the other hand, since we have to
> have an eye on the interests of the national economy, which
> are more important than the interests of the enterprises, it
> is better if the firms do not use lumber, because it is more
> "expensive," etc. Accordingly, the operation of the firms is
> the more economical for the national economy the higher
> the cost of products, the greater the loss—the deficit—and the
> greater the substitution of concrete for lumber.[80]

It is added in a footnote that the Council of Ministers subsequently changed the price ratios of lumber and concrete. The
question arises: Was the irrationality really removed? No definite
answer can be given. In the face of the indeterminacy of prices
there is no guarantee that the planners will chance upon the
"right" price ratios. Furthermore—to introduce world market
considerations for the moment—it is conceivable that under a
more extensive international division of labor the price of lumber would decrease sufficiently to make the substitution of lumber for concrete economical.

The lumber-concrete example is one among many. On the

80. Péter, p. 119.

basis of current prices, choices have been made among alternative methods in production, investment, and export, and it has often not been realized that the arbitrary nature of these prices interferes with the making of rational decisions. It may be objected that in a great number of cases the deviations of current prices from scarcity prices will probably not entail the choice of the "wrong" alternative. Although this is certainly true in some cases, the discrepancies between present prices and prices of the production price type [81] makes one rather skeptical about this point. In view of the large numbers of possible alternatives in exports or investments, these differences may easily turn the balance, especially in choosing between more or less capital-intensive methods. The inference can be drawn that in the limited field of decision-making where current prices are used in making choices among alternatives, the existence of a fairly sizable margin of error renders the calculations to a considerable degree inconclusive. Nevertheless, if Hungary were to shift to the use of a price system of the production price type, the possibility of error would narrow down, although—in view of the considerations presented above [82] —it would not disappear.[83]

81. See above, n. 79.
82. See p. 101.
83. It should be noted that the price reform in 1958 retained the dual price system but mostly dispensed with the undervaluation of investment goods (Csikós Nagy, *Price Policy*, pp. 92–95).

5. The Economics of the Firm

THE MODEL OF INDUSTRIAL ORGANIZATION IN HUNGARY

IN PHYSICAL PLANNING the participants of the economic process enter into two kinds of relationships: vertical (hierarchy of various organizations) and horizontal (relationship between sellers and buyers). In what follows, the vertical and horizontal relationships of industrial organizations will be examined in the framework of the Hungarian economy.

Vertical Relationships

We have already described the hierarchical structure of Hungarian industry.[1] The reader will recall that whereas the Planning Office and the general departments of the ministries are concerned with planning and issue general directives, the directorates of the ministries, besides their function in planning, direct productive activity. In some industries, intermediate organizations—trusts —are interposed between the directorates and the enterprises; in others the directorates are in direct contact with the enterprises, or a mixed form of organization is used where trusts and independent enterprises belong to the same directorate.

In 1956 there were six industrial ministries (including construction),[2] ten to fifteen directorates in each ministry, and ten to twenty enterprises (partly supervised by a trust, partly independent) in each directorate. Enterprises of local importance were subordinated to the local administrative organizations and, indirectly, to the Ministry of City and Town Administration.

The intermediate organizations, the trusts, comprise vertically or horizontally integrated firms. In the former case, the trust combines enterprises which form a single production process (for ex-

1. See above, p. 57.
2. The Ministries for Mining and Electrical Energy, Chemical Industry, Metallurgy and Engineering, Light Industry, Food Industry, and Construction. Other economic ministries were Finance, Agriculture, State Farms, Crop Collections, Domestic Trade, Foreign Trade, and Transportation.

ample, iron foundries, coke ovens, and steel mills belong to the same trust); in the latter, enterprises performing the same productive activity are scattered over a certain area, and the trust is designed to alleviate the task of direction and supervision for the ministry. The two types of trusts can be combined; for example in 1955 the largest Hungarian construction trust consisted of two building construction firms, three civil engineering construction firms, and one firm each for interior installations, prefabrication, and provision for the workers. We shall not deal with the intermediate organizations here but will be concerned only with the relationship between ministry (directorate) and enterprise.

The distinguishing characteristics of the enterprise are its separate plan, separate balance sheet, an account with the National Bank or the Investment Bank, and an allotment of fixed and circulating capital. The chief executives of the enterprise are the director, chief engineer, and chief accountant. The director bears full responsibility for the execution of the superior authorities' orders and the enterprise's performance. The chief engineer is the first deputy of the director. He is the manager of production, being responsible for the technical operation of the firm. The chief accountant is the second deputy of the director and not only is the head of accounting and bookkeeping but also is concerned with the economical operation of the enterprise.

To see the actual operation of the hierarchical structure in Hungarian industry, we have to review the main channels through which the enterprise's work is directed and controlled: [3]

1. The dictated targets of the plan prescribe the production of a number of commodities in quantitative terms, as well as the quality and assortment of the products and the value and cost of production.

2. Most of the materials, and almost without exception the important ones, are allocated centrally, in the framework of the plan of material allocation.

3. In the field of labor, the number of employees in different categories, the wage rates, most of the norms, and the total wages-fund are prescribed partly by the plan, partly through regulations issued by the Planning Office, by the Wages and Labor Department of the Secretariat to the Council of Ministers, and by the ministries.

4. The ministry appoints the chief executives (director, chief

3. Some of these factors are mentioned in Kornai, pp. 166–68.

engineer, chief accountant) of the firm and instructs the enterprise also in connection with the appointment of department heads and other chief employees. The ministry can relieve the chief executives of their posts at its discretion at any time.

5. The allocation, planning, financing, and supervising of investments and renewals are the tasks of the Planning Office, the ministries, and the Investment Bank.

6. The financial and credit system carries on banking functions. The firm keeps an account with the National Bank or with the Investment Bank, and excepting small amounts payments are made through this account only. The bank which holds the firm's account also extends credit to the enterprise and supervises its financial operation.

7. Foreign trade is carried on through the state trading companies; the producer cannot do export or import business directly with foreign purchasers or suppliers.[4]

8. The right of price determination is exercised by the Planning Office (since 1957 by the Price Office) and by the ministries.

9. Given the framework of the plan and the regulations issued by various authorities, the main task of the directorates consists in the operational direction of the firm's productive activity.[5]

10. Control of the enterprise's operation is the task of various organizations such as the State Control Office, the Ministry of Finance, the National Bank, the Investment Bank, and the ministries.

These are the manifold ways in which the productive activity of the enterprise is directed. We now turn to the principal factors that contributed to the extensive centralization of decision-making.

First, in a system of physical planning the main decisions on

---

4. In 1956 some exceptions were made in machine export.

5. The activity of the directorate may be seen by comparing the number of employees engaged in various activities. In 1956 the Directorate No. 1 of the Ministry for Construction, which directed and supervised the operation of three trusts (with fifteen enterprises) and three independent firms—all of them engaged in the construction of projects of national importance—employed the following staff in its various departments: director, 1; planning and statistical department, 5; labor department, 4; department of material allocation, 4; chief engineer and "dispatchers" to direct and supervise production, 11; financial department, 7; administration, 3; total, 35. Only the planning and statistical department was engaged in planning and in collecting data; all other departments were concerned with the direction and control of the enterprise's operations and spent only a small fraction of their time on planning.

production and allocation are made centrally. Although decentralization can be carried out in some fields of decision-making, substantial decentralization in physical planning will be self-defeating, since in the absence of scarcity prices and sufficient incentives for the enterprises to serve the interests of the national economy it may lead to results opposed to the planners' objectives.[6]

Secondly, the supreme role of central orders has ideological implications in Soviet-type economies. Stalin's famous statement according to which "our plans are not plan predictions, not plan guesses, but plan orders," [7] remained, until recently, the fountainhead of the doctrine which exalted central orders (especially those coming from the Party) and snubbed the use of economic incentives to implement the objectives of the national economy. This doctrine was criticized in Hungarian economic journals in 1956 and 1957, but in 1958 the supreme role of centralized decision-making was emphasized again, and the decision-making process underwent no significant modifications throughout the post-Revolutionary period.

Thirdly, the lack of reserves also contributes to extensive centralization. In the absence of sufficient reserves, the planning authorities endeavor to allocate the given (or expected) supply of most materials centrally and attempt to solve the difficulties arising from the short supply of materials through administrative regulations.[8]

At the same time these factors lead to excessive centralization of the economy's management they contribute to the rise of contradictions in centralized decision-making which often defeat its very purpose:

(1) In a developing economy, the increasing complexity of planning diminishes the possible scope of centralized decision-making. As G. Kopácsy observes, "the more developed the productive forces and the social division of labor, the less satisfactory the direction of the economy through plan orders." [9]

6. Marczewski rightly observes that "the absence of a rational price system and interest rate . . . obstructs an effective decentralization of decision-making," *Planification et croissance économique des démocraties populaires*, 2, 519.

7. Report to the Fifteenth Congress of the Soviet Communist Party. Stalin, *Collected Works* (Hungarian ed.), *10* (Budapest, 1952), 350.

8. For additional arguments see above, pp. 85–86.

9. "For the Improvement of Our Planning," *KSz*, No. 2 (1957), 139.

(2) The endeavor to decide everything in the center comes into conflict with the impossibility of seeing every detail, since "the centralized preparation of a detailed program for an entire industry is such a colossal task, that . . . details invariably get lost." [10]

(3) Detailed decisions made in advance are partly defeated by the need for subsequent modifications. It requires a great deal of administrative work, and an apparatus even greater than that at present, to effect the necessary modifications in every part of the plan. As a result, in many cases only some plan indicators are modified, thereby creating disproportionalities between various parts of the ministry's and the enterprise's plan. [11]

(4) Central allocation of materials comes into contradiction with the enterprise's endeavor to pile up materials. Hoarding of materials is induced by a lack of flexibility in the centralized system of allocation in catering to the firm's needs. [12]

(5) The endeavor to bind the enterprise's hands in many fields conflicts with the actual need to disregard some of the regulations for the sake of carrying out others.

The last point brings us to the consideration of the role played by the enterprises in Hungarian planning. It has been said that "the directorate exercises some of the basic functions of the director of the firm." [13] Hungarian economists speak about "the binding hand and foot of the enterprise, the regulation of every kind of essential and nonessential activity from above." [14] Nevertheless, enterprises find leeway in the formal system of comprehensive regulations. Marczewski has aptly characterized the system of centralized regulations in Soviet-type economies as an overdetermined equation system, where "the manager of the enterprise, whose responsibility is theoretically reduced to the execution of the decisions made by the superior authorities, actually assumes a responsibility much more formidable than the capitalist entre-

10. Kornai, p. 43.
11. Ibid., p. 29.
12. See above, pp. 75–76.
13. Kornai, p. 25.
14. S. Balázsi, "Workers' Councils, Autonomy of the Enterprises, Industrial Management," *KSz*, Nos. 11–12 (1956), 1295. Also: "Central decrees have regulated the entire operation of industry in great detail and have made merely executing organizations of the enterprises and their directors": J. Bokor, O. Gadó, P. Kürthy, T. Meitner, S. Sárosi, and J. Wilcsek, "Proposal for a New Method in the Economic Management of Industry," *KSz*, No. 4 (1957), 372.

preneur: to be able to manage the enterprise, he has to disregard knowingly a part of the orders received." [15] In Hungary the managers, "ground between the millstones of a great variety of often contradictory regulations" [16] have shown extraordinary ingenuity in getting around the rigid system of central orders. As Péter notes "We have 'regulated' the operation of the enterprises . . . we have created 'walls,' which in many cases necessarily induced the enterprises to find openings on the 'fences,' on the 'walls'—and such holes were easily found—or induced them to find easy solutions in directions where they faced no restrictions, no walls." [17]

The internal contradictions of excessive centralization coupled with the enterprise's endeavor to circumvent the central regulations have resulted in a rather messy situation. Theoretically, the economy has been directed by itemized plan orders, detailed regulations. Actually, only some of these decisions have been carried out. Deviations from central regulations have partly served the interest of the national economy—avoiding disruptions in production by procuring materials from outside the official allocation system or paying wages higher than permitted—and have partly conflicted with the planners' objectives by bringing about changes in assortment of products, deteriorating quality, etc. Péter, in his capacity as Chairman of the Hungarian State Committee for Industrial Organization, described the tangle created by these contradictory factors: "It is often said that excessive centralization has been the principal fault of the methods applied so far. In reality, however . . . the central decisions have not been effective at all . . . It is not some type of excessive centralization that has been predominant in the management by the state, but the opposite: many elements of anarchy have appeared . . ." [18]

Alongside the inconsistencies in the intricate web of regulations, another reason for the frequent disregard of central orders is that the enterprise resents the ministry's operational direction. The managers dislike any interference with their work and often speak with contempt of the ministerial officials who have never earned their pay. The main motive for disobeying central regu-

15. *Planification*, 2, 485.
16. I. Tatár, "Actual Problems of Our Foreign Trade," *KSz*, No. 2 (1957), 201.
17. Péter, p. 42.
18. *NSz*, February 3, 1957.

lations lies, however, in the enterprise's material interest, a detailed examination of which is presented in the next section.

Horizontal Relationships

In Chapter 3 we examined the formal aspect of the seller-buyer relationship: the drawing up of the enterprise's plan and the system of procurement contracts. Here we shall be concerned with the informal side, the problem of motivation and its impact on the relations between producer and user.

In a free enterprise economy the productive work of the enterprise is realized only if purchasers have been found for the commodities produced. In the Hungarian economy, as in other Soviet-type economies, production results are realized as soon as the production process has been finished. The producer has no interest in catering to the users' needs, but only in fulfilling the plan.[19] He is indifferent whether the buyers are satisfied with the assortment, quantity, and quality of the commodities. His energy is directed toward abstract production results, and toward obtaining bonuses through the fulfillment of the production and profit plan.[20] Although there is a certain moral pressure on the producer to manufacture the needed commodities, his material interest often proves to be stronger. If the commodities produced do not conform to the users' needs, ultimately they may buy them for lack of more suitable products, or the goods will remain unsalable and be discarded at a later date. There is no competition between producers: no producer will undersell or bring the "right" goods on the market if another enterprise fails to do so.

The chauvinism of the producer is not confined to the enterprise but extends to the supervising ministry as well. We have pointed out that for prestige reasons the producing ministries are also interested in fulfilling the production and profit plan. It should be added that a particular form of chauvinism develops when the ministry wants to help its own enterprise against the ministry of the buyer.[21] If the seller and buyer belong to the same

19. See "The Economical Use of Materials," *SSz*, No. 12 (1955), 1053.

20. "Our managers frequently see not the purchaser—whether the consumers, foreign trade, or a big investment project—but only the global figures of the plan" (G. Csatár, "Steady Production," *SzN*, January 15, 1956).

21. "The producing ministries have the task of allocating their products but are

ministry but to different directorates, a similar conflict can be perceived between the directorates. It has been noted that "in the interest of the reputation of the ministry, some leaders of the ministries frequently condone or even encourage the enterprise to produce, for the sake of plan fulfillment, commodities not needed in the national economy." [22]

From the foregoing discussion one can see that the material interest of the producer in abstract plan fulfillment coupled with the lack of incentives to produce commodities in conformity with the purchasers' wishes—and with support from the supervising ministry in these activities—leads to neglect of the users' needs.[23] This is how enterprises behave as sellers; now we turn to the question of how they act as purchasers.

In a free enterprise economy (except during periods of shortages, as in a war) the main concern of an enterprise is to sell its commodities, and it faces little difficulty in procuring the means of production. In the Hungarian and other Soviet-type economies, the reverse is true: the enterprise encounters no problems in marketing but is hampered in procuring materials and intermediate products by the rigidity of its plan, lack of reserves, and the producers' lack of interest in catering to the users' needs.[24] Péter has expressed this by saying that in the Hungarian economy we have competition of buyers instead of competition of sellers.[25] Because of difficulties in material procurement and shortages in many commodities, buyers are in a disadvantageous position in regard to sellers. As a result they cannot control quality, dimensions, and assortment; they must be satisfied with commodities made available by the producers even if these are not quite suitable for their needs. As Kornai says, "the user, whether a factory or a marketing or import firm, cannot set up strict requirements

---

not interested in production and allocation according to actual needs. The interests of the users are frequently the victim of the producers' chauvinism." Sovány, "Theoretical Problems in Simplifying Our Material Allocation System," *KSz*, No. 9 (1956), 1049.

22. G. Csatár, "On Ministry Chauvinism," *SzN*, February 12, 1956.

23. "Objective conditions make it possible for the producer (enterprise, ministry) to organize its production primarily on the basis of its own interests (fulfillment of the plan, profitability, etc.) and not in compliance with other enterprises' needs" (Sovány, p. 1047).

24. Péter, p. 93.

25. Péter, p. 94. In Western economics the concept "sellers' market" corresponds to the term "buyers' competition."

for the supplier . . . The hungry man is not choosy. The enterprise which is hungry for materials does not raise objections about the quality and assortment of the supplied materials." [26]

The Hungarian press often publishes complaints which show that because of the subservient role of purchasers, "frequently defective products and products in dimensions differing from those required are supplied, and the user is often constrained to rework some of the material (for example, to reforge it) in order to avoid more waste and spoilage." [27] And purchasers are reluctant to protest if quality is deficient or the dimensions do not conform to requirements, since in such a case "the factory answers by punishing: it does not deliver for a time." [28] The purchaser has no voice in determining prices either, and must accept higher prices if the producer succeeds in hammering out a price increase at the price-fixing agency which is often his supervising ministry.

The question arises, is the user really interested in high quality, accurate dimensions, low prices, etc.? He is, to a certain degree, since thereby his own plan fulfillment will be served. But he can include the higher price, and in a number of cases also the cost of reworking materials, in the price he charges for his own products. Moreover, if he can claim defective materials, he may be able to conceal deficiencies in his own production. In general, the line of resistance is always weaker at the next stage of production than at the preceding stage. We have a situation in which producers blame one another for every shortcoming in production, and these shortcomings become cumulative in the national economy. It is little exaggeration to say that buyers' competition "is the most expensive method possible, since—as experience shows—it results in deterioration of the quantity, quality, and cost indicators of production and becomes an obstacle to development." [29]

In this section we have reviewed the vertical and horizontal structure of Hungarian industry. In the remaining portions of the chapter we shall examine the workings of the planning mechanism from the viewpoint of the enterprise, and attempt to devise a theory of the firm in Soviet-type economies on the basis of the Hungarian experience.

26. Kornai, p. 145.
27. Sovány, *KSz*, No. 9 (1956), 1047.
28. *SzN*, February 8, 1955.
29. Péter, p. 115.

The Maximization of Bonuses

The Maximization Process in the Enterprise [30]

The directors of a socialist firm manage it under the constraints imposed upon it by the planning authorities. These constraints have been described: the production plan, centralized allocation of materials, operational direction by the directorates, etc. It has been emphasized that managers attempt to break out of the web of regulations, their objective being that the enterprise should serve their own material interest. This is achieved by the maximization of bonuses.

Under conditions of a free enterprise economy, the theory of the firm is built upon the maximization of profit. Although it has been noted that there are objectives other than profit—prestige, power, a quiet life, etc.—and there is much discussion on questions whether short-run or long-run profits should be maximized,[31] the principle of profit maximization continues to be central to the theory of the firm. But in a socialist firm profit is not the main objective. Profits are appropriated by the state, and in present-day Soviet economies the bonuses of the managers are related not merely to profit but to other factors as well. The principle of rational behavior, however, implies a maximization process [32] in the socialist firm as well; here it takes the form of the maximization of bonuses.[33] In other words, the operation of the firm is directed in such a way that bonuses will be maximized over a certain period. This is propelled by the same motive—material interest—that induces the capitalist entrepreneur to maximize profits.

30. On problems connected with the objectives of the firm in the Soviet Union cf. D. Granick, *Management of the Industrial Firm in the U.S.S.R.*, New York, Columbia University Press, 1954; and J. S. Berliner, *Factory and Manager in the U.S.S.R.*, Cambridge, Harvard University Press, 1957.

31. Problems of profit maximization in an economy with oligopolistic market structures are treated in W. Fellner, *Competition among the Few* (New York, Knopf, 1949), chaps. 4–7.

32. Cf. Samuelson, *Foundations of Economic Analysis*, chap. 3.

33. In practice bonuses are paid to chief executives of the enterprise, to most of the technical employees, and to the leading administrative employees on the basis of the firm's performance measured by certain indicators. For brevity's sake we shall use the word "managers" to denote all employees who receive bonuses. In addition to the bonuses received by this group, other groups of white-collar workers also get a small amount of extra remuneration.

To understand the importance of bonus maximization one must realize that in Soviet-type economies the basic salaries of technical and administrative employees are rather low. In Hungary in 1956 an engineer received about 1,600 forints (in U.S. purchasing power approximately $110) monthly; the basic salary of the chief of the financial department in a medium firm was about 1,700–1,800 forints ($120–40); and that of the director in a firm of similar size approximately 2,500 forints ($170). Since the salaries of most of these employees were barely sufficient for the necessities of life, purchases of conveniences and luxuries were tied to receipt of bonuses. The maximum amount of bonuses was quite substantial: in 1956 in high-priority industries (such as heavy and construction industries), bonuses could amount to 75 per cent of the basic salary, in low-priority industries (such as light industry) to 50 per cent. The actual amount of bonuses ranged from zero to the maximum percentage. In heavy and construction industries bonuses averaged 35 to 50 per cent, in light industry 22 to 29 per cent (in different quarters of 1955).[34]

The bonuses have actually become a quasi-permanent part of the managers' income. They regard them as an intrinsic part of the salary. As Kornai observes, managers organize their household, their living in such a way that they definitely expect bonuses. The balance of their family budget will be upset if they have to do without them. Consequently managers of the enterprises regard it as self-evident that they *must* obtain bonuses."[35] In other words, the endeavor to ensure a decent standard of living compels the leading employees of an enterprise to regard obtaining bonuses as their principal goal.

Although maximization of bonuses is the basic objective of management—similarly to a capitalist enterprise—there also are other objectives: promotion, prestige, achieving specific goals, etc. Some of these goals, however, are connected with material interest. For example, the prestige of the enterprise increases as the firm grows; this increase gives occasion to a raise in salary for leading employees and excludes the danger of incorporation into other enterprises, which would mean elimination of some leading positions. Fulfillment of specific targets is often related to special bonuses (for example, extra bonuses can be obtained by

34. Kornai, p. 67.
35. Ibid., p. 69. Italics in original.

finishing the construction of factory buildings of great urgency before the original deadline). The importance of noneconomic motives, such as the endeavor to please Party officials, should not be exaggerated. This consideration is of decidedly less importance than commonly assumed. Besides, in the Hungarian economy Party officials are themselves by and large satisfied with the attainment of objectives necessary for securing bonuses.[35a]

The Premium Conditions

We turn now to the conditions which need to be fulfilled in order to obtain bonuses. (These conditions will be called, using another word for bonuses, premium conditions.) In the first years of planning, up to 1951, these conditions varied according to categories of employees. Premium conditions of chief executives were regulated by the ministry; for other employees the director of the firm determined them on the basis of general regulations. These conditions were highly differentiated, since an attempt was made to fit them to individual cases. This procedure led to a great deal of administrative work (in one construction enterprise an employee had no duties other than to devise premium conditions and calculate the bonuses for fifty people; his principal premium condition was to calculate the bonuses on time), to falsifications (premium conditions were often set only *ex post facto*), and to disproportionate bonuses.

By 1952 the premium conditions had been unified and were based, with insignificant exceptions, on fulfillment of the production plan. In the second half of 1954 this condition was supplemented by fulfillment of the profit plan.[36] Fulfillment of the profit plan was first introduced as a subsidiary condition: if the enterprise failed to show a profit, only 50 per cent of the bonuses calculated on the basis of the production plan fulfillment were paid out; later it became a full condition. Introduction of profitability as a premium condition was not simultaneous in all industries. In the construction industry, for example, fulfillment of the production plan was the sole premium condition until the second half of 1955, when profitability was introduced as a sub-

35a. A similar opinion is expressed in Kornai, pp. 95–96.

36. J. Lacfalvi and R. Wagner, "Bonuses and the Effects of the Bonus System in Industry," *SSz*, No. 7 (1956), 590.

sidiary condition: in case of losses, bonuses were not paid. From the beginning of 1956 bonuses up to 25 per cent of the basic salary were paid on the basis of plan fulfillment in production and, additionally, up to 50 per cent for fulfilling the profit plan.

Calculation of the percentage rate of bonuses has varied in different industries. In some, bonuses have been paid for 100 per cent fulfillment of the production plan, in others only if fulfillment was above 100 per cent. To use the example of the construction industry again, in 1956 a 2 per cent bonus was paid for every one per cent overfulfillment of the production plan above 100 per cent (the maximum being 25 per cent for 112.5 per cent plan fulfillment); a 10 per cent bonus was paid for fulfilling the profit plan, and an additional 5 per cent for every one per cent increase in profits until 50 per cent was reached.

Up to 1955, in most industries, 50 per cent of the bonuses was paid monthly, the remaining 50 per cent at the end of the quarter. In the construction industry, and since 1955 in other industries as well, bonuses have been calculated and paid in every quarter. The calculation of bonuses is not cumulative; every quarter is considered independently.

In the Hungarian economy fulfillment of the production plan and profit plan have been the premium conditions during recent years. *Fulfillment of the production plan* has been measured in different ways in different industries:

1. finished production: value of finished production + services (used in the leather and furniture industry in 1955);

2. full production: finished production ± change in the stock of unfinished and semifinished products (used in the shoe and clothing industry and in most branches of heavy industry);

3. corrected (gross) production: full production + produced or purchased intermediate products (used in the wool, cotton, silk, and paper industries and in some branches of heavy industry); and

4. net production: finished production — cost of materials (used only in the printing industry).[37]

Fulfillment of the production plan as a premium condition was conceived as a device to increase production in every branch of industry and in the entire economy. But increase of production

37. Kornai, p. 31. Fulfillment of the production plan is measured in plan prices.

in every sector does not necessarily lead to a proportionate increase of national income. As is shown in Appendix A, optimization ensues if, in every field, production is extended to the point where the value of the marginal increase in production equals the cost of the additional productive factors used. If fulfillment of the production plan is the sole premium condition, production will not stop at the point where this equality is achieved, but the enterprise will be inclined to produce up to the point where the contribution of the last unit of input to the value of output still exceeds zero, although the additional cost of input is greater than the value of additional production. In other words, the enterprise will squander resources, endeavoring to fulfill the production plan at all costs. It can be added that political agitation for over-fulfillment of the plan has also contributed to making a fetish of 100 per cent fulfillment.[38]

Fulfillment of the production plan as a premium condition appears to be one of the main reasons for the deterioration of efficiency indicated in the last section of Chapter 3. Besides the aforementioned disregard of costs, various manipulations for the sake of higher plan fulfillment also contributes to this result. These practices (examined in some detail later) include increase in material-intensive production, increase in cooperation between the enterprises, production of unneeded commodities, deterioration of quality, narrowing down of variety, increase of prices, juggling with production records between periods, and actual falsification of production results.

Detrimental effects of fulfillment of the production plan as the sole premium condition induced planning authorities to introduce *fulfillment of the profit plan* as a second condition. In pure competition maximization of profits would lead to the optimal allocation of resources. The question is, does this result follow also if fulfillment of the profit plan is made the *only* premium condition? In this case maximization of bonuses would be achieved if profits were maximized. Yet since in physical planning prices are not scarcity prices but are determined arbitrarily by the central authorities, fulfillment of this condition alone does not ensure efficient resource allocation.

The arbitrariness of prices is not the only deficiency of profit maximization in Soviet-type economies. The enterprise can in-

38. P. Erdős, "Some Theoretical Problems of Planning," *Yearbook*, p. 94.

crease its profit not only by reducing costs but also by various manipulations, some of which are also relevant to the fulfillment of the production plan and will be examined in detail at a later point. Fulfillment of the profit plan as a premium condition is certainly conducive to reduction of costs, but the possibilities for cost reduction are rather limited. There are possibilities for improvement of organization and cutting down on unproductive work, but cost cannot be reduced by competitive methods and the enterprise encounters difficulties in its demand for materials and semifinished products of better quality. Moving in the direction of least resistance, it is more likely to increase profits by lowering quality, changing assortment, raising prices, etc. than by reducing costs.[39]

The largest Hungarian construction trust (employing about 10 per cent of the working force under the Ministry for Construction) can be used as an illustration. In 1954 and the first half of 1955, when fulfillment of the production plan was the sole premium condition, the trust operated at a 10 per cent loss. As fulfillment of the profit plan was introduced, first as a subsidiary condition and later as a premium condition in its own right, a decision had to be taken on how to achieve the profitable operation of the trust—in order to obtain bonuses. It was concluded that not much could be done by way of reducing costs, and that efforts should be concentrated on raising prices and improving the billing of the firm's production to the investors. The calculation of individual prices for every project plus various manipulations (to be described in the next chapter) made possible a significant improvement in profitability. In the first three quarters of 1956 the trust showed a 10 per cent profit instead of the 10 per cent loss in former years. The balance sheets show that a similar change has been effected in other trusts and enterprises of the

---

39. Kornai says: "From the point of view of the indicators of cost reduction (likewise those of the value of production), it is a matter of indifference whether the products of the enterprise correspond to consumers' (productive and personal consumption) demand. The cost of production may be reduced also if the enterprise . . . manufactures less needed, less demanded commodities; in such a case, however, from the viewpoint of the national economy it squanders resources" (p. 54). E. Jávorka asserts that "profit and loss here loses its economic meaning . . . This method induces the attainment of 'better' prices rather than technical development and economical production": "Some Problems of the Industrial Price System," *KSz*, No. 2 (1957), 128.

same directorate.[40] It should be noted that enterprises in industries other than construction generally do not have the advantage of individual prices for single products, and although they make use of the manipulations previously mentioned, the scope of these practices is presumably narrower than in the construction industry.

Another deficiency of the bonus system based on fulfillment of the profit plan is the unreliability of planning production costs. Because of frequent modifications in production programs, difficulties in material procurement, lack of precision in cost estimates and costing, etc., profit plans are rather uncertain.[41] This is demonstrated by the considerable differences between plans and actual figures. As an example, take the fulfillment of the profit plan in the enterprises of the cotton industry during the last quarter of 1955: [42]

Percentage	Number of Enterprises
0	1
0–50	2
0–100	4
100–150	4
150–200	4
200–250	1
	16

To avoid excessive fluctuations in fulfillment of the profit plan, as shown in the above figures, the directorates often modify this plan at the end of the second month of the quarter on the basis of the last quarter's balance sheet. These modifications create uncertainty in the enterprises. On the other hand, alteration of the plan does not hinder the managers in the manipulation of the data at the end of the quarter.

We have now examined the fulfillment of the production plan and of the profit plan separately as premium conditions. In Hungary as well as in the Soviet Union,[43] both conditions are

40. This directorate (No. 1 of the Ministry for Construction) employed about one-third of the labor force in the Ministry of Construction.

41. Kornai, p. 58.

42. Ibid., p. 59. Fulfillment of the profit plan is measured here by dividing the actual percentage of profit with the planned percentage. On the other hand, in calculating bonuses, the fulfillment of this plan is measured as the difference between the actual and the planned percentages.

43. Cf. Berliner, *Factory and Manager in the U.S.S.R.*, pp. 73-74.

applied; consequently, maximization of bonuses requires consideration of both. Some actions of the enterprise—for example, the lowering of quality or raising of prices—increase fulfillment of both plans; others result in an increase in one and a reduction in the other. An increase in cooperation between enterprises (cf. below) boosts the fulfillment of the production plan but is likely to result in additional costs and thereby in reduction of profits; on the other hand, restriction of production at the point where additional costs would exceed the value of additional production increases profits but will reduce production. Therefore the maximization of bonuses is not the maximization of one variable with given constraints, but *the maximization of the joint value of two activities* (fulfillment of the production plan and fulfillment of the profit plan) in the face of given constraints, where the two activities are partly of a complementary, partly of a substitutive, character. To maximize bonuses the enterprise must consider the alternative cost of any activity in terms of bonuses.

The term cost is used here in a sense somewhat different from its use in the economics of the firm in a free enterprise system. In the latter case, profit maximization being the main objective, cost denotes expenses of production when, in choosing among alternative methods of production, costs and returns are compared. In the socialist firm, on the other hand, the main consideration is what alternatives cost in terms of bonuses. If bonuses are paid on the basis of profits alone, this criterion leads to essentially the same choice as in the case of profit maximization. Yet—bonuses being paid for fulfillment of the production plan as well as the profit plan—the concept of alternative cost is modified. An alternative may be considered advantageous even if forthcoming receipts do not cover additional costs, when the fulfillment of the production plan is thereby raised to such a degree as to outweigh, in terms of bonuses, the reduction in fulfillment of the profit plan.

As a hypothetical example, let us assume that no bonuses are paid for 100 per cent plan fulfillment and one per cent overfulfillment of the production plan results in a two per cent bonus, whereas one per cent additional profits over planned profits results in a five per cent bonus. The bonus ceiling is 25 per cent for overfulfillment of the production plan and 50 per cent for overfulfillment of the profit plan. An enterprise expects to fulfill its production plan 105 per cent and to achieve profits 3 per cent above the planned figure. The firm can boost its production by purchasing semifinished goods from another firm instead of producing them in its own factory. (Fulfillment of the production plan is measured by the method of "full production.") If the semifinished products in question are purchased from outside, fulfillment of the production plan increases to 110 per cent, while profits decrease by one per cent because of the higher cost incurred in purchasing the commodities instead of producing them (constant average costs are assumed). In this case, the semifinished products will be purchased from outside, since thereby bonuses for fulfillment of the production plan increase by 10 per cent, whereas bonuses for fulfillment of the profit plan are reduced by only 5 per cent, resulting in a net gain of 5 per cent. In reality, various factors, such as nonavailability of certain semifinished goods, increasing marginal costs, etc., complicate the issue; these factors are also taken into account by managers in making their decision.

The Practice of Profit Maximization

The next question is, how does the management of the socialist firm correspond to the principles of bonus maximization described above? Experience suggests that managers actually direct their firms' operations in view of bonus maximization and are aware of the fact that the joint value of the two indicators (fulfilling production and profit plans) should be maximized in order to achieve optimal results. This purpose is kept in view in organizing production and is served by *ex ante* as well as *ex post* manipulations. *Ex ante* manipulations are attempts to change the assortment of production, to raise prices, etc.; *ex post* manipulations consist mainly in doctoring the balance sheet. In the experience of the Hungarian construction trust mentioned above, the profitability of various construction projects was the subject of lengthy discussions, and the managers tried to refuse, for example, to construct farm buildings scattered over a large area—which notoriously meant incurring a deficit—even if thereby the value of future production was likely to be reduced. In general, attempts have been made to get rid of unprofitable projects and acquire others which showed a promise of profit. In

the same construction trust, when the balance sheets were drawn
up, calculations were made measuring how bonuses would be
affected by changing the value of production (modifying production *and* profit) and by changes made in items other than the
value of production (modifying only profit). For example, in the
first quarter of 1955 one of the enterprises belonging to this trust
did not want to reveal production results higher than the 112.5
per cent fulfillment of the production plan which made it eligible
for the maximum bonus of 25 per cent on this count, and so reserved a part of its actual production for the next quarter. The
ensuing reduction in profits was more than counterbalanced by
manipulating other items not affecting production results (for
example, part of the material consumption was not accounted
for).

E. Devons remarks in his book on British aircraft planning
during the second World War [44] that the statistician is bound to
become a prominent figure in planning, since he is needed to
juggle production records. My experience indicates that the key
figure in the process of maximizing bonuses is not the statistician
but the chief accountant. The chief accountant becomes a sort
of business manager who has ideas for raising prices or changing
the assortment of products, and through manipulation of the
balance sheet tries to show the figures needed to obtain the desired
amount in bonuses. The drawing up of the quarterly balance
sheet is an awesome time for the director and leading technical
employees of an enterprise. They visit the chief accountant frequently, inquire about results, and discuss possibilities for modifying various items on the balance sheet. The chief accountant
may obtain a signed statement from the director and the chief
engineer declaring their knowledge of the alterations made; this
statement, enclosed with the balance sheet in the report to the
ministry, will give more credence to the chief accountant's figures.
On the other hand, if the modifications are to be concealed from
the ministry, a secret document may be signed to make the director and the chief engineer the accomplices of the chief accountant.
In some enterprises two balance sheets are drawn up: the official
balance sheet is presented to the supervising ministry and is the
basis of bonus payments; the secret balance sheet contains the
true figures. In connection with this doctoring of balance sheets

44. *Planning in Practice* (London, 1950), pp. 156–57, 164.

comes the question of supervision. Supervision of balance sheets is the task of the directorates. (The balance sheets of enterprises belonging to a trust are supervised by the trust as well as by the directorate; I omit here the discussion of the trust-enterprise relationship, which will be taken up later.) But because of the difficulty of checking the balance sheet in detail, supervisors frequently do not observe the manipulations; even if they do discover them, however, they have no interest in correcting the report in accordance with the true figures: they may actually condone manipulations to help the enterprise in obtaining bonuses; nor is the possibility of bribing excluded.

Various manipulations have been listed above that serve to maximize bonuses. Some of these contribute to the fulfillment of the production or profit plan or to both. Let us examine them one by one.

The enterprise endeavors to get easy plans from the ministry, and for this purpose managers deliberately underestimate the capacity of their firm. Although legal sanctions can be applied against concealment of productive capacity, this regulation is rarely enforced in practice, and the strength of the enterprise's material interest in the easy plan more than outweighs its fear of punishment.[45]

Fulfilling the production plan can be helped by producing material-intensive commodities, since thereby higher production results can be achieved with a given labor force. One encounters many complaints in the Hungarian press of deliberate increases in the weight of materials [46] and changes in assortment of products in the direction of higher weight [47] or larger size.[48] Enterprises refrain from producing labor-intensive commodities and manufacturing spare parts for machines produced by themselves, for the sake of higher production results.[49] Changes in assortment can

45. Kornai, pp. 118–19.

46. A factory is reported to have delivered steel pipes of greater weight than necessary to foreign purchasers for the sake of fulfilling the production plan (SzN, December 27, 1955).

47. In some cases the production process of the user enterprise has been hindered because only the heaviest parts had been delivered (SzN, October 23, 1955).

48. Consumers frequently cannot obtain shoes and clothing of the right size because enterprises favor those of larger sizes (SzN, May 14, 1955).

49. Factories answer the complaints about the shortage of spare parts by saying that they have no time to produce them, for they must produce new machines (SzN, July 10, 1955).

generally be found in the direction of commodities which bring in more forints. Because of the rigidity of the price system, there are wide variations in the prices of commodities with identical labor inputs. Kornai mentions that a square meter of wool fabric can bring in from 20 to 100 forints, and alleges that the value of production in some factories with given capacity and labor force can be subject to variations up to several hundred per cent as assortment changes.[50]

Since in most industries the value of production is measured by the value of "full production," fulfillment of the production plan can be raised also by increased cooperation between firms—that is, an enterprise increases the value of production by purchasing semifinished products previously produced by itself. It has also happened that enterprises have purchased back their own products at the retail price and used them as semifinished products in further production, thereby boosting their production results.[51] Increase in cooperation is one of the main reasons for the widening disparity between the gross and net indices of industrial production in Hungary. On the 1949 basis, the official index shows a 176 per cent increase in gross and a 110 per cent increase in net industrial production by 1955.[52]

Raising the value of production by increased cooperation can be avoided if the value of "corrected production" is used as an indicator of plan fulfillment, although this method can be applied only in industries where the verticality is stable (for example, fibers to raw fabrics to finished fabrics, or iron ore to pig iron to steel) and cannot be employed if the scope of cooperation is very broad, as, for example, in the machine industry or the pharmaceutical industry. However, using "corrected production" to measure plan fulfillment has deficiencies of its own: it makes it possible to fulfill the production plan by concentrating production on those goods (for example, fibers) that give the highest value of production per man hour.[53]

Changes in assortment are also effected by producing commodities with a higher profit rate in order to improve profitability.

50. Kornai, p. 32.

51. Péter, p. 42. Increasing cooperation between firms as a means for increasing production results is also mentioned in *SzN*, September 25, 1956. It is said to be of the greatest importance in the machine industry.

52. *SHK*, No. 6 (1957), 10.

53. Kornai, pp. 37–38.

Prices being rigid and frequently not proportionate to cost ratios, the enterprise will attempt to concentrate on the production of more profitable commodities.[54] For purposes of illustration let us suppose that the planning authority prescribes the production of 100 value units with the following assortment:

Products	Quantity	Price	Cost	Total Value	Total Cost	Price/Cost Ratio
A	20	1	1	20	20	1
B	30	2	1.67	60	50	1.2
C	40	0.5	0.6	20	24	0.83

In such a case the firm will endeavor to concentrate on commodity B, and the assortment will be changed in actual production.

Enterprises often produce unneeded commodities for the sake of plan fulfillment. The criterion of plan fulfillment is that the product shall be accepted by the quality-control department of the factory and be placed in the factory's storage room for finished products. Even if nobody needs the products, they are counted toward fulfillment of the plan.[55] The production of unneeded commodities can result, for example, from deviations in the plan, lack of a contract, changes in demand, production of reserves for export, or refusal of export commodities by foreign purchasers.[56] Trade organizations have in some cases been compelled to accept commodities even if they did not order them.[57] The ministries force stock-piling companies under their supervision to take unneeded commodities from the producer belonging to the same

54. Hoch and Rédei, *Yearbook*, p. 256; Péter, p. 130.

55. M. Somogyi, "Production of Unneeded and Shelved Commodities in Industry," *SSz*, No. 5 (1954), 413. Rákosi's statement of 1954 has retained its validity in later years: "It still happens here that . . . the director as well as the entire personnel of the firm who receive bonuses will be better off if the enterprise overfulfills its plan in the production of a commodity not needed in the national economy than if it achieves smaller production results in commodities important and indispensable to the national economy": *A Magyar Dolgozók Pártja III. Kongresszusának Jegyzőkönye (Minutes of the Third Congress of the Hungarian Working People's Party)* (Budapest, 1954), pp. 52–53.

56. From an official publication: "In many cases, for the sake of fulfilling the production plan enterprises produce commodities not included either in their plans or in their procurement contracts. The greater part of these commodities . . . is not suitable to meet needs in consumption or production" (*Facts and Figures*, p. 125). See also Kornai, pp. 39–40.

57. The Central Arbitration Committee has often compelled trade organizations to purchase commodities not ordered: *Facts and Figures*, p. 124.

ministry because these companies pay only 0.5 per cent for their credits, whereas the producers must pay 3 per cent. It is difficult to estimate the value of unneeded commodities stocked by various organizations, but it is known that, as of the end of 1955, in the clothing industry about 15 per cent of the inventory was considered unsalable.[58]

Enterprises often use deterioration of quality and reduction of variety as a means of improving production results. These practices will be examined in the next section.

The raising of prices also contributes to an increase of production and profit. We have dealt with this problem above.[59]

Hungarian sources mention the actual falsification of production results by the enterprise for the sake of plan fulfillment.[60] In some cases the ministries offered little resistance to the touching up of production results.[61]

All these methods aim principally at the modification of the *absolute* figures of production and profit; maximization of bonuses is also furthered by *temporal* adjustments of production and cost data. Since bonuses are calculated separately for every quarter (or for some time in every month), it is to the enterprise's interest to adjust production and cost records in such a way as to achieve maximization for a longer period, for example a year. For the enterprise the following considerations are important: [62] (1) the degree of plan fulfillment should not be higher than the ceiling necessary and sufficient to obtain the maximum amount of bonuses (75 or 50 per cent of the basic salary); (2) in those periods when the performance of the enterprise does not promise bonuses anyway, data on plan fulfillment should be adjusted downward to create reserves for the next period; and (3) fulfillment of the plan should not be so high that targets are thereby raised in the next period.

Observation of these "rules" by the enterprises has resulted

58. Kornai, p. 41.

59. See pp. 107–9.

60. The official Party paper notes that in one of the largest Hungarian machine factories, the Mávag, as well as in other factories, fraud was used to obtain bonuses (*SzN*, July 3, 1955). The Békéscsaba Machine Tool Factory reported 106.7 per cent fulfillment of its production plan in October 1954 instead of the actual 87.1 per cent: Lacfalvi and Wagner, *SSz*, No. 7 (1956), 588. See also Péter, pp. 39–40.

61. G. Csatár, "Ministry Chauvinism," *SzN*, February 12, 1956.

62. In the following cases we use the expression "plan fulfillment" to mean fulfillment of both the production and the profit plan.

in considerable fluctuation of production and profit records. If an enterprise did not expect to fulfill its yearly plan, it would modify the quarterly results in such a way that the plan would be fulfilled in two quarters and considerably underfulfilled in two other quarters. For example, in 1954 and 1955 production results of the trusts and enterprises under the supervision of Directorate No. 1 in the Ministry for Construction moved largely parallel, showing overfulfillment and underfulfillment of the plan in alternate quarters. Similar fluctuations have been observed in other industries. The Hungarian press frequently deplored the drive for better results at the end of the month during the years when bonuses were calculated monthly.[63] In the machine industry, recorded production in the first decade of the month was in some cases 70 or 80 per cent less than in the last decade of the previous month.[64] The leather industry presents another example: here enterprises did not fulfill the production plan in ten cases during the first half of 1955. On these occasions plan fulfillment never reached 95 per cent; it was between 91 and 95 per cent in six cases, between 80 and 90 per cent in one, and below 80 per cent in three. Apparently if 100 per cent was not reached, the enterprises further reduced production records. With the help of these reserves in the month following the underfulfillment of the plan, it was fulfilled in seven out of the ten cases.[65] In other instances, firms reported 60 per cent plan fulfillment instead of the actual 80 to 88 per cent, so they could shoot ahead in the next period.[66] It should be noted that no deductions have been made from the salary of managers when the plan was not fulfilled, hence the wide application of temporal adjustments in production and cost figures.

Various manipulations are used to adjust the data on cost and production between periods: the value of production or the cost of materials is ascribed to another period, the production of commodities with higher or lower material content is varied between periods, the value of unfinished production and semifinished products is modified, etc. Until bonuses were paid monthly, the managers in many enterprises estimated the production results

63. A. Bródy, "The Drive at the End of the Month and the Inventories," *Yearbook*, pp. 203–18; *SzN*, September 9, 1956.

64. *SzN*, September 2, 1956.

65. Kornai, p. 116.

66. Lacfalvi and Wagner, *SSz*, No. 7 (1956), 598.

in the last days of the month and ordered overtime work or slowing down of production as seemed necessary. In some factories (for example, those where scarce imported materials were used) and in the design bureaus bonuses reached the peak if 100 or 102 per cent plan fulfillment was achieved, and decreased after this point had been passed. Here production results were modified in such a way as to achieve the percentage of plan fulfillment resulting in the highest amount of bonuses. An amusing case came to my attention: in a rubberware factory where fulfillment of the production plan was measured by weight, on the last day of the month if production was too low the management ordered that more air be pumped into the inflated articles to achieve the desired weight. The reverse was applied if the weight was found excessive.

Enterprises have frequently made use of modifications in the value of unfinished production. Kornai reports that in leather factories if production results were not sufficient the management ordered raw hides to be thrown into tubs, an operation that did not require much labor, and the hides in the tubs were valued at 75 per cent of the price of finished leather, contributing to the enterprise's plan fulfillment.[67] Juggling with the reported value of unfinished and semifinished production has also been noted in the machine industry and elsewhere.[68]

Up to this point we have disregarded the possibility of the clash of interests inside the maximizing unit. When enterprises are directed and supervised by a trust, a divergence of interests may appear between the trust and its enterprises. In the Hungarian economy, where premium conditions for the trust and the enterprises are identical, both types of organizations have identical interests with regard to an increase of plan fulfillment in absolute terms. Nevertheless, interests will often differ on the question of temporal adjustments. If a trust's plan fulfillment has already reached a ceiling high enough to secure maximum bonuses, it will endeavor to keep down the plan fulfillment of those enterprises which are below this limit and are striving for a higher figure. On the other hand, if some of the enterprises could not fulfill their plan and are trying to pile up reserves by con-

67. Kornai, p. 38.

68. SzN, September 2, 1956; and G. Bán, "How Do Some Enterprises of the Machine Industry Interpret the Completion of Products?" SSz, No. 6 (1955), 539.

cealing part of their production results, the trust may fight this
tendency in order to avoid an extremely high degree of plan
fulfillment in a later period. While supervising the balance sheets
of the enterprises belonging to the largest Hungarian construction trust in 1953–56, I took an active part in such negotiations
between the trust and its enterprises. Before embarking on the
work of balance-sheet supervision, representatives of the trust
estimated the probable results and agreed on the figures to be
aimed at for purposes of bonus maximization on the trust level.
On this basis, substantial modifications of both production figures
and profit figures were often made. The enterprises frequently
complained—half-jokingly, half-seriously—that no matter what
their balance sheet showed, the results were determined in advance by the figures projected by the trust. Although this is
certainly an overstatement, modifications in the value of production in some cases reached 5–8 per cent. In the last quarter of
1955, for example, when new premium conditions were introduced, the trust could not obtain bonuses to fulfill the production
plan except by avoiding losses. Production fulfillment seemed
assured; hence the trust's efforts were concentrated on profits.
Three of the trust's enterprises had operated at a profit, two others
showed losses. The latter enterprises had wanted to increase their
accounting losses as much as possible in order to create better
possibilities for plan fulfillment in the next quarter. Yet the
trust considerably modified the profit-loss statement of these enterprises and thereby achieved a small margin of profit on the trust
level, assuring substantial bonuses for the trust personnel.

Similar tendencies have been observed in other trusts and also
in cases where the directorates received bonuses for plan fulfillment. The trust (or directorate) often uses coercion, persuasion,
and exhortation to implement its interest, even at the expense
of the material interests of the enterprise.

A clash of interests may also ensue within the enterprise. The
situation here is analogous to that described above: the managers
of the enterprise may endeavor to increase the degree of plan
fulfillment when the plant or workshop (which receives bonuses
on the basis of fulfilling its own plan) is opposed to any further
increase, and vice versa. It has been observed that the director
may force a workshop to produce to its disadvantage in order to

increase plan fulfillment on the enterprise level.[69] Kornai is of the opinion that "those indicators have the dominant role, the greatest influence in the factory's life, which are related to the bonuses of the employees, above all the chief executives, whose bonuses are calculated on the basis of plan fulfillment of the firm as a whole." [70]

We have disregarded so far premium conditions other than fulfillment of the production and profit plans. In some industries subsidiary premium conditions have been introduced from time to time, the lack of fulfillment of which may have resulted in the reduction of bonuses calculated on the basis of fulfillment of the production and profit plans. Such conditions were, for example, fulfilling the assortment plan in the textile industry and completion of projects at the prescribed date in the construction industry. In practice, these conditions have often been disregarded if the production and profit plans have been fulfilled: in the construction industry, although in every quarter several projects had not been finished in time, this condition was disregarded until 1955 on the basis of the often spurious explanations given by the enterprises on the causes of delays, while in the second half of 1955 and in 1956 unsubstantial deductions were made from the amount of bonuses. In general, the existence of subsidiary conditions has not diminished the central importance of the fulfillment of the production and profit plans.

Special Bonuses

Besides the regular bonuses there are special bonuses, which are tied to the fulfillment of special targets. The director's fund as well as bonuses paid for exceptional performance of the enterprise, reduction of inventories, completion of some construction projects, and production of selected commodities come under this heading.

The director's fund is determined on the basis of fulfillment of the production and profit plan and increases as the profit plan is overfulfilled. A part of the director's fund is used for social and cultural purposes, another part for rewarding individual em-

69. Kornai, p. 72.
70. Ibid., p. 73.

ployees of the firm. The importance of this fund should not, however, be exaggerated; the amounts in it have been rather insignificant. In 1955, for example, in light industry the entire director's fund amounted to 2.1–2.3 per cent of the wages fund, and the amounts which could be used for rewarding individual employees reached only 1.2–1.3 per cent.[71] Furthermore, since chief executives do not share in the director's fund, they are not especially interested in its increase; [72] and after fulfillment of the profit plan has been introduced as a premium condition, the director's fund cannot be a separate incentive but can only reinforce the maximization of bonuses, since its conditions are roughly the same as the premium conditions.

The enterprise receives special bonuses for exceptional performance, awarded if it wins the competition for the title of "leading firm." Competitive conditions are rather intricate [73] and do not seem to have much impact on the management of the firm, except in those cases where the prestige motive considerably influences the director. The smallness of the prize given with the title (less than one per cent of the wages fund, the percentage decreasing as the size of the firm grows) [74] is a further reason for its unimportance.

From time to time bonuses have been paid for reduction of inventories. We have noted the tendency of enterprises to pile up materials. Target bonuses paid in case of reduction in stocks have been designed to counteract this tendency. In 1955 the amount of these bonuses was less than 0.1 per cent of the wages fund in light industry [75] and not much higher in others. More will be said about this below.[76]

In the construction industry bonuses have been paid by investor firms for the completion of some construction projects of exceptional importance. These bonuses were significant primarily in 1950–52. At that time an exceptionally strong drive for the speedy

71. Ibid., p. 89.

72. This regulation has been circumvented in some cases when a director gave special bonuses from the director's fund to some "reliable" employees who returned a portion of them to the director or other chief executives.

73. Fulfillment of the production and profit plans, decrease of material consumption, increase in labor productivity, avoidance of wage payments in excess of the planned wages fund, increase of the number of stakhanovite workers, etc.

74. In light industry 5–10 forints per capita (Kornai, p. 85).

75. Ibid., p. 89.

76. See pp. 160–61.

completion of certain projects—especially those serving military goals and purposes of heavy industry—was manifest. The bonuses often amounted to 100 per cent or more of the salary of technical employees (calculated for the period of construction) working on the project, and the managers also shared in it. As a consequence, the material and labor supply of these projects was considerably better than for other projects, and the "cost and effort should not be spared" principle reigned. Although this method contributed to the observance of the planners' priority scale, it also reinforced the detrimental effects of using fulfillment of the production plan as a primary premium condition on efficiency. Furthermore, it was not just a question of priorities set by the planning authorities, for various ministries tried to overbid one another to achieve their own objectives; in other words, a form of bargaining was noticeable. After the launching of the New Course, the role of these bonuses was greatly reduced, but in 1955 and 1956 it regained some of its importance. At that time a clash of interests developed on the question of costs between the management of the firm and the technical employees of projects where special bonuses were paid, as also among technical employees working on projects with and without target bonuses on the question of obtaining material, labor, and machines.

Bonuses for the production of some commodities are of two kinds: those paid for producing consumer goods out of refuse, and those paid by other enterprises for speedy delivery. The first kind (amounting to a high percentage of profit from the goods involved) was introduced after the inauguration of the New Course to ensure better provision for consumer needs. In practice, it served another objective also: to create additional funds for rewarding employees where accounts might be doctored if otherwise profits would not be forthcoming in the production of these commodities.[77] Target bonuses paid by the user to the producer for speedy delivery are more important. This is an outgrowth of the shortage of goods, of the competition of the buyers. It affects production by giving priority to the production of commodities for which target bonuses are paid and neglecting others. As a form of buyers' competition it also results in deviations from

77. In one construction enterprise a considerable sum was obtained by showing great profit in the production of kindling from refuse—with some manipulation of the accounts.

the national material allocation plan. Finally, it gives opportunity for corruption. It has been said that in the machine industry before a new and urgent order is taken the first question is: how much target premium will be paid? Date of delivery and other conditions are made dependent on the amount of bonuses.[78] Similar methods have been used in factories producing construction materials.

In connection with bonuses, fulfillment of the wages-fund plan [79] should also be mentioned. In some industries if the planned amount of wages is exceeded, the chief executives must pay a penalty, in others the regular bonuses are reduced. The endeavor to fulfill the wages-fund plan gives further incentive to material-intensive production which leads to a reduction of the percentage share of wages.[80] In industries where fulfillment of the wages plan was a subsidiary premium condition, the rigid planning of wages sometimes resulted in curious situations. For example, in a warehouse with 170 employees where the absolute amount of the wages fund was planned, the plan called for 537,000 forints in wages to be paid, with 30,000 forints in wage reductions planned for absences. Now if the planned-for number of people did not become sick, the wages fund was exceeded and a deduction was made from the bonuses of the management.[81]

The various kinds of special bonuses described above can be regarded as qualifications to our theory of the maximization of bonuses, since the management will maximize not only the amount of regular bonuses but the sum of the regular and special bonuses. Yet in view of the relatively small amounts paid in the form of special bonuses, this modification is not of great significance.

In this section we have presented a theory of the socialist firm based on maximization of bonuses. In the following we shall examine various aspects of the firm's activity, such as the quality

78. Kornai, p. 74.

79. It usually determines the amount of wages on the assumption of 100 per cent fulfillment of the production plan. In the case of overfulfillment, proportionately higher wages can be paid in most industries. In some, however, fulfillment of the wages plan is measured in absolute terms rather than relative to fulfillment of the production plan, and no allowance is made for overfulfillment.

80. Péter, p. 41.

81. *SzN*, April 22, 1956.

problem, the procurement of materials, and the use of capital goods, in their relation to the maximization of bonuses.

THE QUALITY AND VARIETY OF PRODUCTS

We have already mentioned the quality deterioration of consumer goods in the Hungarian economy. Not only consumer goods are affected, however, but all kinds of products. It has been said that "there are no incentives of any importance which induce an enterprise to improve quality, and at the same time there are a series of factors which entice it to reduce quality." [82] Here are a few of these factors:

First, the endeavor to maximize bonuses induces the enterprise to deteriorate the quality of the products. Kornai observes that "this is the simplest method [of cost reduction] which has been applied regularly during recent years." [83] The possibility of quality deterioration is augmented by, secondly, buyers' competition. Instead of creating resistance to reduction of quality, the competition of buyers induces the producer to reduce quality, since even products of lower quality will be taken.[84] The low quality of many materials and intermediate products not merely results in the production of goods of lower quality, because of defective materials, but also serves as an excuse for additional deficiencies in the next stage of the production process. As has been seen, producers like to blame the immediately preceding stage of production for any deficiency in their own products and "the enterprise does not consider itself responsible for the manufacture of products of inferior quality." [85] Thirdly, raising labor norms contributes to a deterioration of quality. One of the main forms of worker resistance against higher norms has been less accurate work: negligence in the handling of materials, omission of a manipulation, carelessness in finishing. The impact of the drive for higher earnings on the reduction of quality has been generally recognized, and in the case of defective products the

82. Kornai, p. 56. A similar conclusion is reached by I. Friss, "The Application of the Principle of Material Interest in the Building of Socialism," *TSz*, No. 1 (1956), 19.

83. Kornai, p. 55.

84. Péter, p. 47.

85. Ibid., *SzN*, February 9, 1956.

slogan "This is the product of socialist emulation" has been widely (and derisively) quoted.[86]

The methods used by the producer to bring about deterioration of quality can be classified into two groups: deterioration of quality of a certain product, and exploitation of price differences. Deterioration of quality of a given product has been effected by use of poorer materials (as in the cotton industry), by reduction of actual working time expended on the product (as in precision manufacturing), and by omitting a manipulation in the process of manufacturing (as in the shoe industry).[87] In some factories reduction of costs through deterioration of quality has been considered a real accomplishment and a successful method for effecting savings.[88] Insufficient differentiation of prices also creates a possibility for quality reduction. The Hungarian production-price system, lacking sufficient differentiation to reflect quality and cost differences, induces the enterprise to manufacture commodities of relatively poorer quality. In the Uniform Product and Price List, products of different quality can be found listed under the same price; in other cases price differences do not adequately reflect differences in costs. In the interest of bonus maximization, loopholes of the system are exploited in both cases.

The planning authorities have endeavored to stop the process of quality deterioration by instituting quality-control departments in the producing enterprises. It has been generally recognized that this regulation falls short of its objective. The official Party paper notes that "the managers of the enterprises frequently look upon quality controllers as obstacles to plan fulfillment." [89]

86. According to Rákosi, in some cases rejects were manufactured to help toward the fulfillment of labor norms (*Minutes of the Third Congress*, pp. 52–53).

87. The process of quality deterioration is aptly described by Hoch and Rédei: "The fixed price, adapting itself with difficulty to gradual change in quality, not only hinders the improvement of quality but encourages a gradual deterioration of quality. For although the basic character of a product will not change if it is less carefully processed and finished, if from time to time some step in its finishing is omitted—if to some extent inferior material is used, or if wrapping is less careful and tasteful—all this does not change the character of the product (assuming that on any one occasion deterioration of quality is not considerable) and there is no need to reduce the fixed price—nevertheless such deteriorations in quality, even though carried out only occasionally and on a small scale, can, after a certain time, alter the character of the product, and then we have an inferior commodity which is functionally of less value. But the price remains the same, as if the quality had not deteriorated" (*Yearbook*, p. 259).

88. *Facts and Figures*, p. 125.

89. *SzN*, May 28, 1956.

But the quality controller cannot be much of an obstacle, since he is not independent of the enterprise—he gets bonuses from the director, and "for the sake of plan fulfillment and bonuses he will relax the discipline in inspection." [90] Constant pressure is exerted on him to classify inferior commodities in higher categories. From time to time a campaign is launched by the Party to improve the quality of products, the quality controllers become more exacting for the moment, only to resume their lax attitude after the campaign has run its course. Consequently, the same commodity may be classified as of different quality at different times.[91]

Besides the deterioration of quality, reduction of variety also serves the purpose of bonus maximization. Two reasons can be given: (1) since unit costs are assumed to be decreasing as production expands,[92] decreasing the number of commodities produced results in cost reduction for the enterprises; and (2) the maximization of bonuses, apart from inducing the enterprise to lessen the number of commodities produced at a given point of time, also exerts influence on the enterprise to avoid the introduction of new commodities. New products need retooling; there are costs for the new pattern; some new tools may be needed; the workers are accustomed to the production methods used in the manufacture of the old products; etc. These additional costs dissuade the enterprise from introducing new products.[93]

As a result, hand in hand with deterioration of quality a certain drabness has become noticeable in the assortment of commodities manufactured for both domestic and export purposes.[94]

PROCUREMENT OF MATERIALS AND THE INVENTORY PROBLEM

The objective of bonus maximization demands a steady supply of materials in the required quantity, assortment, and quality. We have already reviewed the system of material allocation in Hun-

90. Ibid.
91. Kornai, p. 47.
92. Ibid., pp. 56–57.
93. We noted above, p. 109, the inclination of enterprises to create "new" products by making insignificant changes in old ones, in order to raise prices. In the present section we deal with "genuine" new products, the introduction of which requires additional costs.
94. Similar conclusions are reached by Kornai, p. 67.

gary and reached the conclusion that the applied method of physical allocation does not ensure that enterprises receive the needed materials. Because of shortcomings of the material allocation system, enterprises often do not obtain the needed material in time; in many instances they receive less than the required quantity; the materials procured may not correspond to the assortment needed for production; and they are frequently of poor quality.

To a degree, the firm can avoid disturbances in production by changing the assortment of the commodities produced. But this can be a stop-gap measure only, since in the case of periodic shortages in basic materials, as experienced in Hungary, no change in product assortment could save the enterprise from disturbances in production. Shortages have often arisen also in some subsidiary materials of strategic importance for the production process (for example, ball bearings), the lack of which would lead to interruptions in production even if the basic materials were available.

Since the enterprise aims at the maximization of bonuses, it must find ways to overcome the deficiencies and shortcomings of the system of material allocation. If the physical allocation of materials by the planning authorities does not satisfy the needs of the enterprise, it must get around the system. This activity of the enterprise serves not only its own interests but also (at least partly) the interests of the national economy, since by procuring materials from outside the official channels disruptions in production are avoided which might have resulted in chain reactions throughout the entire economy. In other words, by contravening the regulations in planning, the firm may serve the very objectives of the plan.

There are two principal methods for ensuring the steady supply of material to the enterprise: the informal process of material procurement outside the system of material allocation, and the hoarding of materials for fear of future shortages. These methods will be the subject of the present section.

The Informal System of Material Procurement

Because of the inadequacies in the material allocation system, the enterprise tries to find ways outside the official channels to procure the necessary materials. The development of an informal system of material procurement is described by Sovány:

> The enterprise—by reason of its primary responsibility for the fulfillment of the production plan—breaks through the rigid framework of the system of material allocation. There begins and proceeds, on an increasing scale, the barter, the purchase, and the sale of material stocks at the enterprises, to such a degree that it actually develops, parallel to the official . . . system of material allocation, into a necessary but informal trade . . . which serves as a substitute for the absence of trade.[95]

This informal system of material procurement has a parallel in similar institutions of the Soviet Union: the *blat,* defined as "the use of personal influence for obtaining certain favors to which a firm or individual is not legally or formally entitled," [96] and its agent the *tolkach,* the pusher, who "pushes for the interests of the enterprise in such matters as the procurement of materials." [97] This similarity is not due to imitation of Soviet methods; the informal system of material procurement is a necessary corollary of the system of physical planning. Since, in the absence of the equilibrating function of prices, the method of physical allocation cannot ensure avoidance of discrepancies between the supply of and demand for products, an informal system of material procurement will necessarily develop to serve the objectives of the enterprise.

It is difficult to evaluate the cost of the informal methods of material procurement in terms of working time and other expenses. But it is well known that "the managers of the enterprises spend a great part of their time and energy not on the solution of problems in production but on material procurement." [98] To give an actual example: the Construction Trust of Sztálinváros in 1956 stationed a group of pushers, consisting of about twelve to fifteen people, in the capital, and the enterprises of the trust employed two to three agents for the same purpose. There was

95. Sovány, p. 1048.
96. Berliner, *Factory and Manager in the U.S.S.R.,* p. 102.
97. Ibid., pp. 209–10.
98. Péter, p. 49.

a permanent fight between the Ministry for Construction and the trusts and enterprises which did not have their main office in the capital, since the ministry repeatedly forbade its trusts and independent enterprises to station pushers in Budapest. The orders have never been carried out: the trusts and enterprises changed the location of the material expediters rather than to discontinue their activity. When the ministry found the new place, it was changed again, sometimes to private apartments. If the enterprise in question had a building site in Budapest, the pushers were put on the staff of this building site. A game of "hide and seek" developed between the ministry and its enterprises, the ministry searching for places where the expediters were hiding and the enterprise looking for new hiding places when the old ones were discovered.

It is certain that from the point of view of the enterprise, the pushers have certainly earned their money. For the enterprise, procurement of materials from outside the official channels helps to avoid—sometimes at insignificant cost—interruptions in production costing millions in production value and thousands in bonuses forfeited. In view of the maximization of bonuses, the "marginal productivity" of the pushers has probably been quite high. This is not necessarily so on the national economy level, if comparison is made with an economy where trade methods are used for acquiring materials.

The pusher has its place in the official system of material allocation as well, by influencing officials of the ministry to increase the material allotments of the enterprise and by attempting to obtain a favorable allocation for the enterprise in means of production distributed in intervals shorter than a month, such as wagon capacity, trucks, and horse-drawn carts. But the main task of the pusher is to create and maintain good relations with the suppliers. This is necessary not only to obtain materials in excess of the allocated quota but also to make certain that the allotted materials arrive in time. The producers supply materials over and above the quota partly from above-plan output, partly at the expense of other users' quotas or by exploiting the loopholes of the material-allocation system. In the case of a large firm, the material expediters are highly specialized and have been working in their fields for years. Their methods consist of friendly persuasion, recompense in products manufactured by the enterprise in question, offering target bonuses, and in some cases outright bribing. Some pushers work for more than one firm and enjoy a considerable income, paid under various disguises, as, for example, "hauling materials." In general, the description of the blat and tolkach in the Soviet Union given in chapters 11 and 12 of Berliner's book fits the Hungarian situation, although I am of the opinion that these phenomena have been found to a lesser degree in the Hungarian economy, perhaps because of difference in size of the two economies, and differences in distances.

Inventory Policy

In evaluating the firm's inventory policy three factors must be considered: scarcity of materials, uncertainty of future deliveries, and cost of holding inventories. The scarcity of materials has been mentioned before; shortcomings of the material allocation system —creating uncertainty about the satisfaction of the enterprise's future material needs—have also been noted.[99] In making its decision on inventory holding, the firm must consider the cost of interruptions in production and compare it with the cost of holding inventories. For the sake of maximizing bonuses that alternative will be chosen which costs less in terms of bonuses.

Up to 1954, when bonuses were paid on the basis of plan fulfillment in production, the cost of inventory holdings was left out of consideration. Since profit or loss did not affect bonuses, the alternative cost of holding inventories was nil in terms of bonuses, while the avoidance of interruptions resulted in higher production and higher bonuses. After 1954, bonuses being paid on the basis of fulfillment of the production and profit plans, the alternative cost of holding inventories had to be taken into consideration. Nevertheless, the cost of inventories has remained negligible.

Inventories are financed from two sources: the circulating fund (working capital) of the enterprise, and credits. The circulating fund (allotted by the ministry) is destined to cover the financing of the firm's average inventory needs. Although its allotment of working capital is calculated on the basis of inventory/output coefficients, there is often room for bargaining to raise the amount apportioned. The circulating fund is adjusted periodically to meet seasonal needs. There is no interest charge for the use of

99. See pp. 70 ff.

this fund. Since the predominant part of the enterprise's inventory is financed by its circulating fund allotment, the cost of holding the major part of the inventories (excepting the cost of storage) is nil. The minor part of the enterprise's inventory is financed out of credits. The interest charge on credits is extremely low; in 1958 it was shown to be, on the average, yearly 2.3 per cent, amounting to only 0.4 per cent of the enterprise's cost.[100] In view of the low cost of holding inventories, the enterprises have been inclined to hoard materials, since the penalty for not having materials has been considered greater than the penalty for storing them.[101] At this point it should also be considered that the cost of holding inventories reduces bonuses paid for the fulfillment of the profit plan only, not bonuses for fulfillment of the production plan.

The planning authorities have endeavored to check the drive for accumulating inventories at the enterprise. The simplest way to do this is to control the size of stocks in particular materials by reducing allotments when inventories are high. This practice can be applied successfully in the case of continuous production when only a limited number of inputs is used (for example, cotton and wool in the textile factories); it is less successful in the case of more complicated production processes where a great number of materials are used. Because of this last factor, an indirect method for inventory reduction has been applied: target bonuses have been paid for the reduction of stocks as compared to a base period.

In connection with these special bonuses, a clash of interests has developed in the firm between various groups of employees. Reduction of inventories is usually directed by financial employees, for whom the amount of expected bonuses coming from this source may be quite considerable. On the other hand, technical employees who directly experience the consequences of the

100. J. Kornai, "The Enterprise Should Become Materially Interested in the Realistic Planning of Circulating Funds," *PESz*, No. 8. (1958), 289. Interest charges were of similar magnitude in 1956.

101. According to Péter, "the enterprise will suffer no disadvantage if, fearing difficulties in material procurement, it hoards materials, perhaps for some years" (p. 58). Kornai notes that "the cost of the interest paid for credits is dwarfed by the additional costs arising from disturbances in production. Consequently, the enterprise endeavors to pile up as much material as possible" (p. 157).

lack of inventories, resist the reduction of stocks. In some cases materials which would have been needed to avoid disturbances in production have been sold without the knowledge of the technical employees. On other occasions the technicians have blocked the way of called-for reductions by citing possible (but never realized) future needs.

It has also been reported that enterprises have frequently got around the regulations on the reduction of circulating funds by reducing their inventories through the temporary transfers of stocks.[102] In the experience of the construction industry, materials were sold to a marketing organization (so-called stockpiling firm), or, more commonly, to an investor firm with a repurchase agreement.[103] The transferred stocks were repurchased either immediately following the deadline for the reduction of inventories or later as need for the materials arose. In the case of periodical payment of bonuses for reducing circulating funds (these bonuses do not constitute part of the regular bonus system but are calculated apart), inventories were increased in one period and reduced in another. For the purpose of reducing inventories, materials were also sorted out as useless but were in some cases used at a later date. The enterprises have been inclined to avail themselves of the possibility of sorting out materials, since the here-experienced loss is not taken into account in calculating bonuses paid for fulfillment of the profit plan. These losses were sometimes quite considerable. In the last quarter of 1955, at the Construction Trust of Sztálinváros, losses due to the sorting out of materials amounted to 2.5 million forints, more than 2.5 per cent of the value of production in that quarter.

In view of these manipulations by the enterprises, the efforts of the planning authorities have met with only partial success,[104] and hoarding of materials has remained an important part of the strategy in the enterprise's endeavor to maximize bonuses.

102. S. Gergely and V. Wessely, "Stocks Out of Use Are Important Reserves," *KSz*, No. 2 (1956), 187.

103. It should be noted here that the investor firms do not pay carrying charges, because they purchase materials at the expense of their investment-fund allotment, and the carrying charges of stockpiling companies are extremely low (see above, p. 145).

104. Sovány contends that "measures for reducing inventories of the enterprises have not been successful" (p. 1048).

USE OF CAPITAL GOODS

Another problem arising in connection with bonus maximization is the use of capital goods.[105] In Hungary, capital goods used by state enterprises are the property of the state and are given to the enterprise for use through so-called book transfer. The capital goods appear in the books of the enterprises as both assets and liabilities. Faithful to Marxist dogma, no charge is made for the use of fixed funds; the enterprise pays depreciation charges only. The rate of depreciation is low—about 1 to 2 per cent for buildings, 7 to 8 per cent for machines, and 20 to 25 per cent for means of transportation, in most industries.[106] About half the depreciation charge paid by the firm is considered to cover renewal, and an amount approximately corresponding to this figure is returned to the enterprise for this purpose. The other half of the depreciation charge goes into the national investment fund. It has been pointed out in the literature of recent years that the depreciation rates are unduly low, one of the reasons being that no charge for obsolescence has been included.[107]

The economic consequences of the absence of an interest rate and low depreciation charges are that the enterprise will attempt to obtain as many capital goods as possible, it will be unwilling to part with the capital goods in its possession, and will not have sufficient incentive to take good care of its equipment.

As we shall see in Chapter 6, capital goods, including new investments, are given gratuitously to the enterprise. Consequently, the firm endeavors to grab as many capital goods as possible, especially machines and means of transportation. It is characteristic that, as the national machine-balances show, enterprises have demanded in many cases three times as many machines as the available supply.[108] From the viewpoint of bonus maximization, the alternative cost of equipment is so low that the equilibration of

105. In the Soviet orbit the expression "fixed funds" is used.

106. Two per cent for buildings and 7.5 per cent for machines are informative rates, according to Üzemgazdaság (Business Economics) (Budapest, 1950), p. 80.

107. G. Rejtö, "Some Problems Related to Depreciation Rates," PSz, No. 6 (1955), 445; L. Bors, "Economic Aspects of Obsolescence in Articles of Voproszi ekonomiki," KSz, No. 2 (1957), 219–20; A. Kunvári, "Economic Problems of Technical Obsolescence of Machines," KSz, No. 3 (1957), 249–61.

108. A. Máriás, "Some Problems in the Allocation of the Means of Production," KSz, No. 4 (1958), 383.

supply and demand is not possible except by central allocation. But in the absence of economic incentives restricting the demand for capital goods, and in the absence of calculations on investment efficiency, the decisions on the allocation of machines and other equipment do not have a sufficient economic basis. The national economic plan can decide the main proportions of the allocation of capital goods, but it becomes increasingly inadequate as we approach the enterprise level.

The enterprise is unwilling to transfer its equipment, once obtained, to another firm.[109] Because of the low cost of possessing capital goods, the enterprise is inclined to stock as many machines as possible, for the sake of future needs which may never arise. This is noticeable not only between enterprises but also between plants or construction projects within the same firm. The endeavor is to achieve maximum security in regard to machines, since the cost of this security is judged to be lower than the cost of accidental disturbances in production. It has been observed that on many construction projects twice or even three times as many machines are found as are actually needed, and machines are often procured months ahead of their actual use.

There is no serious incentive to take good care of machines and other equipment.[110] In many factories there is a presumption that if a machine becomes unserviceable, the planning authorities will provide another one. This attitude is one of the reasons for the considerable deterioration that can be noted in the machine parks of many industries.[111] Moreover, at some places not even the loss of machines is taken seriously. In 1955 the loss of machines and other equipment to the amount of about 10 million forints has been accounted for in the balance sheet of the Construction Trust of Sztálinváros.[112] All equipment being the property of the state, this item was not debited to the profit and loss statement of the trust, but the book value of these capital goods was deducted from both the asset and the liability side of the balance sheet.

It can be concluded that the extremely low cost of the use of

109. Kunvári, p. 261; Péter, p. 59.
110. Péter, p. 59.
111. F. Jánossy, ME (July 20, 1956), p. 3.
112. This amount (about 3 per cent of the value of yearly production) covered the losses for about two to three years. Considerable amounts were accounted for in the balance sheets of some other construction enterprises as well.

capital goods not only distorts price relations (as has been seen
in Chapter 4) but also hinders the economical use of the machines
and other equipment in the enterprise.

INCENTIVES AND COMPETITION

Examination of the effects of material incentives in the Hungarian economy fails to present a clear-cut picture. In the process
of maximizing bonuses the managers endeavor to fulfill (and
overfulfill) the production and profit plans. The first objective
leads to an over-all increase in production and—at the same time
—to the neglect of cost considerations and to various practices
employed for the sake of plan fulfillment; the pursuance of the
second objective offers an inducement to cost reduction but results also in price increases, quality deterioration, and other
manipulations. The increase in production and the reduction in
costs correspond to the objectives of economic policy, but the use
of various practices described in the foregoing sections entails
a clash between the interests of the firm and those of the national
economy—the latter being pushed into the background. But one
should not forget that some of these manipulations, such as increase in prices and doctoring accounts, do not involve direct
harm to the economy, since the quantity and quality of the commodities produced will not be reduced thereby. Nevertheless,
even in these cases indirect harm is being done: some people
receive unduly high bonuses, and the decision-making bodies get
a distorted picture of actual achievements. At the same time, disregard of the users' needs, neglect of labor-intensive commodities,
deterioration of quality, etc. cause direct damage to the national
economy. Although there is no way to ascertain their magnitude,
experience indicates that these deleterious results have been fairly
strong in the Hungarian economy.[113]

The harmful effects of the material incentive system in Hungary have been frequently deplored.[114] The question remains to

113. Cf. the discussion in the preceding sections of this chapter. It should be
noted here that because of obvious efforts of the firm (and even of the ministry)
to cover up malpractice, information on such cases is evidently very incomplete.
See Péter, p. 99.

114. To quote a characteristic statement: "Encouragement of indifference to demand . . . and of deterioration of quality and narrowing down variety—these are
the common characteristics of such indicators as the value of production and the

be answered: is it possible to remove the deficiencies of the incentive system in the framework of the presently employed system in planning? Different ways can be followed in searching for such a solution. Some people maintain that it should be made impossible for the firm to get around the regulations by tying its hands even more than at present. Application of this method does not seem very promising; we have seen before that in attempting to direct the economy by itemized central orders one encounters certain contradictions that run counter to the very purpose of centralization. Moreover, no matter how closely knit the regulations are, ways can always be found to elude them. In view of the Hungarian experience, one is bound to agree with Kornai's statement that "as soon as a new regulation appears to close a loophole, shortly thereafter a new loophole is found." [115]

Another way to bring the firm's and the national economy's interest into harmony is said to be to simplify the planning process and apply a single indicator: profitability, as a guiding rule for the firm's operation. This method certainly has its advantages over the present system, yet is deficient primarily in two respects: [116] as long as prices are not scarcity prices, profit maximization does not lead to efficient resource allocation; and in the absence of competition among sellers, producers have no incentive to comply with the users' wishes.

The first deficiency has been examined extensively in the foregoing chapters; here we shall concentrate on the second. The application of administrative methods in the management of the economy finds one of its major shortcomings in the lack of opposing interests between the participants of the economic process. Administrative methods are not sufficient to compel the enterprise to produce the commodities actually demanded, or to improve quality. Absence of trade methods puts the buyer at a disadvantage, for—although the producer has considerable latitude in determining the assortment in production—the user can make his choice neither among producers nor among products. As we have previously seen, this situation leads to considerable

---

cost of production" (Kornai, p. 60). Cf. also Lacfalvi and Wagner, *SSz*, No. 7 (1956), 589–90; Péter, pp. 99–100.

115. Kornai, p. 38.

116. Cf. also the shortcomings of a bonus system based on profitability, indicated above, pp. 136–38.

waste and to a deterioration of quality. On the other hand, if the buyers are given the opportunity to choose among the products of different enterprises, a powerful incentive is given to economical production. The competition of the sellers—in contradistinction to the competition of the buyers—is conducive to more careful work, to reduction of costs, and to development of technological methods in production.[117]

The discussion in the years 1956 and 1957 has demonstrated the understanding of the detrimental effects of administrative methods in directing the economy.[118] It has been pointed out that by extending the use of economic incentives, the efficiency of the system could be greatly improved.[119] Yet little has been published of the proposals put forward on the reform of the planning system. Only the solution advocated by Péter has been articulated: (1) instead of directing the economy by itemized central orders, the planning authorities should determine the basic directives only, and should make the decisions on investment; (2) prices should equilibrate supply and demand and should be changed if necessary; and (3) in place of the presently existing buyers' competition, the competition of the producers should be established.[120]

Péter was strongly rebuked by holders of orthodox views, not

117. Sellers' competition is contrasted by Péter with the methods presently used in Hungarian planning. He maintains that at present "the buyers . . . are at the mercy of the producers. They must try to please the producers, the sellers, to compete for their favors, in some cases by bribery . . ." On the other hand, "the competition of the sellers tends to improve the quantity, quality, assortment, and cost of production; consequently this system is cheaper" (p. 115).

118. The editorial in the first issue of *KSz* (Nos. 11–12, 1956) published after the Revolution, concludes: "The presently known form of socialist economy in Hungary has been much less sensitive to botchery than a capitalist economy, partly because the state has played an extremely large role in financing the economy, through the budget, partly because enterprises have not been exposed to an economic mechanism making use of the motives of economical production and material interest" (pp. 1288–89).

119. G. Kopácsy contends that "whereas the direct administrative management of economic life is relatively simple as a method but operates with low efficiency and ultimately leads to smaller results, the employment of economic incentives is rather complicated as a method, requiring great theoretical and practical preparation; but in its use considerable problems and contradictions do not arise, and it works with very great efficiency": "For the Improvement of Our Planning," *KSz*, No. 2 (1957), 140.

120. Péter, pp. 60–61, 64–65, 75, 115. One may note the similarity of Péter's proposal to that of W. Brus for Poland: "On the Role of the Law of Value in Socialist Economy," *Oxford Economic Papers*, 9 (1957), 209–20.

so much by economic arguments as by ideological weapons. It was charged that "placing the enterprises in conditions of competition . . . would bring back the anarchic effects of the law of value to the socialist economy." [121] Péter in his answer emphasized again that "there is competition in our system as well, but competition turned on its head: it is not the sellers who compete with each other for winning customers, but the customers for the favors of the sellers," and argued that there is not much logic in the opinion of Hevesi, "who regards the buyers' competition as 'socialist method' and the sellers', the producers', competition as 'capitalist method.' " [122] Nevertheless, Péter's recommendations have not been applied, and during 1957–58 there has been a return from the criticism of centralized planning to its praise, the opposite views frequently being branded as reactionary and counterrevolutionary. It is likely that future developments will also be greatly affected by shifts in the relative weights of economics and ideology.

121. G. Hevesi, Secretary of the Hungarian Academy of Science, quoted in Péter, p. 79.
122. Ibid., p. 142.

6. Investment: Plans and Realization

INVESTMENT IN PHYSICAL PLANNING

IN CHAPTER 3 we reserved for later discussion the problem of determining planned targets. Our assumption was that the final bill of goods is determined *prior* to the allocation process. By making this simplifying assumption we abstracted from the fact that the rigid separation of the two types of decisions—on the final bill of goods, and on the allocation of resources among these targets—cannot be carried out in practice, since the final bill of goods is constrained by resource availabilities and production possibilities. As we turn to problems connected with the determination of planned targets, this interrelationship between the two types of decisions should be kept in mind.

In determining planned targets, a macroeconomic decision on the proportion of national income to be used for consumption and for investment purposes has first place. It is widely held that in a comprehensive system of planning (not only in its centralized form but also in market socialism) the determination of the amount saved (and invested) is a "political decision" [1] made "arbitrarily" [2] by the planning authorities.[3] A different view has been taken by Barone [4] and E. Atkinson,[5] who maintain that the entire national income should be distributed among the population and the decision of how much to save should be left to each individual. Since in our definition of physical planning the absence of consumer sovereignty is postulated, we shall proceed

1. A. P. Lerner, *The Economics of Control* (New York, Macmillan, 1944), p. 262.
2. O. Lange, "On the Economic Theory of Socialism," in Lippincott, ed., *On the Economic Theory of Socialism*, p. 85.
3. This is the official view in the Soviet orbit as well. See *Soviet Textbook of Political Economy*, p. 460.
4. *Collectivist Economic Planning*, pp. 278–79.
5. "Saving and Investment in a Socialist State," *Review of Economic Studies*, *15* (1947–48), 78–83.

under the assumption that the proportion of national income saved is determined by the central authorities.

After the share of national income to be used for consumption and investment purposes has been decided, the bill of consumer and investment goods must be determined, taking into account existing resources and production possibilities. Of these decisions, the planning of consumer goods for individual consumption has already been dealt with,[6] and the planning of collective consumption is not our concern here. On the following pages, therefore, we shall deal exclusively with problems related to investment activity.

Given the share of investment in national income, the decision-making process on investment activity consists of three steps: (1) allocation of investment funds among various sectors of the economy, (2) decision on individual investment projects, and (3) choice among technological variants in implementing a particular investment project.[7]

Let us assume for the moment that, instead of physical planning, price-planning is used, hence prices reflect the scarcity relationships of the economy. Now interest appears as a price, the price of capital, which gives expression to the scarcity of capital. The rate of interest will be equal to the productivity of the last unit of capital invested in a given period, when—according to our previous assumption—the amount of investment is determined by the central authority.

The use of the interest rate serves dual purposes: it is a costing device (the interest rate as a price reflects the cost of alternatives sacrificed and is an element in price determination), and it is an allocative device (it is used in making a choice among alternative investment possibilities).

Consequently, in the planning of investment activity the rate of interest would be used in allocating the available investment funds among sectors and among projects, and in choosing among

6. See above, pp. 110 ff.

7. In the following discussion we must keep in mind the highly complex nature of the process of decision-making on investments. This process includes long-run targets (such as development of various sectors of the economy) and investment projects extending from five to ten or more years (such as electrification of a backward region) as well as short-run decisions (such as purchase of machines from abroad during the next year). On the role of economic balances in investment decisions see below, p. 175.

technological variants as well.[8] In the realm of static theory existing prices are employed in the valuation of investment alternatives, since it is assumed that the present factor prices, product prices, and interest rate will continue to prevail. This assumption implies unchanged scarcity relationships in the economy. Actually, scarcities will change as a consequence of the very act of investment as well as for other reasons, such as technological change, exhaustion of mineral resources, etc. Therefore, in appraising investment alternatives, the planners should take the expected changes in relative scarcities into account.[9] The error of using existing prices may be greater for an economy in an early stage of industrial development (for example, China) and smaller in a developed country (for example, Czechoslovakia). Another qualification is that the use of present prices implies the acceptance of the present valuation scheme. Yet the planning authority may set certain long-term targets for the economy, the fulfillment of which requires and presupposes modifications in the valuation of factors and products. The central authority may aim at achieving the maximum growth rate, increasing military production, developing backward regions, or some of these and other objectives may be combined. Setting long-term targets for the economy implies a new valuation scheme which corresponds to the planners' objectives.

In the above discussion we assumed the existence of rational prices, prices reflecting the scarcities of the economy, as in price planning. We have had opportunity to see that in physical planning prices are not rational but arbitrary. Prices being arbitrary, an element of arbitrariness will be introduced also in the evaluation of investment alternatives. For example, if the commodities produced by industry W are undervalued and those of industry Z overvalued, investment will stop short of the necessary amount in the first industry, whereas it will be excessive in the second. Nevertheless the arbitrariness of the price structure does not imply that we should shun the use of an interest rate in physi-

8. Investment alternatives are evaluated by comparing the returns and costs of investment alternatives discounted by the rate of interest.

9. For example, in an aluminum-producing project, use of present prices of bauxite, electrical energy, and aluminum may be misleading if present price relations are likely to change because of atomically powered generation of electrical energy or an increase in demand for aluminum.

cal planning.[10] In Chapter 4 [11] it was concluded that by charging interest for the use of capital, we move toward a more rational price structure. Absence of interest (in other words a zero interest rate) implies that capital is regarded as a free good. As a result, labor-intensive products will be overvalued and capital-intensive products will be undervalued; and in the choice among investment alternatives there will be a bias toward capital-intensive investments and toward projects with a long construction period and a long period of recoupment (amortization).[12]

To avoid these inefficiencies, one needs to use interest in physical planning. Yet, in view of the qualifications given above, we cannot jump to the conclusion that investment alternatives should be evaluated solely on the basis of existing prices and interest rates. To repeat: existing prices do not reflect, or only imperfectly reflect, scarcities in physical planning; existing prices may change, because of changes in scarcity relationships; and the planning authority may set certain basic targets for the economy, thereby modifying the existing valuation scheme.

This formidable list of qualifications can overturn the results reached by the traditional valuation methods. Before embarking upon an examination of the three steps in the process of decision-making in investment activity, we shall make some general observations on these points.

Although we would move toward a rational price structure by recalculating prices on the basis of marginal costs, taking into account interest, rent, and quasi-rent, rational prices (as we have pointed out) cannot be achieved until prices are considered also in allocating resources. As a consequence, the endeavor to make

10. It could be argued that, prices being arbitrary, we do not need to use an interest rate if prices of future products are set appropriately to reflect the valuation of the planning authority. See F. Malinvaud, "Capital Accumulation and Efficient Resource Allocation," *Econometrica*, *21* (1953), 252. But this method also entails the implicit use of an interest rate, since the future prices of those goods whose relative valuation undergoes no change will equal the present price augmented by the (implicit) interest rate.

11. Above, pp. 92 ff.

12. Nevertheless, at a certain point in time the use of capital-intensive methods is constrained by the total amount of available capital. Consequently, in the short run the absence of an interest rate cannot lead to application of higher capital-intensive methods for the entire economy; rather, it leads to higher capital intensity in some processes at the expense of others.

rational investment decisions will probably induce the planning authorities to advance toward a system of price planning. On the other hand, if the physical allocation of resources is retained, planners will more frequently overrule or even leave out of consideration calculations on the efficiency of alternative investment possibilities, maintaining that prices are irrational anyway.

Even if we assume that existing prices are rational, future prices cannot be calculated with certainty. The planning authority may estimate the effect of certain investments on future prices, but an element of uncertainty is created, for example, by unforeseen future technological changes, by the discovery of mineral deposits, etc.

The most important qualification is the setting of basic targets for the economy, which necessitates a change in the existing scheme of valuation. But these considerations do not lend themselves easily to numerical expression and are not likely to be incorporated in calculations on the efficiency of investments. Consequently, a further element of vagueness is added to the evaluation of investment alternatives.

One more point should be mentioned. In our discussion on prices in Chapter 4 we omitted consideration of foreign trade relations, postulating that prices should correspond to the domestic scarcity relationships of the national economy. We shall now introduce the possibility of international trade. It is taught in the theory of international trade that prices of traded commodities are formed on the world market, thereby reflecting scarcity relationships in countries participating in world trade rather than scarcities in individual countries. Domestic prices of these commodities will correspond to world market prices after an appropriate conversion on the existing exchange rate and an adjustment for transportation costs have been made.[13] In the development policy of an economy participating in the international division of labor, prices on the world market and thereby production possibilities of other countries will be given con-

13. Nevertheless, the state may cause domestic prices to deviate from world market prices for transitional periods by using appropriate taxes (tariffs) and subsidies, if it is expected that the inherent production possibilities of the economy can be realized thereby (infant-industry argument). Domestic prices can be made to differ from world market prices also, in order to smooth out fluctuations on the world market or to avoid the destruction of an industry needed for military purposes, etc. (For a discussion of Hungarian foreign trade see below, Appendix C.)

sideration. As a result, we will expect changes of lesser intensity in the existing valuation scheme.

The effect of international trade relations on domestic prices and on investment decisions of different economies will depend on various circumstances. In a large economy, such as that of the Soviet Union, which is in possession of most of the needed resources, world market relations may be given less consideration than in an economy such as Hungary's, where many basic resources are lacking. Yet even in the latter case, political motives and military goals might lead to autarky and hence to disregard of trade possibilities in making investment decisions.

Having examined these qualifications, we may now consider in detail the three types of decisions made in investment planning.

1. In allocating investment funds among various sectors of the economy, long-term targets set by the planners play a salient role. Yet in this connection the problems we face in an autarkical economy are different from those of an economy that is expected to participate in the international division of labor. In the latter case the task of investment planning is simpler, since world-market price relations can be used in evaluating investment alternatives, and adjusting the structure of production to world market conditions may be one of the major goals. It can be said that in this case the long-term targets of the economy are constrained by prices on the world market and by the resource endowment of the country in question. In an autarkical economy the planners have one more degree of freedom, since in deciding basic objectives they do not consider world market prices. Consequently, in the absence of the guiding role of world market prices, calculations on investment efficiency are likely to play a lesser role than in a country entering into trade relations with other economies, and will be more frequently overruled by giving consideration to long-term goals.

Investment decisions that would be considered irrational on the basis of calculations on investment efficiency may become rational from the viewpoint of the basic targets set for the national economy. Nevertheless, as efficiency calculations recede into the background in allocating investment funds, investment decisions will become more vague. Because of the difficulty in giving numerical expression to long-term objectives, the possibility of misallocation of resources increases, and bargaining for investment funds

may assume considerable importance. Yet this may be the necessary price paid for achieving certain objectives.

Many intermediate stages can be imagined between the two
situations described above, where political and military considerations may considerably affect the allocation of investment funds.[14]
It should be added that even if adjustment to conditions on the
world market is assumed to be one of the major objectives, the
strategy of development must be decided by the planning authorities, and different strategies imply different rates of development
for various industries.[15]

2. After the allocation of investment funds among various
sectors of the economy has been decided on, the next step is the
decision on individual investment projects. For example, if an
increase of electrical energy is planned, a choice must be made
among alternatives such as production of energy by atomic
power, water power, or coal. In such a case, calculations on
efficiency should assume primary importance. Yet if the choice
is to be made among projects with different end products, calculations on investment efficiency may be overruled by consideration of long-run targets of the economy. In this connection,
military considerations and the endeavor to develop backward
regions may be mentioned. The first case is a prototype of noneconomic objectives; the second is an example for external
economies in a dynamic sense. Expected changes in scarcity rela-

14. Besides Marxist theology, the drive for autarky and political and military
considerations are the main reasons for neglecting calculations on investment
efficiency in the Soviet Union. A good exposition of this policy can be found in
T. S. Khachaturov, *Osnovy ekonomiki zheleznodorozhnogo transporta* (*The Economic
Principles of Railroad Transportation*), Pt. I (Moscow, 1946), quoted in H. Hunter,
"The Planning of Investments in the Soviet Union," *Review of Economics and
Statistics, 31* (1949), 58: "The allocation of investment funds among industries and
the choice of projects to be carried out, are made as the outcome of considerations
related to the task of socialist construction, industrialization of the country, the
policy towards the nationalities and the strengthening of national defense." Or more
strongly: "Propositions which consist in submitting capital construction in the
U.S.S.R. to the bourgeois principle of 'efficiency' are in contradiction to the policy
of the Party and the State in their work of planning capital investment and in
contradiction to the Soviet method of industrialization"—*Planovoe khozyaistvo*, No.
4 (1949), 85, quoted in P. Wiles, "Scarcity, Marxism and Gosplan," *Oxford Economic
Papers, 5* (1953), 306.

15. On the problem of the strategy of development in underdeveloped countries
see A. O. Hirschmann, *The Strategy of Economic Development*, New Haven, Yale
University Press, 1958.

tionships present another qualification. Nevertheless, the objectives being narrowed down, calculations on the efficiency of investments should assume a much larger role in choosing among investment projects than in the allocation of investment funds among sectors.[16]

3. In the choice among technological variants for implementing a particular investment project, calculations on the efficiency of different variants should give guidance.[17] Since the long-run targets of the economy have already been taken care of at the preceding stages, the problems have narrowed down sufficiently to give numerical expression to the factors determining the decision. The choice among technological variants should be made on the basis of information on initial cost, operating expenses, period of recoupment, and productivity of the new investment, with consideration given also to anticipated changes in scarcity relationships. For example, in the choice between a single- or double-track railroad, estimates on future transportation needs are necessary; and in designing new machines, attention should be paid to expected changes in technology.

In making the above decisions, the planners should consider the consistency of these decisions. In a free enterprise economy, investment decisions are made on the basis of expected prices and demand conditions when information on the decisions of other investors is rarely available. It is an advantage of a planned economy that overlapping and inconsistency in investment decisions can be avoided. Consistency can be achieved by the use of long-term physical balances which contain the quantities of various commodities produced in future years as a result of investment activity.

16. This is not so in the Soviet Union, where calculations on the efficiency of various investment projects are apparently not used in choosing among alternative projects; see Khachaturov's statement quoted above, n. 14.

17. As G. Grossman describes, the choice among technological variants is the task of the project maker in the Soviet Union. The project makers (mostly engineers) have often calculated the efficiency of the variants and in some cases have also used an interest rate in the calculations on the basis of which the choice among technological variants is made. Yet the attacks from exponents of Marxist orthodoxy have resulted in a partial retreat from the use of the interest rate: G. Grossman, "Scarce Capital and Soviet Doctrine," *Quarterly Journal of Economics,* 67 (1953), 311–43. The discussion has flared up again in recent years, but the official Soviet position has not yet been revealed.

Investment Decisions in Hungary

In Chapter 2 we reviewed the economic policy of the Hungarian government during the postwar period. It was shown that since 1951 frequent changes have been made in economic policy and consequently in investment policy. In the following discussion we shall consider the 1950–55 period as a whole.[18]

Hungarian economists who have examined the planning of investments agree that efficiency considerations had been largely neglected in shaping investment policy.[19] Neither were changes in investment policy based on an objective economic examination of the issues involved.[20] It has been pointed out that "in the preparation of long-term investment plans the role of the conditions of efficiency was not clarified; consequently efficiency considerations were neglected in determining the goals of investments."[21] Awareness of some basic difficulties in investment planning can also be spotted in these writings. Turánszky notes the impossibility of giving numerical measure to the vaunted principle of "consideration of the national economy's interest."[22] One can also notice awareness of the fact that the arbitrary nature of prices creates arbitrariness in calculations on the efficiency of investment alternatives as well.[23] The absence of rational prices has even led some economists to the conclusion that "in the present situation it is impossible to imagine calculations which would give an unequivocal answer to the efficiency of investments."[24] It can be inferred from these writings that the predominance of noneconomic considerations, the vagueness of the

18. For policy modifications during this period see above, pp. 32 ff.

19. F. Deák, "The Preparation and Economic-Technical Planning of Investments," SSz, No. 4 (1956), 298; F. Deák, D. Sóky, and G. Szende, "The Efficiency and Planning of Investments," SSz, Nos. 1–2 (1957), 61; J. Tar, "Changes in the Length of the Construction Period," SSz, Nos. 7–8 (1956), 620; M. Turánszky, "Some Problems in Investment Planning," SSz, No. 12 (1957), 1026–27.

20. "General directives changed several times during these three years (1953–56), each modification resulting in a loss of some hundred million forints . . . With regard to the planning of investments, the common characteristics of the Rákosi and Imre Nagy policy was to disparage objective economic considerations and make subjective decisions" (Turánszky, p. 1036). A similar conclusion was reached by Deák (p. 298) regarding the entire Five Year Plan period.

21. Turánszky, pp. 1026–27.

22. Ibid., p. 1027.

23. Deák, Sóky, and Szende, p. 62.

24. Ibid., p. 65.

concept of the national economy's interest, and the irrationality of the price structure contributed equally to the neglect of efficiency considerations.

Furthermore, shortcomings have been experienced in regard to the consistency of investment decisions. An official source reveals that insufficient attention was paid to the interrelationships of various investment projects and to changes in capacity resulting from investment activity; and no provision was made for procuring materials to be used in many of the newly built plants. In general, investment planning was in forints rather than in physical units—which impeded the establishment of consistency.[25]

We turn now to changes in the share of investments in national income.[26] In 1938, 6 per cent of the national income (slightly higher than the 5 per cent experienced in 1934–37 [27] went for fixed investment; the figure reached 10 per cent when increase in stocks was included.[28] During the Three Year Plan, 15 to 17 per cent of national income was invested, and this percentage increased further during the Five Year Plan: as Table 1 shows, on 1949 prices it averaged 26 per cent in the 1950–55 period. The data used to calculate these figures include a turnover tax on consumer goods; if this item is deducted from the value of national income, the share of investments in 1950–55 is between 28 and 29 per cent; and if undervaluation of producer goods—already noticeable in 1949—is considered, it reaches 35 per cent.[29] This per-

---

25. "There has been no estimate how the new investment projects will increase fixed capital in particular economic sectors or how the capacity of particular economic or industrial sectors will increase as a result of new investments. Investment plans have not taken into account whether materials needed for the new plants are available at all, and if so, whether they can be procured from domestic production or must be imported. Investment plans have usually been prepared only in global terms, in forints. This means the project outlines contained no deadline, no capacity, no material needs, no cost of investment projects—only the forint amount to be spent for various investment purposes" (*Facts and Figures*, p. 45).

26. In Chap. 2 the investment figures, in accordance with Hungarian usage, referred to gross fixed investment. In this chapter distinction is made between net investment and gross fixed investment, where net investment = gross fixed investment + renewals ± changes in inventories − depreciation. In the following discussion the share of investment in national income will denote the share of *net* investment in *net* national income. Here and throughout, the Marxist conception of national income (net value of material production) is used.

27. Matolcsy and Varga, *National Income of Hungary*, p. 75.

28. J. Judik, "The Three Year Plan," *KSz*, Nos. 1–2 (1947), 32–33. There are no estimates on changes in inventories prior to 1938.

29. See below, p. 217.

centage greatly exceeds the "25 per cent rule" which, according to
Strumilin, corresponds to planning practice in Soviet-type economies.[30]

Given the share of investments in national income, investment
decisions can be examined in the framework delineated above,
where we distinguished three steps of allocating investment funds:
(1) among sectors, (2) among projects, and (3) the choice among
technological variants of a particular project.

TABLE 1. *Share of Investment in National Income*

	percentage
1949	21.0
1950	26.7
1951	34.0
1952	26.5
1953	28.8
1954	19.6
1955	20.0
1950–55 average	26.0

Source: Corrected figures of official statistics (below, p. 214).

The apportionment of investment funds among sectors can be
seen in Table 2. Two matters should be considered in this connection: allocation of investment funds among various branches
of industry; and allocation to industry as distinct from other
productive sectors.

The figures of Table 2 show the disproportionate development
of heavy industry. In the 1950–55 period, heavy industry received
91 per cent of the funds devoted to industrial investment. If
we inquire into the reasons for this policy, political[31] and military[32] motives become apparent. In the Hungarian economy, as
in other satellite countries, there was a tendency to imitate
Soviet methods. Arguing from the presupposition that the example

30. S. Strumilin, "The Balance of the National Economy as an Instrument of
Socialist Planning," *Voprosy ekonomiki*, No. 11 (1954), 38, quoted in *Economic Survey
of Europe in 1955*, p. 199.

31. An editorial in *KSz* states that "in forming economic policy itself, the political
point of view has been decisive": Nos. 11–12 (1956), 1287.

32. I. Friss, Director of the Economic Institute, revealed that "most of the investments were basically of such a kind that they served armament, directly or indirectly": "Our Problems in Economic Policy and the Plan for 1957," *KSz*, No. 7
(1957), 702.

of the Soviet Union indicates the "unique road to socialism," the conclusion had been reached that the satellite countries should follow Soviet economic policy in developing their own heavy industry.[33] Rearmament and the endeavor to disengage economic ties with the West were also conducive to this policy.

TABLE 2. *Allocation of Gross Fixed Investment*

	Five Year Plan (1950–54)		1955	1950–55
	Original Plan	Augmented Plan	Actual Figures	
	BILLIONS OF CURRENT FORINTS			
Heavy industry	18.3	40.5	27.5	3.9	31.4
Light and food industries	3.0	3.5	2.3	0.8	3.1
All industry	21.3	44.0	29.8	4.7	34.5
Agriculture	8.0	11.0	9.3	2.6	11.9
Transport and communications	7.5	10.0	8.6	0.9	9.5
Trade	0.9	1.0	1.7	0.4	2.1
Housing, health, cultural, social	7.4	13.0	10.0	2.4	12.4
Other	3.3	3.4	8.0	0.2	9.2
Reserve	2.5	5.0	—	—	—
TOTAL	50.9	85.0	67.4	11.2	78.6

Sources: On the original plan: *The Five Year Plan of the Hungarian People's Republic,* pp. 6–7.
On the augmented version of the plan: *ST,* No. 2 (1954), 8–9.
Figures refer to gross fixed investments. Data on net investments are not available in this breakdown. If no other reference is given, investment figures cited in this section are taken from the above sources.

The available evidence suggests that economic preparation of the allocation of investment funds among sectors was lacking in two important respects: the efficiency of investments in various sectors was not evaluated, and in some instances—especially in

33. It was said to be the duty of every people's democracy to develop its heavy industry. Objections were silenced with arguments that do not indicate a profound understanding of pricing methods applied or of the law of comparative advantage. A quotation from the official Communist party paper will serve as an example. A rhetorical question is asked: "Is it possible to suggest to a people's democracy having favorable conditions for raw-material production that it should develop only its heavy industry, while we develop only light industry and agriculture? It is known that development of heavy industry is more costly than that of light industry. How can we demand of a friendly country that it invest a substantial part of its national income in coal-mining, metal production, and other branches of heavy industry and leave us to develop only the 'cheap' branches of the national economy?" (*SzN,* July 31, 1955).

the iron and steel industry—insufficient provision was made for
procuring raw materials.[34] These deficiencies have been forcefully expressed in Imre Nagy's words:

> Industry, and especially heavy industry, was not developed
> on the basis of scientific analysis, with due regard for economy
> and practicality. At the same time when it was decided to
> build great industrial establishments a complete lack of in-
> formation prevailed as to their cost or the amount of imported
> material that would be required to establish them . . . All
> this became evident only after the great industrial establish-
> ments had already been put into operation. By then it was
> too late to do anything but import the necessary basic and
> raw materials, unless we wanted to close down the establish-
> ments.[35]

Two particular cases will be examined here: coal-mining and
iron and steel production. Investments in these two fields
amounted to 38 per cent of funds devoted to industry as a whole.

Hungarian coal-mining compares unfavorably with that of
Poland, for example. Labor productivity in Hungarian mines
is only one-third of Polish productivity. While the Hungarian
miner produces 0.6 tons per man-day in hard coal equivalent,
the Polish miner produces 1.8 tons.[36] Hungary had to pay a high
price for the 65 per cent increase in coal production (hard coal
equivalent) during the 1949–55 period.[37] The original version
of the Five Year Plan envisaged a 61 per cent increase in coal
production with an investment of 2.5 billion forints, and the
augmented version projected an increase of 139 per cent in
production and an investment of 4.8 billion forints. Actually,
up to 1955, 7.0 billion forints were spent for this purpose, and
coal production increased by 65 per cent.[38] These figures indicate
that the sacrifice necessary to achieve the original production
targets was considerably larger than expected, and the planning
authorities had to encroach upon investment funds originally

34. Friss, p. 703, and sources cited above, n. 19.
35. *Imre Nagy on Communism*, p. 186; see also pp. 107, 136.
36. *Economic Bulletin for Europe*, No. 2 (1955), 93.
37. *SHK*, No. 4 (1957), 39.
38. Data on investments refer not merely to coal-mining but also to other branches
of mining. Yet the numerical importance of investments in these other branches
is relatively small and can be overlooked in comparing the figures.

allotted to other industries to increase coal production.[39] In view of the comparative disadvantage of the Hungarian coal industry, it is doubtful that these funds were used efficiently in the long run; nevertheless, the immediate fuel need of the economy for achieving given targets, coupled with difficulties in importing fuel, made these investments necessary. It is another matter that the production targets in some coal-intensive industries (such as the iron and steel industry) can be judged excessively high, and that the import difficulties were largely the effect of the regime's foreign-trade policy.

Less can be said for the development of the iron and steel industry. In a country which imports 80 per cent of its iron ore, more than 90 per cent of coking coal, and 50 per cent of its scrap iron, iron and steel production is not likely to be efficient. The inefficiency of the extension of iron production in Hungary can be seen from data compiled by a Hungarian economist, J. Fáy. Table 3 shows the cost (per one ton of pig iron) of importing pig iron and of producing it from imported materials.

According to Fáy's estimate Hungary spends (per one ton of pig iron) 23 per cent more on the import of iron ore, coking coal, and other raw materials necessary for iron-smelting than on the import of pig iron. If domestic production costs are added, the cost of producing pig iron exceeds the cost of importing it by 88 per cent.[40]

In view of these figures, the 6.1 billion forints invested in metallurgy appears to have been used inefficiently. A large part of this amount was devoted to constructing iron and steel works at Sztálinváros.[41] This investment exemplifies some of the characteristic errors committed in developing heavy industry. The establishment was originally scheduled to use Yugoslav pig iron and Hungarian coking coal (from Komló). After construction was begun, for military considerations the building site was moved

---

39. Investment in mining as a percentage of investments in the entire industry:

> Five Year Plan, original version (1950–54)   12 per cent
> Five Year Plan, augmented version (1950–54)   11 per cent
> Actual (1950–55)   20 per cent

40. Fáy, SSz, Nos. 7–8 (1957), 558. The indirect losses (due to undervaluation of coal and electrical energy) were also added to actual cost.

41. The entire cost of the investment in Sztálinváros, including the construction of dwellings, roads, etc., amounted to 3,751 million forints in 1950–55.

eighty miles north of its original site near the Yugoslav border. The breaking of economic ties with Yugoslavia and the non-fulfillment of expectations for the cokeability of Komló coal necessitated importing iron ore from the Soviet Union and procuring coking coal from various Western and Eastern European countries.[42] The investment was considered unproductive

TABLE 3. *Cost of Importing Pig Iron and Materials Necessary for Iron Smelting*

	Price and Cost of Transportation Paid to Foreign Suppliers		Cost of Inland Transportation	Together
	FOREIGN EXCHANGE FORINTS	DOMESTIC FORINTS		
Pig iron	580	760	40	800
Materials for iron production	559	923	117	1040
Difference	−21	+163	+77	+240

Source: J. Fáy, "On the Problem of Efficiency in Metallurgy," *SSz*, Nos. 7–8 (1957), 559.

"Foreign exchange forint" denotes the unit of account used in Hungarian foreign trade. The difference between the cost of importation expressed in "foreign exchange forints" or in "domestic forints" is due to differences in valuation of foreign currencies. It has been estimated that one foreign exchange forint corresponds to 1.31 domestic forints for pig-iron imports from the Soviet Union and to 1.65 domestic forints for imports of raw materials needed for iron-smelting (these materials come partly from hard currency areas such as Belgium and Germany). The valuation of foreign currencies was effected by calculating the domestic value of the commodities to be given up for one unit of a particular currency. It should be noted that this calculation (based on 1954 data) has a considerable margin of error, since the country of procurement for pig iron, and for iron ore, coking coal, and other materials necessary for iron-smelting may change, and the composition of trade in general may alter.

and construction of the plant was interrupted during the period of the New Course, though it was resumed upon return to the policy of accelerated industrialization.

The situation in regard to a few other industries may be briefly noted. An important achievement of the Hungarian economy is the increase in production of electrical energy from 2.52 million MW-hours in 1949 to 5.43 million MW-hours in 1955,[43] as a

42. Fáy's article, published in 1957, took no note of the possibility of future iron ore imports from Yugoslavia.

43. *SE*, p. 74.

result of an expansion in electrical generating equipment. Yet it can be objected that production costs of electrical energy are higher in Hungary than in any neighboring country, and it may prove cheaper to import electrical energy than to produce it domestically.[44] In view of the production records, it seems that economical production was better served by investments in the chemical industry.[45]

Parallel to the accelerated development of material-intensive branches in heavy industry, labor-intensive sectors which succeeded in establishing a competitive position on the world market before World War II (such as precision mechanics, electrical instruments, telecommunications equipment) have been largely neglected in investment programs.[46] This policy has certainly deprived the Hungarian economy of potential foreign-exchange earnings and impeded the development of its industry along the lines of comparative advantage.

Besides the neglect of some labor-intensive branches in heavy industry, the failure of the investment policy to provide adequate investment funds for purposes of light industry should be emphasized. In the period 1950–55 only 1.6 billion forints were devoted to investments in light industry. Since the funds allotted to renewal of equipment were considerably less than depreciation charges,[47]

44. See *Economic Bulletin for Europe*, No. 2 (1955), 93.
45. For the machine industry see below, pp. 268–69.
46. The following table shows the allocation of investment funds among various branches of heavy industry in 1950–55:

	Million Forints
Mining	6,996
Metallurgy	6,114
Electrical power	5,116
Building materials	2,008
Chemicals	4,212
Machine industry	3,397
Electrical machinery and electrical instruments	879
Precision mechanics and hardware production	2,212
Transport repair shops	371
	31,305

Out of the 2,154 million forints spent on investments in precision mechanics and in the hardware industry in 1950–54 only 412 billion were devoted to the first purpose: *Economic Survey for Europe in 1955*, p. 244 (this breakdown of data is not available for 1955). It has been reported that a considerable part of investment in the hardware industry directly served military purposes (munitions production, etc.).

47. In the 1951–55 period depreciation charges exceeded the amounts spent

the machine stock of light industry deteriorated rather than improved during the period under discussion. Insufficient attention paid to developing light industry is another case which shows the effects of neglecting efficiency calculations. It is now widely accepted that modernization of equipment would have considerably improved the competitiveness of Hungarian light industrial products in the world market.[48]

In general, in allocating investment funds among industries, the development of material-intensive branches were emphasized at the expense of labor-intensive sectors. This choice is justified if autarky and increase of military production are considered the main goals of the economy. Different conclusions will be reached if participation in the international division of labor is taken into consideration. In such a case, in view of the lack of industrial raw materials and the favorable past record of the labor-intensive branches of manufacturing, allocation of investment funds among various industries cannot be regarded as economical.[49] Besides disproportions in this allocation, it has also been charged that industry as a whole had been given an unduly high proportion of investment funds at the expense of agriculture.[50] We cannot pass judgment on this question here; we shall return to it after examining national income data in Chapter 7.

---

on renewal by 5.9 billion forints in industry as a whole (SE, p. 45; data not available for 1950). Since renewal activity was considerably less in light and food industries than in heavy industry, it is likely that the main part of this discrepancy pertains to these industries.

48. It has been held also that the required increase in capacity to achieve a certain increase in production is much less in light industry than in heavy. The following figures are given by J. Drecin, "Some Questions in Regard to Investments," MSzKSz, Nos. 8–9 (1954), 717, on the required increase in capacity for a production increase of 100 forints:

	1950	1951	1952
Heavy	67	76	93
Light and food	5	8	12

Drecin does not give the source of his figures, and it is possible that although he speaks about capacity requirements he is really comparing actual changes in capacity and production. In the latter case his findings must be strongly qualified, since in light and food industries better utilization of capacity also contributed to an increase in production.

49. Facts and Figures, p. 113.

50. I. Farkas, "New Features of Our Investment Policy," KSz, No. 11 (1958), 1150.

The discussion presented above indicates the neglect of efficiency considerations in apportioning investment funds among sectors. Calculations were not prepared to compare the efficiency of alternative investment projects either. The only exception was in the field of electrical power generation, where the efficiency of various possibilities for producing electrical energy was compared.[51] There is no evidence, however, that this calculation was actually put into use, and there is general consensus that the efficiency of investment alternatives was not considered in selecting investment projects.[52] It was held that the basic objectives of the economy can be served without relying on efficiency calculations. This practice has led, nevertheless, to neglect of economic considerations and to the increased importance of bargaining in allocating investment funds among projects.[53]

Consonant with Soviet practice, estimates were prepared on divers occasions on the efficiency of technological variants for carrying out a particular investment project. The Hungarian Ministry for Transportation availed itself of methods employed in the Soviet transportation industry and also made use of an interest rate, disguised under the name "coefficient of effectiveness." The design bureaus, the project-maker organizations in Hungary, prepared estimates on the cost of technological variants for some investment projects but without using an interest rate. Such estimates were employed at times in choosing among technological variants of a particular investment project.[54]

Having reviewed the main aspects of making investment decisions in Hungarian planning, in the next section we shall give a short description of the process of project-making and shall characterize the respective role of the investor, the design bureau, and the contractors (that is, the enterprises which carry out the investment project). This discussion will prepare the ground for considering the cost and actual realization of investments.

51. T. Liska, "Experimental Calculations on the Efficiency of Investments and of Our Participation in the International Division of Labor," *KSz*, No. 5 (1956), 521–29.

52. Deák, Sóky, and Szende, *SSz*, Nos. 1–2 (1957), 64.

53. On the administrative process of project-selection see the next section.

54. "During this period [the Five Year Plan] productivity considerations were entirely neglected. Estimates on efficiency (if they were made) were used (if they were used) only in the next step: to decide in what form a particular investment should be carried out" (Deák, Sóky, and Szende, p. 64). Cf. the relevant passages in the next section, below.

ORGANIZATIONAL STRUCTURE IN THE PLANNING AND CARRYING OUT OF INVESTMENT PROJECTS [55]

Investment projects may be initiated by various organizations. Projects of national importance are initiated by the Planning Office, some projects by the ministries, and reconstruction or enlargement of an existing plant frequently by the enterprises. As in production planning and allocation, the method of "planning from above" applies also to planning investment projects. On the basis of directives received from the Party and the Council of Ministers, the Planning Office apportions investment funds among various sectors. Furthermore, with the approval of the Council of Ministers, the Planning Office also decides on the amounts allotted to large investment projects and on investment funds made available to various ministries for implementing smaller projects. In allotting funds among ministries, the previously mentioned bargaining process plays a considerable role. The ministries, in specifying the use of amounts allotted for smaller investments, take into consideration requests of the enterprises for investment funds. The final list of investment projects is approved by the Planning Office and ultimately by the Council of Ministers.

The actual planning of investment projects consists of three steps: the investment program, the project outline, and the technological plan documentation.

The investment program is prepared by the organization which initiates the investment. It contains informative data on the objective of the investment and on the expected capacity and location of the project. The investment program for projects above the five-million forint limit is approved on recommendation of the Planning Office by the Council of Ministers, and below this limit by the ministry supervising the investor.

The project outline is drawn up by a design bureau, which will also prepare detailed technological plans for the project.

55. This section is based mainly on my "Cost Estimate and Calculation," in *Workshop Administration in the Construction Industry*, pp. 150–80. It will be concerned with investments financed from the state budget. It should be noted that only an insignificant part of industrial investments was financed from other sources, such as the director's fund or bank credit (A. Schmidt, "The Financing of the Investments of State Enterprises," *Yearbook*, p. 224).

This outline supplies data on the operation of the project if completed. It contains a description of technological methods to be used in carrying it out, a rough calculation (on the basis of aggregate norms) of expected material needs and costs, and the time schedule of the investment. The process of approval is the same as for the investment program.

The technological plan documentation (prepared by a design bureau) contains a detailed description (with drawings) of the location of the project, detailed technological plans, and a cost estimate. This documentation is designed to supply all technological plans and calculations necessary for carrying out the investment. The design bureau may subcontract to specialized design bureaus the parts of the documentation which require special skills to prepare. The plan documentation is approved by the ministry supervising the investor.

Except for the supervising organizations, participants in the process of planning and executing an investment project are the investor firm, the design bureau, and the contractors. Some factors affecting the behavior of these organizations will be examined below.

If the investment project entails constructing a new factory or substantial reconstruction or enlargement of an existing one, an investment firm is established to implement the project. Upon completion of the investment project this firm merges with the producing enterprise. In the case of smaller reconstruction or enlargement, the investor is the firm operating the plant. In the following we shall use the term "investor" to denote both.

It is characteristic of the financing of investments from the state budget that the investor regards the investment funds as gratuitous; [56] the centralized planning of investments assumes the character of a grant, where the investment funds appear as given "from above." Absence of interest charges on the fixed capital of the firm points in the same direction. Another factor influencing the investor's behavior is that the planning authorities do not use any appropriate method for evaluating the efficiency of various investment projects. The behavior of the investor, resulting from these factors, can be characterized as follows: [57]

56. Turánszky, SSz, No. 12 (1957), p. 1026.
57. Some of these points have also been made by Schmidt, pp. 218–41.

1. the enterprise endeavors to obtain as much in investment funds as possible;
2. these investment funds are demanded (and often obtained) even without sufficient justification;
3. the enterprise is inclined to demand an expensive variant even if a modest one would suffice;
4. the investment frequently appears as the most convenient solution for the enterprise's problems in the sphere of plan fulfillment and profitability;
5. the gratuitous character of the investment funds tempts the enterprise to cover some of the costs of current production at the expense of the investment account;
6. investment funds being appropriated yearly and not transferable for the next year, needed or unneeded, the investor will spend the available funds at the end of the year, since otherwise these would be lost (in general, funds are often spent even if their use is unjustified, in order to fulfill the investment plan in forint terms);
7. since additional funds can generally be obtained to complete the project, the investor is unconcerned if actual costs exceed planned costs.

Points 1–4 have an effect on exaggerated demands for investment funds; 5–6 result in the misuse of these funds; and 6–7 indicate lack of concern on the part of the investor for cost increases brought about by the enterprises carrying out the project. The last factor, which is of great importance in the realization of investments, will be dealt with in more detail later.

The investor engages a design bureau (which may subcontract portions of the technological plans) to prepare the project outline and the technological plan documentation for the project. In preparing the technological plans, the design bureau may compare technological variants, but it has no incentive to do so: since the employees of the design bureau receive bonuses for speedy completion of the plans, painstaking comparison of alternative variants would reduce their chances for bonuses. In like manner, the managers' chances for higher bonuses are reduced if they employ more people on the preparation of a particular plan. Furthermore, most design bureaus receive their remuneration calculated as a percentage of the cost of the project; thus they are materially interested in a high price.[58] As a counteracting force, the professional spirit in searching for better solutions may be mentioned. This spirit, however, does not necessarily lead to cost reduction; it may well lead to employment of new but costly technological methods.

The supervising ministry (mostly the Ministry for Construction) designates a design bureau to prepare the technological plans of a particular investment project, and construction enterprises and other firms which are to carry out the project. Thus the investor has no choice among design bureaus or construction enterprises and cannot compare alternative cost estimates or bids; it must engage the enterprise designated. As a consequence, competition for contracts cannot operate as a force leading to reduction of investment costs.

Investment projects are carried out by construction enterprises, by factories supplying machines, and in the case of some agricultural investments (for example, reforestation) by the investor firm itself. In 1950–55 about 56 per cent of investment funds were spent on construction, 21 per cent on procuring machines, and 23 per cent for other purposes (the last item includes the cost of technological plans, the administrative costs of investment firms and some agricultural investments).[59] In this section, we shall be concerned with construction enterprises only.

Like any other firm, the construction enterprise endeavors to maximize bonuses. For this purpose it frequently avails itself of such devices as price increases, charges for nonperformed work, and deterioration of construction quality. The first step in the price increase for construction work is a countercalculation prepared by the construction firm in opposition to the design bureau's cost estimate. The design bureau is not materially interested in the approval or rejection of the countercalculation, but experience suggests that the professional pride of the designing engineers has often stood in the way of modifying the original estimate. An important exception is that since 1955 the construction enterprise participates in drawing up the basic cost-determining estimates, and thereby costs can be increased *before* the

58. The material interest of the Design Bureaus in a high price in order to over-fulfill their production plan is emphasized by Turánszky, pp. 1042–45, and *Facts and Figures*, p. 87.

59. *SE*, p. 46.

detailed cost estimate is prepared by the design bureau. In these cases the construction firm has a better chance to hammer out higher prices. Furthermore, if the countercalculation is partly or entirely rejected by the design bureau, the firm can apply to its own supervising ministry, the Ministry for Construction (in the case of road and railroad building, the Ministry for Transportation) to revise the price. The enterprise encounters less opposition here, since the ministry has a moral interest in plan fulfillment on the ministry level and in the well-being (materialized in terms of bonuses) of the employees in its enterprises. As a result, decisions by the Ministry for Construction (and the Ministry for Transportation) have become an important factor in the cost increase of investments in the experience of Hungarian planning.

The investor's chances of preventing price increases in construction work are limited, since the decision of the Ministry for Construction is final and cannot be appealed. Yet in view of the foregoings, the investor does not even have much incentive to keep down costs. In Hungary cost considerations have been of little importance to the investor, his main objective being the completion of the investment project. For this purpose he has been willing to make concessions to the construction firm in the form of price increases and in accepting charges for nonperformed work. This tendency was especially strong during 1950–54, when the employees of the investment firm received bonuses for fulfilling the investment plan expressed in forints. Consequently, the interest of the employees of the investment firm was identical with that of the construction enterprise in spending investing funds. Even if an invesment firm had been thrifty during the year, the remainder of the allotted funds was usually spent in the last month. As a result, the value of construction activity in December exceeded the monthly average by 20 to 30 per cent, although—because of cold weather and the Christmas holidays —actual production was probably 30 to 40 per cent less than usual.[60] In 1954 this bonus system was discontinued, but the new system does not give incentive to cost reduction either, and no significant change has been experienced in the investor's behavior.[61]

60. To fulfill the investment plan, in December most unsettled items which accumulated in previous months were accepted. This practice is mentioned in Deák, Sóky, and Szende, p. 61.

61. Turánszky, p. 1041.

In 1954 the Investment Bank increased the personnel of its control groups in an attempt to prevent squandering of investment funds. The controllers reviewed cost estimates as well as the amounts actually charged by the construction enterprises. Excessive charges were revealed to the amount of 200 million forints in 1954, 76 million in 1955, and 84 million in the first three quarters of 1955.[62] Yet the Bank's activity was necessarily limited by the impossibility of reviewing more than a fraction of the accounts, and especially by the common resistance displayed by the investor, the construction firm, and the Ministry for Construction.

Cost of Investment

We saw in the last section that investment funds are spent on construction, procurement of machines, and other items such as cost of technological plans and reforestation. Increases in the price paid for the various categories will be estimated here in order to give a measure to the rise of investment costs during the period under examination. It should be noted that the price charged by the contractors to the investment firm is considered as the cost and, at the same time, the value (price) of the investment, hence the expressions "cost" and "value" (price) of investment are used interchangeably.

Construction activity is the first item to be dealt with. We have pointed out before that the endeavor to maximize bonuses induces the construction enterprise to employ various devices to achieve high plan fulfillment. It should be emphasized here that—in the face of rising construction costs in 1949–55—the increase in prices was a compelling necessity, not only to increase profitability but simply to avoid losses. The rise in construction costs can be estimated as follows:

In 1949–55 average wages in the construction industry increased by 85 per cent,[63] and allowing for the 3 per cent rise in labor productivity measured by using a corrected production index, labor costs rose by 79 per cent.[64] In the same period the price of

62. Schmidt, p. 229.

63. *SE*, p. 58.

64. The number of workers in state construction enterprises increased by 92 per cent. According to official statistics, the value of production in the state sector rose by 182 per cent (*SE*, p. 139), whereas the corrected production index shows a 97

construction materials increased by 6 per cent [65] and a similar
rise is assumed also in other direct costs. Overhead costs, if expressed as a percentage of the value of production, are estimated
to have stayed unchanged.[66] Other indirect costs, the so-called
"costs arising from special circumstances of the working place"
(costs of lodging, traveling costs of workers whose domicile was not
at the working place, cost of protective clothing and food, etc.)
increased from about one per cent of the value of production to
six per cent.[67] If we take into consideration all these factors, the
increase in the cost of construction activity may have amounted
to 26–28 per cent.[68]

Inflation in the value of construction activity has been higher
than the increase in construction costs, since after profitability was
introduced as a premium condition in the second half of 1954,
many enterprises previously producing with a deficit have become
profitable [69]—primarily by various manipulations. Nevertheless, in
the official statistics the value of construction accounted for in
the cost of investment was said to have been calculated on constant
prices. Abonyi and Tar advance the opinion that "the constant
prices designed for measuring the volume of production in the
construction industry . . . have ceased to be constant prices and
have become useless for this purpose . . ." [70] The same authors

---

per cent increase (for the correction applied see below, p. 194). The rise of labor
productivity, then, appears to be 3 per cent.

65. *Prices*, p. 12.

66. About 30–35 per cent of the overhead costs consists in the salaries of employees
other than workers. We have seen above, p. 87, that in the construction industry the number of these employees amounted to 10–12 per cent of the number
of workers in 1949, and to 37 per cent in 1955. No data are available for the rise of
salaries in this group, but average earnings may have risen proportionately to the
earnings of the corresponding employees in manufacturing, where the increase was
85 per cent (*SE*, pp. 88–89). If other overhead costs are considered unchanged, the
percentage of overhead costs in production value is not likely to have increased
substantially.

67. Cf. below, p. 192.

68. The following breakdown of construction costs was used for 1949 (my estimate):
material cost, 53; labor cost, 26; other direct costs, 5; overhead costs, 15; other indirect costs, 1; total, 100.

69. This problem has been discussed above, p. 137. It should be added here that
in the state construction industry the deficit for construction activity amounted to
3.4 per cent in 1954, whereas 1.8 per cent profit was accounted for in 1955: *SHK*,
No. 3 (1957), 57.

70. I. Abonyi and J. Tar, "Problems of the Calculation of a Production Index and
a Price Index in the Construction Industry," *SSz*, Nos. 8–9 (1957), 705.

COST OF INVESTMENT   193

reach the conclusion that "the comparison with the 1949 basis has lost its reality." [71] In the following, various estimates will be presented to indicate the numerical magnitude of inflation in the value of production of construction activity.

In 1956, in conjunction with a high official of the Price Department in the Ministry for Construction, I prepared an estimate on inflation in the value of construction activity since January 1, 1952. According to the estimate, the following factors contributed to this increase:

1. Partial inclusion of increases in costs in the calculations of the design bureaus may have amounted to 6–8 per cent.

2. Increase in prices achieved through participation of the construction enterprises in preparing some cost estimates and through the countercalculations of the enterprises, aided by favorable decisions of the Ministry for Construction as the price-fixing authority, may have reached 5–7 per cent.

3. Gradual introduction of a surcharge for "costs arising from special circumstances of the working place" and the general application of this surcharge in 1955 resulted in a 9 per cent increase in the value of production.[72]

4. In 1955 the price of construction work was also increased on many large projects by a special surcharge for "impediment of construction work" by the parallel operation of the plant.[73] By that time many of the large investment projects had reached a half-finished stage and some of their plants began producing. This circumstance actually resulted in some excess costs for the con-

71. Ibid., p. 708.
72. The policy of building large investment projects (and partly in newly established towns) resulted in a 92 per cent increase in the labor force of the state construction industry, accompanied by a multiple increase in the number of workers not employed at their domicile. The additional cost of employing these workers may have amounted to one per cent or less of the value of production in 1949 and reached (according to the consolidated balance sheet of the Ministry for Construction) 6 per cent in 1955. The difference between the 9 per cent charged to the investors and the 6 per cent actual cost was a net gain for the construction enterprises. The "costs arising from special circumstances of the working place" were originally accounted for in overhead costs, charged as a percentage of calculated direct costs. When the new surcharge was introduced, the overhead mark-ups were not reduced.
73. B. Balassa, Épitöipari önköltségvizsgálat (Cost Audit in the Construction Industry) (Sztálinváros, 1956), p. 48. In the construction of Sztálinváros an average of 6–7 per cent of surcharge was accepted by the investor on a yearly value of construction amounting to 100 million forints. On some other projects the surcharge was as high as 10–12 per cent.

struction firm, but it has also become a cover for price increases. On some projects the surcharge for impediment of construction work exceeded the actual surplus costs by 100–200 per cent and became the subject of bargaining between the investor and the construction enterprise. On the national economy level, the additional cost to the investors because of this surcharge may be estimated at 2–3 per cent.

5. Increase in the value of production was also served by the practice of charging the investor for nonperformed work.[74] This item is estimated at 3–4 per cent.

In view of these figures, the total increase in the value of production in the construction industry may have reached 27–30 per cent between 1952 and 1955.

Abonyi and Tar compared the cost estimates of some typical construction projects and calculated the price increases at 2–4 per cent in 1951–52 and 26–38 per cent in 1951–55. The same authors compared the difference between the cost estimates and construction cost actually charged to the investor on individual buildings and found discrepancies amounting to 12–96 per cent.[75]

G. Bartalis examined the rise in the cost of road-building on the basis of detailed figures and concluded that the rise in costs between 1951 and 1953 amounted to 16–31 per cent in various types of road construction.[76]

Relating these three estimates to the 1949–55 period, we can put the inflation in value of construction activity at approximately 30 per cent.

Another large item is the procurement of machines. The practice of pricing machines on the basis of current costs was mentioned in Chapter 4. The increase in average wages in the machine industry is known to have been 92 per cent between 1949 and 1955.[77] According to the official index, labor productivity rose by 41 per cent,[78] which would entail a 37 per cent increase in labor costs.

74. This practice is mentioned also in I. Abonyi, "Problems of Invoicing in the Construction Industry," *SSz*, No. 10 (1955), 862.

75. Abonyi and Tar, *SSz*, Nos. 8–9 (1957), 707.

76. G. Bartalis, "Examination of the Rise of Costs in Road Construction," *SSz*, No. 5 (1955), 437. Bartalis, as well as Abonyi and Tar, implies the absence of price changes between 1949 and 1951.

77. *SE*, p. 90.

78. *SHK*, No. 1 (1958), 17.

But this index was calculated with inflated prices; the real index may show a considerably lower figure. It appears, therefore, that the increase in labor costs was larger.[79] In the same period the cost of energy rose by 4 per cent, while the price index of industrial raw materials shows a 20 per cent increase.[80] Although one must admit that available information is not sufficient to present an accurate calculation on changes in costs, a crude estimate can be ventured; on the basis of the above data the increase in the costs of the machine industry may be put at 25–30 per cent between 1949 and 1955. The increase in the price of machines is likely to be of similar magnitude.

We come lastly to the other items in investment activity. Among these the price paid for the preparation of technological plans is an important item.[81] The cost of project-making is largely determined by the salary paid to employees of the design bureau. No data are available on the increase in the earnings of these employees, but it is likely that the rise is at least as much as in light industry, which was considered a low-priority sector. The earnings of technical employees in light industry were 57 per cent higher in 1955 than in 1949.[82] The cost of reforestation might have increased nearly proportionately with wage costs; according to official statistics, in the state sector of agriculture wages rose by 128 per cent between 1949 and 1955.[83] Another item is investment in livestock. Here we can refer to the price index of livestock, which reached 192.2 in 1955.[84] The administrative costs of investment firms also belong in this category. These consist primarily of wages to personnel of the investment firm, and the increase corresponds to the rise in the earnings of technical personnel mentioned above. On the other hand, the price paid for land appropriated for investment purposes has increased only slightly.

On the basis of these estimates of increases in different cate-

---

79. If we assume, for example, that production figures were inflated by 25 per cent, the index of labor productivity would stay at 106 and the increase in wage costs would amount to 81 per cent.

80. *Prices*, p. 18.

81. In 1954–55 the cost of technological plans amounted to 4.4 per cent of gross fixed investment: *SHK*, No. 5 (1957), 28.

82. Kornai, p. 77.

83. *SHK*, No. 4 (1957), 17.

84. *Prices*, p. 42.

gories of investment cost, the inflation of the value of investments can be put at approximately 30 per cent for 1949–55.[85] Although this estimate leaves a considerable margin of error, the increase in investment costs is more likely to have been under- than over-estimated. In the following, this estimate will be used.

ACTUAL REALIZATION OF INVESTMENT PROJECTS

The lack of long-term investment plans lies at the root of the difficulties encountered in carrying out investment projects.[86] As a result of this deficiency in planning, lack of technological plans has plagued construction work since the beginning of the first Five Year Plan. During 1950–52 technological plans were prepared mostly parallel to construction itself.[87] In 1953 among 182 large investment projects under construction, eighty-five did not even have a project outline,[88] and the situation has not greatly improved in the years following.[89] In 1955, only ten big investment projects out of 250 possessed completed technological plans.[90] Finally, in 1956, 60 per cent of the large projects lacked complete technological plan documentation.[91] It has also been reported that technological plans were frequently modified during the period of construction. In 1955 18,000 modifications were made of the technological plans of 4,300 investments.[92]

Lack of technological plans and their frequent modifications have impeded the economical organization of construction work and resulted in excess costs. Similar consequences have ensued from the frequent shortcomings in the coordination of different projects. A good example is the electricity plant at Tiszapalkonya, where it was learned only after construction had been almost

85. The reader is reminded here that in the above period 56 per cent of investment funds was spent on construction, 21 per cent on procuring materials, and 23 per cent on other items. Further breakdown of the last group has not been published.

86. According to Turánszky, "The long-term and the yearly plans have no reliable basis" (SSz, No. 12, 1957, 1027). Deák also deplores the fact that "the yearly plans have not been based on economic and technological investment plans": SSz, No. 4 (1956), 299. See also above, p. 60.

87. Deák, pp. 302–3.

88. Ibid., p. 304.

89. Ibid., p. 305.

90. Turánszky, p. 1030.

91. Schmidt, p. 228.

92. Ibid., p. 229.

finished that the envisaged water transportation of coal could not take place because no action had been taken on constructing the canal connecting the coal mine and the electricity plant. Lack of sufficient coordination coupled with the drive for speedy completion of investments resulted in the derangement of the normal sequence of construction work on the largest investment projects, such as Sztálinváros and Kazincbarcika. On these projects roads, waterworks, and lodgings for the workers were built parallel to the construction of the plant itself; nor was the electricity supply assured. As a consequence, transportation, water, and electricity problems prevailed during the construction period and daily transportation of workers from great distances was necessary. Moreover, some of the underground workings had to be rebuilt two or more times as construction proceeded.

It should also be mentioned that enforced speeding up of construction in some projects gave rise to imaginary accomplishments and additional costs. It was widely publicized that in Sztálinváros the first iron was smelted on November 7, 1951, to honor the anniversary of the Soviet Revolution, but less publicity was given to the fact that afterward repair work on the furnaces, which were not yet in a state satisfactory for smelting, lasted for about a year. Under similar circumstances, three years of repair work were needed in the Kazincbarcika Chemical Works to pay for the premature commencement of production.[93]

The aforementioned deficiencies in planning and carrying out investment projects, alongside the frequent shortages of materials, considerably lengthened the construction period of investment projects, increased costs, and reduced the actual accomplishments of investment activity in Hungary. Only 28.5 per cent of the new factories planned in the original version of the Five Year Plan were finished by 1954. Of these seventy-five factories put into operation, completion was delayed in almost every case. In metallurgy the average delay was thirty months, in the textile industry sixteen months, in other industries eight to thirteen months. Extreme examples are a blast furnace at Sztálinváros with four years, and a textile factory at Kaposvár, with two and a half years of delay.[94] It has been reported that on the whole the average period of construction was twice as long as planned, and some

93. NSz, August 20, 1958.
94. Facts and Figures, pp. 91–92.

of the buildings with standardized designs needed three years to reach completion instead of the five to six months envisaged originally.[95] An interesting study was made comparing the construction period of apartment houses before 1945 and after 1951. Whereas construction lasted for seven to twelve months before the war, thirteen to sixteen months were required to construct buildings of similar type during the period of the Five Year Plan.[96]

In addition to the delay in completing most projects, the majority of investment projects actually finished did not reach planned capacity. In 1954 production reached 18.4 per cent of the planned figure in the Balinka coal mine, 65.1 per cent in the Mály brick factory, 38.4 per cent in the Inota electricity plant, and 36.7 per cent in the Tisza chemical works.[97]

To turn to the question of investment costs, it was estimated that actual investment costs of new factories were twice as much as planned in the original version of the Five Year Plan.[98] In other words, if we wish to ascertain the fulfillment of the original investment plan, we should reduce the actual investment figures by 50 per cent. Whereas the Five Year Plan envisaged new investments to the value of 50.9 billion forints, the comparable value of actual investments in the same period would be 33.7 billion forints, instead of the 67.4 billion in the official statistics. In searching for the causes of the 100 per cent increase in investment costs, the following factors deserve consideration:

1. In the absence of technological investment plans, the calculations used in drawing up the Five Year Plan seriously underestimated the cost of the investment projects planned.

2. In the preceding section we put the increase in the cost of an investment project, disregarding changes in the carrying out of investments, at 30 per cent.

3. If the actual realization of investments is compared with the carrying out of investments under hypothetical ideal conditions, excess costs arose because of lack of technological plans during the construction period, unsatisfactory coordination of the

95. Schmidt, p. 237. The results drawn from a sample of fifty investment projects showed the average construction period to be 470 days instead of the planned 219 days (*Facts and Figures*, p. 92).

96. Tar, "Changes in the Length of the Construction Period," p. 610.

97. Deák, Sóky, and Szende, *SSz*, Nos. 1–2 (1957), 56.

98. Ibid., p. 55.

projects, a drive for speedy completion of the investments, and actual delays in completion of the construction work.

Although it is not possible to estimate the magnitude of items 1 and 3, the estimated 100 per cent difference between planned and actual costs may not be exaggerated. It should be noted, however, that items 1 and 2 do not entail excess costs on the national economy level, and only item 3 burdens the national economy.

DYNAMIC EFFICIENCY IN HUNGARIAN PLANNING

It will be recalled that we have defined dynamic efficiency as the hypothetical growth rate of national income achievable in different economic systems, under identical resource use and saving ratio. Under these assumptions dynamic efficiency depends on efficiency in resource allocation, the organizational structure, the technology applied, and the planning and realization of investments. In the following, these questions will be taken up in turn.

Efficiency in the allocation of resources affects dynamic efficiency in two ways. On the one hand, if resource allocation is efficient, the fund of accumulation will be higher; on the other hand, dynamic efficiency may be served also if static efficiency is neglected. In Chapter 3 we examined static efficiency in the Hungarian economy and concluded that the allocation of resources has been inefficient to a considerable degree. Consequently, the fund of accumulation has also been less than under ideal conditions. On the other hand, dynamic efficiency might have been served at the expense of efficient resource allocation. The so-called quantitative point of view which has been deplored in connection with static efficiency gives an inducement to growth that is less strong if the enterprises are profit-maximizers rather than production-maximizers. This method may lead to a higher degree of utilization of existing resources and to employment of hidden reserves, human and material. Nevertheless, the more intensive use of resources may result in their abuse as well, and as the full utilization of resources is reached, the quantitative point of view ceases to have any advantage with regard to growth. In Hungarian industry this method might have served growth in the first years of planning when a higher degree of resource utilization could have been thereby achieved, but it soon became an obstacle to further development, as we have had occasion to see.[99] It should be added that in the Hungarian economy virtually full utilization of existing resources had been achieved in the early years of planning, and except for transitional idleness of resources this has been maintained throughout the period under consideration. This high degree of resource utilization partly counteracted the shortcomings found in regard to static efficiency and raised the fund available for accumulation.

The dynamic efficiency of an economy is also affected by organizational factors. Up to this point we have used the concept organization in a narrower sense, denoting the structure of planning that consists of various decision-making and decision-implementing units. It has been seen that the organization of production in Hungary is not conducive to static efficiency. Nevertheless, the deficiencies of the organizational structure are less important from the point of view of growth. Centralized decision-making is advantageous for achieving specific goals, which, in turn, may serve the growth of the economy.[100]

If we understand the concept of organization in a wider sense, the problem of apportioning resources among various sectors will also be included. Hungarian economic policy has contributed to growth by redirecting a part of the labor force from other occupations (primarily handicraft and agriculture) into manufacturing. Rosenstein-Rodan's well-known article indicates the existence of disguised unemployment in the agriculture of Eastern and Southeastern Europe in prewar years.[101] The prewar Hungarian economy was no exception; [102] we can safely assume that the marginal productivity of labor in agriculture was quite low. Hence, its redirection from this sector into manufacturing has increased national income in recent years.[103]

The next question, which will be explored in more detail, is technological change. Here, Hungarian experience differs a great

99. Above, pp. 89–91.
100. We shall return to this problem in Chap. 7.
101. N. Rosenstein-Rodan, "Problems of Industrialization of Eastern and South-Eastern Europe," *Economic Journal, 53* (1943), 202–11.
102. M. Matolcsy, *Mezőgazdasági munkanélküliség Magyarországon (Agricultural Unemployment in Hungary)*, Budapest, 1933.
103. For a numerical estimate see below, Chap. 7.

deal from the alleged "technological bias" of the Soviet Union.[104] One of our sources lists coal production, electricity generation, electrical industry, machine industry, production of artificial materials, chemical industry, and transportation as sectors characterized by backward technology.[105] Various branches of light industry could be added to this list. The following reasons can be given for the unsatisfactory developments in the field of technology: low technological level of many new investments, neglect of renewals, and lack of incentives for technological change in the enterprises.

Imre Nagy has stated that "the first Five Year Plan made no basic changes in the technological backwardness of our industry; while great investments were being made in increasing production capacity, almost nothing has been done to perfect production and improve technology. Even a good many new establishments are no exception to this." [106] The available information gives support to this assertion. Among the seventy-five factories put into operation during the Five Year Plan, forty-six are equipped with modern, twenty-three with partly outdated, and six with outdated technology.[107] Modern technology has been introduced, for instance, in production of ball-bearings and transportation equipment, but in other fields many new investments are less productive than old ones. This can be seen, for example, in electricity generation and iron production.[108] The following figures show the use of coal per 1 MW-hour of electrical energy:

Old Plants		New Plants	
Ajka	1.65 kilogram	Mátravidék	1.91 kilogram
Bánhida	1.22 "	Inota	1.91 "
Budapest	1.20 "	Sztálinváros	2.06 "

In iron production the coking-coal consumption per ton of pig iron was 1.025 tons in the old Diósgyör plant and 1.180 tons in the new Sztálinváros plant. In 1955 the cost of producing pig iron in Sztálinváros exceeded that in Diósgyör by 17 per cent.[109]

Hungarian sources give these reasons for the low technological

104. Cf. G. Grossman, "Some Current Trends in Soviet Capital Formation," *Capital Formation and Economic Growth* (Princeton University Press, 1955), pp. 192–95.

105. J. Lacfalvi, "Raising the Technical Level in Industry," *SSz*, Nos. 7–8 (1956), 587–89.

106. *Imre Nagy on Communism*, p. 187.

107. Deák, Sóky, and Szende, p. 52.

108. Ibid., pp. 59–60. Data refer to 1954.

109. G. Rejtö, "The Cost of Certain Products in 1955," *SSz*, No. 10 (1956), 871.

level of the new investments: [110] unsatisfactory planning of technological change, isolation of design bureaus from practical experience, lack of satisfactory technical personnel, difficulties in material procurement and in cooperation between factories, and opposition of material interests to technological development. It should be added that political motives are also responsible for this phenomenon. In many instances (for example, the steel mill at Sztálinváros) Hungary purchased machinery from the Soviet Union, although more advanced machinery was available in Western countries. It has been reported that this decision was forced upon Hungary by the Soviet Union, which often supplied outdated machinery.

Another reason for technological backwardness is neglect of renewals.[111] In 1950–55, in industry as a whole, renewals amounted to 7,010 million forints, whereas depreciation was 12,990 million.[112] Actually the discrepancy was much larger, since depreciation rates were set too low, while renewal charges were valued at current costs and the value of equipment was not adjusted as investment costs rose. As a consequence of this policy, the average age of machines increased in many industries. In the machine industry, for example, between 1951 and 1954 it rose from 17.6 to 18.4 years.[113] The situation is even worse in the textile industry, where the majority of machines are obsolete.[114] As an example, in the largest Hungarian textile factory most machines are 70 to 80 years old.[115] The excessive drive for quantitative results has also contributed to deterioration of fixed capital in many areas.[116]

We turn now to the question of incentives for the development of technology in the firm. Available information suggests that the enterprise is opposed to technological change if its fruits cannot be reaped in the immediate future. I. Friss contends that "the primary obstacle to technological development is . . . that the interest of the enterprise is essentially against technological

110. Lacfalvi, pp. 594–600.

111. P. Erdös has observed that "it is not surprising that we remain behind technically if we go for years without creating adequate material preconditions for renewing equipment" ("Some Theoretical Problems of Planning," *Yearbook*, p. 95).

112. *SE*, p. 45.

113. A. Nyilas, "Problems of Fixed Funds and Renewal," *SSz*, No. 11 (1954), 871.

114. M. Simán, "The Economic Problems of Light Industry," *KSz*, Nos. 8–9 (1958), 912.

115. Nyilas, p. 871.

116. F. Jánossy, *ME* (July 20, 1956), p. 3.

improvements." [117] Two reasons are offered for this phenomenon: employees working on new technological methods are considered unproductive, since their activity does not add to the value of production; and experimental production leads to underfulfillment of the production plan and to temporary losses.[118]

The conflict between technological development and short-run bonus maximization appears in many writings.[119] This behavior implies that maximization of bonuses in a socialist firm extends over a considerably shorter time-horizon than in a capitalist enterprise. In the Hungarian experience the cause may be found in the frequent changes of leading employees and a feeling of insecurity on the part of many managers about the future. Another important consideration is that, unlike a free enterprise system, competition does not exist as a force inducing technological development. J. Lacfalvi has described differences in motivation: "In a capitalist economy, the drive for profit and competition compels the capitalist to endeavor unremittingly to develop his products . . . He is *forced* to keep step with general technical development . . . there are no such *inner* forces to keep stimulating and urging the [socialist] firm in this direction." [120]

In spite of advantageous developments in some fields, the aforementioned factors have resulted in an absolute deterioration on the technological level of equipment in several industries and a relative deterioration in comparison with Western economies. As Imre Nagy expressed it, "progressive techniques elsewhere left us further and further behind." [121]

Another factor influencing dynamic efficiency is the planning and realization of investments. The detailed analysis in the foregoing sections demonstrates that the various shortcomings in the planning of investments and the carrying out of investment projects have considerably impaired dynamic efficiency.

It can be concluded that, among the various factors influencing

117. According to him, "frequently the introduction of new techniques and technology which would increase productivity has been hindered by the fact that thereby bonuses would temporarily decrease": "The Application of the Principle of Personal Interest in the Building of Socialism," *TSz*, No. 1 (1956), 20.

118. J. Kornai, *SzN*, October 14, 1956.

119. Lacfalvi, p. 594; T. Lányi, "The Value of Production and Technological Development," *SSz*, No. 9 (1956), 789–92; *SzN*, July 25, September 27, 1956.

120. Ibid., p. 595. Italics in original.

121. *Imre Nagy on Communism*, p. 187.

dynamic efficiency, organizational factors have had an advantageous effect; whereas inefficient resource allocation, deficiencies encountered in the planning and realization of investments, as well as laggardness of technical change pull in the other direction. All in all, it appears that the shortcomings found with respect to dynamic efficiency have been of decidedly greater importance than the favorable factors.

7. Achievements of the
Hungarian Economy

NATIONAL INCOME IN 1949–1955 [1]

THERE has been much discussion on the reliability of Soviet national income statistics. With few exceptions the consensus among Western scholars appears to be that Soviet official data expressed in current rubles are by and large reliable and can be used in analyzing the Soviet economy at a certain point in time (for example, in a particular year). On the other hand, figures expressed in so-called constant prices are less useful for measuring the growth of national income.[2] The question of reliability arises also in connection with Hungarian national income figures. Nevertheless, before embarking upon a consideration of various shortcomings in the Hungarian national income statistics, two conceptual problems should be dealt with. One is the definition of national income in Soviet-type economies, the other, the meaning of national income figures expressed in the arbitrary prices of physical planning.

In Hungary as well as in other countries of the Soviet orbit, the Marxist concept of national income is applied. According to Marxist terminology, national income includes only the net value of material production. Material production comprises agriculture, industry (manufacturing and handicraft), transportation of goods, trade (domestic and foreign), and domestic industry; excluded are passenger transportation, personal services, house rent, public administration, and defense. Yet in its practical application the concept of national income used in Soviet-type economies differs much less from Western concepts than is usually assumed. To begin with, the value of materials used in providing these "unproductive" services and production of military goods are in-

1. 1955 rather than 1956 has been chosen as the closing year because production results in 1956 were greatly affected by the Revolution.

2. On these problems the locus classicus is A. Bergson, *Soviet National Income and Product in 1937* (New York, Columbia University Press, 1953), pp. 6–11.

cluded in any case. Furthermore, wages paid to public administration officials and military personnel are included in the use of national income as private consumption,[3] whereas on the production side the corresponding item is the turnover tax levied for financing these expenditures.[4] Consequently, the entire cost of public administration and defense appears in the national income figures. Depreciation of dwellings is also included on the consumption side, and in Hungary the low house rent is not likely to exceed the depreciation charges. As a result, only wages, profits, and turnover tax in passenger transportation and personal services are excluded from national income. For the sake of comparison it may be mentioned that the total value of these services amounted to 5.3 per cent of personal consumption in 1949 and to 5.7 per cent in 1955,[5] part of which is included in national income as material consumption.

We have had occasion to comment on the arbitrariness of prices in physical planning. Prices being arbitrary, the national income figures will be greatly affected by the rules (and hazards) of price determination.[6] For instance, if the production of overvalued commodities rises the most, the growth of national income measured in constant prices will be overestimated, and vice versa. Another example involves the pricing of consumer goods. Let us assume that from one year to another the planners want to reduce the real value of consumption by 20 per cent without affecting money wages. If shortages are to be avoided, consumer prices should be raised by 25 per cent to maintain the nominal value of consumption, which is assumed to equal the wage bill. Now the share of consumption will be substantially higher on the new prices than if calculated on prices of the previous period. Hungarian national income statistics can also be used to illustrate this

3. The income of the wage-earners may be taken equivalent to their consumption because of the insignificant amount of personal savings. This assumption is made also in Hungarian official statistics (*National Accounts*, p. 58).

4. We neglect here direct taxes which amounted to 10 per cent of the turnover tax in the 1954 budget (*SzN*, June 16–19, 1954).

5. *National Accounts*, p. 9.

6. For a recent discussion of this problem in connection with the national income statistics of the Soviet Union the reader is referred to the following articles: P. Wiles, "Are Adjusted Rubles Rational?" *Soviet Studies* (1955), pp. 143–47; D. Granick, "Comment," ibid. (1956), pp. 46–49; D. R. Hodgman, "Measuring Soviet Industrial Expansion: A Reply," ibid. (1956), pp. 34–45; P. Wiles, "A Rejoinder to All and Sundry," ibid. (1956), pp. 134–47.

point. According to official figures, the share of private consumption in 1954 amounted to 58 per cent if national income was measured on 1949 prices and 70 percent if expressed in 1954 prices. In the same year the contribution of agriculture to national income was 19 per cent on 1949 prices and 28 per cent on 1954 prices.[7]

The arbitrariness of prices in Hungary, then, has created a corresponding arbitrariness in national income statistics.[8] Nevertheless, I believe that with certain corrections and qualifications 1949 prices can be used in measuring changes in national income, mainly because the two distorting factors of greatest importance—the turnover tax on consumer goods and undervaluation of producer goods—in 1949 had relatively less effect on the price structure than in later years.[9] In the following, changes in Hungarian national income expressed in 1949 prices will be examined, and those factors will be subjected to scrutiny which have contributed to inflation of national income date. To begin with, motives for exaggerating production results should be considered.

Such motives can be found in the enterprises, ministries, and highest planning authorities. We have seen in Chapter 5 that the objective of bonus maximization induces the managers to adopt various practices in order to increase production and/or profits. It has also been established that prestige considerations and the ministry's partiality toward its own enterprises often leads to silent approval of these manipulations.[10] On the national economy level, exaggeration of the economy's achievements [11] is due to political reasons: to prove the alleged superiority of a socialist system and, for the population, to show the actual accomplishments of the

7. *SE,* p. 33.

8. J. Fáy observed: "because of the present structure of producer prices, planning and statistics have become uncertain, and, in a certain degree, unscientific": "Effects of the New Production Price System on Foreign Trade," *SSz,* Nos. 9-10 (1956), 98.

9. The total amount of turnover tax was about 15 per cent of consumption in 1949 and increased approximately sevenfold between 1949 and 1955. *GT,* No. 2 (1949), 104-6; *SE,* p. 39; *SzN,* June 16, 1954.

10. Cf. above, pp. 129-30.

11. In Eckstein's opinion, "after the middle of 1948 there was a gradual clamping down on publications and from 1948 onward there began what appears to be a systematic effort at statistical camouflage. As a result of this and for propaganda purposes, accomplishments were presented in a rather misleading and exaggerated form": "Postwar Planning in Hungary," *Economic Development and Cultural Change,* 2 (1954), 382.

economy in a favorable light. Nevertheless, in conformity with Bergson's assumption concerning the Soviet Union,[12] the absence of a double bookkeeping system in Hungarian national accounts (one set of figures for the population, another for the planners) will be assumed.[13] Such being the case, the following propositions will be made with regard to the planners' behavior on questions of statistical accuracy: first, the drive for higher production records reduces the authorities' resistance to the enterprises' endeavor for price increases and other practices; second, there is a deliberate attempt to use statistical methods which magnify the achievements of the national economy;[14] and third, a selective use of statistics is made, and the methods employed in estimating natural income have not been published, in order to render a thorough check of official figures impossible.

After having dealt with the motives for exaggerating production results, we now turn to the various ways inflation of production records actually occurs:

1. Plan prices are based on current costs for commodities not produced in the base period (p. 103).

2. The enterprises endeavor to achieve disguised price increases through introduction of "new" products (p. 109).

3. In the case of group prices, those commodities are manufactured which have the lowest production cost (p. 109).

4. Plan prices of nonstandardized products in the machine industry, in mounting, assembling and construction, are based on current costs (p. 104).

5. The renewal of capital goods is measured in current prices (p. 212).

12. *Soviet National Income and Product in 1937*, p. 7.

13. In connection with this assumption it should be noted that there are some examples of known falsifications effected by the highest authority. The reader will recall the untrue statements made in 1951 and 1952 on the alleged increase in the standard of living during those years (above, p. 34). It has been reported that statistical data on the production records of the collective farms were touched up during the prerevolutionary period to give an embellished picture on the performance of these farms. Nevertheless, in view of the paucity of information, we shall neglect the possibility of outright falsifications on the volume of national income. This assumption does not exclude the juggling with data on the use of the national income, for example, for the purpose of disguising the magnitude of defense effort.

14. For instance, current prices are accepted for new products and are also used in measuring investment activity and reckoning a part of industrial production. Another example is the use of the weights of the last period (Paasche index) in the calculation of the consumer price index to minimize the extent of price increases in the estimation of changes in the standard of living (cf. below, p. 221).

6. Current prices are used in reckoning the production of artisans' cooperatives and of domestic industry.[15]

7. Quality deterioration during the period under consideration has led to a reduction in the real value of the commodities produced (pp. 153–55).

8. Depreciation charges are insufficient, partly because depreciation rates are unrealistically low, partly because investment goods are undervalued.

9. Actual falsification of production records in enterprises sometimes occurs.[16]

The impact of some of these factors on national income figures can be estimated more or less accurately. In other cases either the nature of the problem (for example, falsifications) or lack of sufficient information (for example, depreciation charges) does not permit numerical estimates. No adjustment will be made in the latter cases. The examination of national income statistics will be based on the breakdown of the use of national income, since in view of the available information this grouping lends itself more easily to making corrections. The official data on the use of national income are given in Table 4. The various items of this table will be subjected to scrutiny below.

Private consumption. This item includes all consumer goods purchased by the population and commodities consumed by the private producers themselves. Purchased consumer goods are valued at retail prices, including turnover tax. Assuming that the proportion of the taxed commodities did not change during the period under examination, the existence of turnover taxes does not distort temporal changes in the level of consumption valued at plan prices. On the other hand, turnover taxes on consumption goods affect the estimation of the share of consumption in national income. We shall return to this problem at a later point. The

15. *SE*, pp. 71, 127.

16. See above, p. 145. In regard to the insufficiency of checks on the enterprise's production records the following statement by A. Bródy deserves consideration: "Besides the distortions due to material interest [on the part of the enterprises] the discipline of statistical work and the reliability of data are seriously undermined by the lack of control of the figures from two sides: from the side of production (distribution) and from the side of use. The few material balances compiled since 1952 have frequently shown the expected deficiencies of production reports" ("Changes in Some Quantitative Indicators of Heavy Industry," *Yearbook*, p. 153). The same author reveals that statistical material balances on the production and use of commodities have been prepared for a limited number of intermediate products only (ibid.).

value of food produced and consumed on the farm is valued at producer prices.[17]

TABLE 4. *Use of National Income in 1949–55 (Unadjusted)*

IN BILLION FORINTS

	1949	1950	1951	1952	1953	1954		1955	
	IN 1949 PRICES						IN 1954 PRICES	IN 1954 PRICES	IN 1949 PRICES
Private consumption	24.9	26.4	27.5	26.5	27.3	32.8	60.0	64.2	35.1
Material consumption of nonproductive organizations	4.2	5.9	7.0	10.7	12.9	9.9	10.3	8.9	8.6
CONSUMPTION	29.1	32.3	34.5	37.2	40.2	42.7	70.3	73.1	43.7
Increase in fixed funds	4.8	5.8	9.0	10.7	11.7	9.5	9.5	10.1	10.1
Increase in variable funds	3.1	6.4	9.1	4.1	6.9	4.6	5.7	8.0	6.3
INVESTMENT	7.9	12.2	18.1	14.8	18.6	14.1	15.2	18.1	16.4
Use abroad	0.7	1.0	0.6	0.2	0.3	−0.1	0.0	1.9	1.9
NATIONAL INCOME	37.7	45.5	53.2	52.2	59.1	56.7	85.5	93.1	62.0

Source: SE, p. 39. The official publications do not estimate the national income of 1955 in 1949 prices. This calculation was carried out by dividing the 1955 data expressed in 1954 prices by implicit price indices computed from the official data which estimate the national income for 1954 in both 1949 and 1954 prices. Implicit price indices were computed for various components of national income by dividing the figure expressed in 1954 prices by the figure reckoned in 1949 prices. This method has obvious shortcomings because of changes in the composition of the various components between 1954 and 1955, but it can be used for the measurement of growth with a small margin of error. The only exception is the item "Use abroad." Here the summation of positive and negative figures gives the final result and—in the absence of the necessary breakdown—it cannot be established whether price changes or changes in the magnitude of the positive and negative elements affected the 1955 figure. Consequently, in the columns bearing the heading "in 1949 prices" the absolute figure given in 1954 prices was used.

An official publication of the Hungarian Statistical Bureau estimates the reduction in the value of consumer goods caused by deterioration of quality and disguised price increases between 1949 and 1955 at 10.5 per cent. This estimate is accepted here and the value of private consumption is corrected accordingly.[18] After this correction is made, the increase in the value of consumer goods between 1949 and 1955 appears to be 26 per cent and the increase in per capita consumption 19 per cent. Calculations on changes in living standards indicate, however, that consumption per inhabitant is not likely to have increased by more than

17. *National Accounts*, p. 56.

18. *Prices*, p. 70. For the intervening years the following index is given: 1949, 100.0; 1950, 99.2; 1951, 98.1; 1952, 95.2; 1953, 91.6; 1954, 90.5; 1955, 89.5 (ibid.).

8 per cent.[19] The discrepancy between the per capita consumption figures in the national income accounts and in the statistics of the standard of living may be the result of using different price weights, erroneous classification of expenditure, or overvaluation of the increase in private consumption in the national income accounts.[20] In the latter case, the growth of national income would be exaggerated in the figures above. Nevertheless, in the absence of sufficient information, no correction will be made in the national income figures on this count.

Material consumption of nonproductive organizations. This item covers the material consumption of public administration, culture, social, and health organizations, and probably some of the cost of armament as well. The breakdown of the data is not given in official statistics. It will be assumed here that the 10.5 per cent quality deterioration and disguised price increase noted in private consumption applies to this item also.

Increase in fixed funds. This entry corresponds to the concept of net investment in fixed capital. Its breakdown is finished gross investment + renewals — depreciation.[21]

19. Cf. below.

20. Another reason for the discrepancy may be a reduction in the share of those items in consumer expenditure which are not included in the national income accounts but enter into the statistics on living standards. Nevertheless, the depreciation of dwellings (which in Hungary roughly corresponds to rent) and the material consumption of the various services being included under private consumption in national income accounting (*National Accounts*, p. 56), the remaining item (wages, profits, and turnover tax on these services) is only a small fraction of consumer expenditure. At any rate, the share of services has increased (from 5.3 to 5.7 per cent) rather than decreased (ibid., p. 9). Changes in personal savings cannot offer an explanation either, since they were negligible throughout the period.

21. The breakdown of the increase in fixed funds is given in the statement on fixed funds (*SE*, p. 45). For the earlier years there are great differences between the two sets of data, as can be seen from the following figures:

	Increase in Fixed Funds according to		Discrepancy
	NATIONAL INCOME ACCOUNTS	STATEMENT ON FIXED FUNDS	(1)—(2)
	million forints		
	(1)	(2)	(3)
1950	5809	5333	476
1951	8936	7647	1289
1952	10726	9836	890
1953	11679	11404	275
1954	9525	9492	33
1955	10131	10159	—28

According to the same publication (p. 44), such items as the expenses for training skilled workers for newly established enterprises and the cost of technological plans

1. The value of finished gross investment in fixed capital is given in the statement of fixed funds. In accordance with our results in regard to the increase in the cost of investment (pp. 191 ff.) the 1955 data will be deflated by the estimated 30 per cent overvaluation.[22]

2. In Hungarian statistics the value of fixed capital is augmented by the cost of major repairs effected (renewal). Correspondingly, the rate of depreciation is said to include an allowance for this purpose. Renewals were carried out mostly by the repair departments of factories themselves and by machine-repair shops. Renewal activity has been priced at current costs.[23] According to my estimate, the cost of renewal increased by approximately 45–60 per cent between 1949 and 1955.[24] In the national income accounts the 45 per cent figure will be used in deflating the value of renewal expenditure.

3. Depreciation rates are intended to cover wear and tear and the cost of major repairs. We have seen above that depreciation rates were too low. Another reason for the insufficiency of depreciation charges is the undervaluation of investment goods. This, coupled with the increase in the cost of new investment, prompted

---

subsequently not used are not included in the statement on fixed funds but only in the national income accounts. But these items cannot be responsible for more than a fraction of the discrepancy. It is suggested here that erroneous data of national income accounts, allowed to go uncorrected, are primarily responsible for the discrepancies in 1950–52. Consequently, the figures of the statement on fixed funds is accepted here. This modification does not affect the growth rate of national income (calculated from the 1949 and 1955 data) but only the figures of some intervening years. (It should be noted that the statement of fixed funds is expressed in current prices and the national income accounts are reckoned in plan prices. Yet the discrepancy due to this factor is negligible since, in general, current prices served for plan prices. The implicit price index shows only a 0.4 per cent discrepancy between 1949 and 1954 prices.)

22. It will be assumed here that there was a steady increase in prices of construction activity between 1951 and 1955 (cf. p. 194, above), whereas for other items the even distribution of price changes during 1949–55 is surmised.

23. G. Rejtö, "Some Problems Related to Depreciation Rates," *PSz*, No. 6 (1955), 446. K. Ambrus, "Pricing Problems of Machine-Investments and Renewals," *PSz*, No. 12 (1955), 874.

24. In estimating the rise in the cost of renewals the increase in wages and material costs is taken into account. Between 1949 and 1955 average wages in manufacturing rose by 83 per cent (*SE*, pp. 88–89), while the rise in the price index of the means of production was 8 per cent (*Prices*, p. 6). Repair work being labor-intensive, the share of labor costs may have amounted to 50–70 per cent. The corresponding increase in the cost of renewals would be 45–60 per cent.

the revaluation of fixed capital in 1957. Up to now this revaluation has been accomplished in light industry only; there the value of fixed capital has been increased by over 100 per cent, so that from 1958 depreciation charges in light industry will rise 122 per cent.[25]

Although both above-mentioned factors indicate that depreciation charges in the period under examination were insufficient, in the absence of information on the gross value of fixed capital in the necessary breakdown no attempt will be made here to modify the figures, and the data on increase in fixed funds will be corrected only by adjustments effected in the value of finished fixed investment and renewals.[26]

Increase in variable funds. This entry contains the increase in the value of unfinished investments in fixed capital and the increase in inventories. The breakdown of the latter item is partially known for 1955 but no comparable information has been released for previous years. It has been reported that military goods are also contained in this figure. With regard to the increase in stocks, the 10.5 per cent correction applied to consumer goods will be used, and the unfinished investment-component will be modified by the deflator used in adjusting the value of finished gross capital investment.[27]

25. B. Polgár, "The Revaluation of Fixed Funds in Light Industry in 1958," *SSz*, No. 11 (1958), 1118.

26. The unadjusted and adjusted data on the increase of fixed funds can be seen from the following table (the original data are from *SE*, pp. 45–46):

Increase in Fixed Funds

	UNADJUSTED			ADJUSTED			
	finished gross investment	renewals	depreciation	finished gross investment	renewals	depreciation	total (4) + (5) −(6)
	million forints						
	(1)	(2)	(3)	(4)	(5)	(6)	(7)
1950	8067	1143	3877	7906	1063	3877	5092
1951	10471	1352	4166	10071	1177	4166	7082
1952	12447	2251	4863	11261	1838	4863	8236
1953	13395	3612	5602	11434	2779	5602	8611
1954	12467	3248	6224	10084	2362	6224	6222
1955	12587	4616	7044	9682	3183	7044	5821

27. The breakdown of the increase in variable funds is as follows (the original data are from *SE*, pp. 39, 46):

Use abroad. Reparation payments and the trade balance are included in this item. There is no information how this figure has been arrived at, and therefore no adjustment can be made.

Taking into account the above modifications, the adjusted figures of Hungarian national income appear in Table 5. It should

TABLE 5. *Use of National Income in 1949–55 (Adjusted)*

IN 1949 PRICES, BILLION FORINTS

	1949	1950	1951	1952	1953	1954	1955
Private consumption	24.9	26.2	26.9	25.2	25.0	29.7	31.4
Material consumption of non-productive organizations	4.2	5.9	6.8	10.2	11.8	9.0	7.7
CONSUMPTION	29.1	32.1	33.7	35.4	36.8	38.7	39.1
Increase in fixed funds	4.8	5.1	7.1	8.2	8.6	6.2	5.8
Increase in variable funds	3.1	6.3	8.9	3.8	6.1	4.1	5.7
INVESTMENT	7.9	11.4	16.0	12.0	14.7	10.3	11.5
Use abroad	0.7	1.0	0.6	0.2	0.3	−0.1	1.9
NATIONAL INCOME	37.7	44.5	50.3	47.6	51.8	48.7	52.5

Source: SE, p. 39, and above, notes 17–27.

be noted that a considerable margin of error exists in regard to the estimates presented, especially in the figures for 1950–52. The main sources of possible error are the following:

1. Because of lack of information, some of the aforementioned factors which inflate the value of national income (pricing part of industrial production at current prices, low depreciation charges, etc.) could not be given sufficient expression in the adjustments of national income figures, or are omitted entirely from consideration. The discrepancy between consumption figures in the na-

	Change in the Value of Unfinished Fixed Investment		Change in the Value of Inventories		Increase of Variable Funds (2) + (4)
	UNADJUSTED	ADJUSTED	UNADJUSTED	ADJUSTED	ADJUSTED
	(1)	(2)	(3)	(4)	(5)
	million forints				
1950	1000	980	5387	5344	6324
1951	2781	2675	6354	6233	8908
1952	2802	2535	1284	1222	3757
1953	2996	2559	3903	3575	6134
1954	−144	−117	4714	4264	4147
1955	−462	−355	6762	6051	5696

tional income accounts and the statistics of the standard of living is not accounted for either.

2. It has been reported that in 1950–52 the achievements of the economy were exaggerated for political reasons.[28] Part of the overestimation of national income might have resulted from valuing military goods at current prices. Although there are no estimates on this expenditure, it appears to be by far the greatest in these years.

3. Our corrections have been worked out for 1955. For intervening years the adjustments were effected by interpolation, on the assumption of steady changes in factors resulting in the corrections. The application of this method leaves the possibility of considerable error in adjustment for intermediate years.

The adjusted figures given in Table 5 show a 39 per cent increase in the volume of national income between 1949 and 1955, corresponding to a growth rate of 5.6 per cent. Although the qualifications given above—especially the discrepancy found in regard to private consumption—would imply a lower growth rate, in the absence of satisfactory estimates on these factors the 5.6 per cent growth rate will be used as a basis for further comparison.

The growth of national income in the 1949–55 period compares favorably with the experience of the interwar years, when it took ten years to achieve a comparable increase.[29] Nevertheless, the latter period includes a severe depression; in the postdepression years the growth rate was only slightly lower than the growth of national income calculated for 1949–55.[30]

The results appear to be less favorable by comparison with the planned increase. It was seen in Chapter 2 that the original version of the Five Year Plan projected a 63 per cent rise in national income, whereas in the augmented version a 120 to 140

28. With regard to this period Imre Nagy states: "Although the results calculated on the basis of incorrect value indices show a significant growth, the facts and the existing difficulties plainly contradict such data" (*Imre Nagy on Communism*, p. 188).

29. Using the presently employed concept of national income, the volume of national income increased, in comparison to the period 1924/25–1926/27, by 32.5 per cent up to 1936/37. Matolcsy and Varga, *The National Income of Hungary*, p. 73.

30. Between 1933/34 and 1937/38 national income increased by 20.5 per cent, which corresponds to a growth rate of 4.8 per cent. *A Magyar nemzetgazdaság fejlödésére vonatkozó adatok (Data on the Development of the Hungarian National Economy)*, Hungarian Institute for Economic Research (Budapest, 1938), p. 15.

per cent increase was envisaged. The actual increase fell rather short of the planned targets.

GROWTH OF THE ECONOMY

The data of the preceding section show that in the 1949–55 period the Hungarian economy attained a growth rate twice as high as in 1924/25–1936/37 and slightly higher than in the post-depression years of the thirties. In former chapters we have described certain inefficiencies in resource allocation and various shortcomings in respect to dynamic efficiency in Hungarian planning, which would all point in the direction of a lower growth rate. The task which awaits us here is to analyze those factors which have counteracted the described inefficiencies and short-comings in static and dynamic efficiency and contributed to the attainment of the 5.6 per cent growth rate. In this connection the high rate of investment, organizational factors, and the increase in the working force will be examined.

We saw in Chapter 1 that the planning authorities can increase the growth rate by overruling consumer preferences in regard to saving vs. spending and enforcing a higher saving ratio. The importance of this factor in the planning period becomes manifest if we compare the proportion of national income invested and the growth rate in the postdepression years of the thirties and in 1949–55. During the period 1933/34–1937/38 the growth rate of national income was 4.8 per cent, whereas between 1949 and 1955 it amounted to 5.6 per cent. The price paid for growth in terms of the invested part of national income was quite disproportionate in the two periods; in the first, it probably did not exceed 10 per cent; it was 26 per cent in the second if estimated on the basis of the corrected national income figures of Table 5. National income figures include turnover taxes on consumer goods in both periods. If, in accordance with Bergson's view that turnover taxes should not be regarded as factor payments, we disregard these items, the share of investment increases by about one per cent in the first period and 3–4 per cent in the second.[31] A further ad-

31. *Soviet National Income and Product in 1937*, pp. 50–52. Data on turnover taxes in Hungary are from *The National Income of Hungary*, p. 31, and *GT*, No. 2 (1949), 204–6. The absence of the necessary breakdown of data does not permit making precise calculations.

justment can be made if the undervaluation of investment goods in the planning period is taken into account. On the 1939 basis the price index of investment goods increased to 443.5, that of consumer goods to 705.6, by 1949.[32] In this discrepancy both the increase in turnover taxes and the undervaluation of investment goods in 1949 played a role. We can abstract from the effect of these distorting factors if we deflate the national income data of 1950–55 (measured in 1949 prices) by these price indices; thereby we can estimate the share of investment reckoned in 1939 prices. By doing so, we arrive at a 35 per cent figure.[33] It should be noted that using the same argumentation (but without publishing detailed calculations) official Hungarian sources estimated the share of investment, "taking into account prices reflecting the true value-relations," at 35–40 per cent.[34] The figures show that in the 1949–55 period a rate of investment three times as high as in 1934/35–1937/38 was needed to achieve a slightly higher growth rate. These results imply the existence of considerable inefficiencies in the planning period. In other words, the deficiencies and shortcomings in planning made a disproportionately higher rate of investment necessary in order to achieve a given growth rate.

In Chapter 7 we commented on the importance of such organizational factors as the central direction of the economy and the reapportionment of resources among various sectors for dynamic efficiency. These matters are taken up again now, since we can make use of the national income figures given in the foregoing section.[35]

32. *Prices*, p. 23. It is noted here that the discrepancy between the prices of investment and consumer goods has further increased between 1949 and 1955; in 1955 the price index of investment goods reached 479.6, that of consumer goods 1275.4. Nevertheless, since the national income figures used here are expressed in 1949 prices, these changes do not concern us in this discussion.

33. In deflating the investment figures, the assumption has been made that about one-third of the increase in inventories (9 billion forints) refers to consumer goods. In making this estimate data on the absolute size of inventories in consumer goods given in *SzN*, March 31, 1957 have been used.

34. *Facts and Figures*, p. 113.

35. The reader is reminded that according to our definitions in Chapter 1 the *actual* growth rate differs from the *hypothetical* growth rate under identical resource use and saving ratio (dynamic efficiency) only if the planning authority overrules individual preferences in regard to saving vs. spending and leisure vs. work. Since organizational factors are at work even if there is no change in the amount of resources used and in the saving ratio, in our terminology they belong to problems connected with dynamic efficiency.

In time of war the central direction of the economic process assumes considerable proportions even in a free enterprise system. This is apparent not only in sectors immediately related to the war effort but—through centralized allocation of many materials and central control of prices and wages—in the entire economy as well. It is understood that for purposes of war when a limited number of objectives enjoy absolute priority, centralized decision-making is of great importance, since it is essential to avoid the use of resources for subordinate purposes. War economies are also characterized by an imbalance between the required performance of the economy and the supply of existing resources. This imbalance appears as a result of rechanneling resources from peaceful to war purposes. It is contended here that Soviet-type economies are, broadly speaking, similar in character to a war economy.[36] The similarity can be seen in the application of the method of physical resource-allocation, in the apparent overloading of the economy,[37] and in the fact that developing heavy industry and increasing military production are in both cases first-priority targets. In spite of the inefficiencies found in these systems,[38] centralized decision-making may contribute to fulfill-

36. A similar view is expressed in a recent article by O. Lange (*Zyczie gospodarcze*, no. 14, 1956) with regard to the planning methods applied in Poland until 1956 (quoted in *Economic Bulletin for Europe*, No. 2, 1956, 33). In regard to Hungarian planning this point has been made by Péter (pp. 105–6).

37. Overburdening the economy is described as one of the main characteristics of Hungarian planning in the writings of several Hungarian economists: A. Máriás, "Some Problems in the Allocation of the Means of Production," *KSz*, No. 4 (1958), 388; S. Ausch, "Some Major Problems in the System of National Economic Balances," *KSz*, No. 6 (1958), 562; Kornai, p. 159. It should be noted here that overloading the economy is not so much a characteristic of centralized planning as a result of policy decisions and errors committed in the planning process.

38. Péter gives the following testimony on the similarities between a system of physical planning and a war economy, and the inefficiencies of both: "The notion that the directives of the central plan must include everything, that they should precisely prescribe the quantity, assortment, and cost of the commodities, material consumption, planned preventive maintenance, technical indices, etc., etc.—furthermore, that they should regulate how much various enterprises obtain from the available materials and products (in the form of central allotments)—suits the conditions of a beleaguered castle, of a war economy. In a war economy no economic laws are working, there is no demand, no supply (but there is bureaucracy and corruption); there are not sufficient stocks and reserves, every commodity is in short supply, everything must be accurately and minutely apportioned and centralized allocation or rationing must be used, etc. But in a socialist economy the maintenance of such a system is unnecessary, and—since it results in excessive centralization and bureaucracy—it is injurious" (p. 106).

ment of a limited number of objectives. It can be claimed that, for example, an increase in coal production or electricity generation can be served better by central orders allocating more investment funds, material, and labor to high-priority sectors than by use of the free market mechanism. Now, if these high-priority sectors have a key role in the growth of the economy, this method gives an edge to a planned economy over a free enterprise system. For example, in a free enterprise system the profit motive may well channel a large part of the economy's resources in investments serving consumer needs, such as better housing, luxury hotels, and private airplanes, whereas under centralized planning the same resources may be employed in producing machines and other equipment which in turn can be used for further investments. These considerations have been of importance in the Hungarian economy too. Here, besides the neglect of investments in consumer durables, the importance of organizational factors can be seen also in the reapportionment of the labor force among the various sectors of the economy, coupled with the making of appropriate investments to provide the increased labor force of certain sectors with tools and equipment.

Reallocation of the labor force and increase in the number of workers in the economy as a whole can be given numerical expression by estimating the hypothetical value of national income for 1955 under the assumption that the working force of each sector was identical to that of 1949. In the calculation, 1955 labor-productivity figures are used for each sector. The hypothetical value of national income then appears to be 39.3 billion forints (Table 6). In other words, from the 14.8 billion forint increase of national income between 1949 and 1955, only 1.6 billion forints can be attributed to increase in labor productivity in each sector, whereas the 13.2 billion forint increase appears to be caused by the reapportionment and numerical increase of the labor force.

Using the same method, the hypothetical value of national income can also be estimated, taking into account the increase of the labor force and assuming an unchanged percentage distribution of labor among the various sectors. Under these assumptions national income is estimated at 44.6 billion forints. On the basis of these figures, from the 14.8 billion forint increase in national income—given the labor productivity attained in 1955 in each sector—5.3 billion forints can be attributed to the increase of the

TABLE 6. *National Income under the Assumption of Unchanged Labor Force*

	1949		1 9 5 5			Net Product Assuming Unchanged Labor Force in Each Sector (in billion forints)
	Working Force (in thousands)	Net Product (in billion forints)	Working Force (in thousands)	Net Product (in billion forints)	Net Product per Laborer (forints)	
	actual			a c t u a l		
					(4):(3)	(1):(5)
	(1)	(2)	(3)	(4)	(5)	(6)
Manufacturing	520	15.6	904	35.1	43.2	22.5
Handicraft	250	3.2	213	4.3	20.2	5.0
Agriculture	2121	9.9	1972	12.5	6.3	13.4
Trade	212	5.4	272	5.6	20.6	4.4
Transportation	163	1.5	241	3.8	15.7	2.6
Construction	97	2.3	212	4.2	19.8	2.0
TOGETHER	3363	37.9	3814	65.5	17.9	49.9
Trade balance and other items		−0.2		−3.5		−3.5
National income (official statistics)		37.7		62.0		46.4
National income (corrected figures)		37.7		52.5		39.3

Source: Available information does not make it possible to correct the official figures in sector breakdown. Consequently, the calculations presented are based on official data and only the final figures of national income have been corrected in conformity with the adjustments made in the previous section. In making this correction it was assumed that the hypothetical value of national income calculated here is overestimated in the same degree as the actual value of national income. Data on the working force and on national income are from *SE*, pp. 39, 57. The breakdown of the net production of industry into manufacturing and handicraft was calculated on the basis of data on gross production given in *SE*, p. 71. The possible discrepancy between the shares in gross and net industrial production was neglected.

working force and 7.9 billion to its reapportionment among sectors. The latter item corresponds to the reallocation of labor from the low labor-productivity sectors, such as agriculture and handicraft, to sectors of high labor-productivity, such as manufacturing and construction.[39]

39. In reallocating the labor force, marginal rather than average productivity is relevant. Our calculations are based on average productivity figures, and it is

The discussion of this section shows that the high rate of investment, the increase of labor force, and the reorganization of the economy have been the major forces instrumental in the growth of the Hungarian economy. In view of the actual results, the impact of these factors on growth has proved greater than the shortcomings found with regard to static and dynamic efficiency, which factors pulled in the opposite direction.

STANDARD OF LIVING

In evaluating developments in the standard of living we must consider changes in real wages and incomes, social benefits, and the housing situation. This section will be devoted to examining these factors.

Table 7 shows changes in real wages and real incomes between 1949 and 1955 on the basis of official data.[40] It should be·noted that the Hungarian cost of living index is an index of the Paasche type (weights of the last period are used), which is known to underestimate the rise in prices. Furthermore, the index reportedly includes in an unduly high proportion commodities whose prices increased relatively less. As a consequence, the official estimate on real wages and per capita real incomes has an upward bias. To correct this, an appropriate price index should be employed which rightly reflects changes in consumer prices. Three alternatives will be presented here:

1. For 1954 we can calculate an implicit price index of con-

---

assumed that sectors with low average productivity display also low marginal productivity.

40. By real income, the real value of personal income is meant. Personal income includes wages and salaries, income *in natura*, and nonwage benefits, such as children's allowances, pay for the period of sickness, clothing allowances, and contribution to the cost of meals consumed at the working place. The derivation of the per-capita real income figures from the data on real wages for the workers' and other employees' group are given in the official statistics:

	1949	*1955*	*1955/1949*
	(IN 1954 FORINTS)		(*index*)
Real wages	12,339	13,084	106.0
Nonwage benefits	2,293	2,531	110.4
Real income per worker	14,632	15,615	106.7
Ratio of workers to dependents	42.4%	50.3%	118.6
Real income per capita	6,208	7,855	126.5

Source: Facts and Figures, p. 364.

sumer goods on the basis of consumption data in the national income statistics, where the commodities consumed in 1954 are valued at both 1949 and 1954 prices.[41] This index gives an 83.0 per cent price increase between 1949 and 1954. If we estimate changes in consumer prices between 1954 and 1955 on the basis of the official cost of living index, we arrive at a figure of 181.5 for 1955.

2. An article in *Statisztikai Szemle* gives information on the cost

TABLE 7. *Real Wages and Incomes in 1949–55* (*Unadjusted*)

	1949	1950	1951	1952	1953	1954	1955
Workers and other employees			1 9 4	9 =	1 0	0	
1. Index of normal wages	100	107.1	114.5	147.4	155.0	173.5	178.3
2. Index of per-capita nominal income	100	111.6	125.6	169.2	176.7	203.7	212.7
3. Cost of living index	100	105.7	127.7	179.1	178.3	169.6	168.2
4. Correction for quality deterioration and implicit price increases	100	99.2	98.1	95.2	91.6	90.5	89.5
5. Index of real wages without correction under (4), (1):(3)	100	101.3	89.7	82.3	87.0	102.3	106.0
6. Index of real income per capita without correction under (4), (2):(3)	100	105.7	98.4	94.5	99.2	120.2	126.5
7. Index of real wages corrected by (4)	100	100.5	88.1	78.3	79.7	92.6	94.9
8. Index of real income per capita corrected by (4)	100	104.9	96.5	90.0	90.9	108.8	113.2
Peasants							
9. Index of real income, per capita without correction under (4)	100	101.7	117.8	66.0	107.4	109.7	120.5
10. Index of real consumption per capita without correction under (4)	100	112.7	118.8	106.6	100.6	111.0	127.2
11. Index of real income per capita with correction under (4)	100	100.9	115.6	62.8	98.4	99.3	107.8
12. Index of real consumption per capita with correction under (4)	100	111.8	116.5	101.5	92.2	100.5	113.8

Source: SE, p. 296; *Prices,* p. 70.

41. *SE,* p. 39.

of living index based on 1949 weights (Laspeyres index). This index shows an 82.8 per cent increase in the cost of living between 1949 and 1955.[42]

3. For 1953 the Central Statistical Bureau estimated the rise in cost of living on the 1949 basis by using both 1949 and 1953 weights. The price rise was 99.0 per cent in the former case and 94.6 per cent in the latter. Modifying these figures by the price change between 1953 and 1955 as given in the official index, we find the increase of consumer prices to be 87.7 per cent with the first method and 82.9 per cent with the second.[43]

The three indices presented above amply indicate the downward bias in the official cost of living index. To avoid the error due to the use of the latter index, in the following calculations on real wages and real incomes of workers and other employees the implicit price index of consumer goods will be applied. No adjustment will be made in real income figures given for the peasantry, because in this case the underlying calculations have not been disclosed.

TABLE 8. *Real Wages and Incomes of Workers and
Other Employees in 1955 (Adjusted)*

	Wages	Income per Head
	1949 = 100	
1. Nominal value index	178.3	212.7
2. Consumer price index	181.5	181.5
3. Correction for quality deterioration and disguised price increases	89.5	89.5
4. Real value index without correction under (3)	98.2	117.2
5. Real value index with correction under (3)	87.9	104.9

Source: Table 7.

The corrected index of real wages for workers and other employees shows a 12.1 per cent reduction in real wages between 1949 and 1955 (Table 8). The reduction in real wages served as an inducement to increase the number of workers in many families. As a consequence of the increase in the proportion of the working population, real income per head rose by 4.9 per cent in the workers' and other employees' group as a whole. This average increase disguises the deterioration of living standards

42. L. Drechsler, "The Problem of Weighting Price Indices," *SSz*, No. 7 (1958), 629.
43. *Facts and Figures*, p. 343.

in those families where the number of workers could not be increased.

For the peasantry the official figures show a 7.8 per cent increase in real income per head and a 13.8 per cent rise in real consumption per head. The increase in real consumption was larger because in 1955 the peasants spent a lower proportion of their income on inventory accumulation than in 1949.

Changes in real income of the "others" group (handicraftsmen, private traders, physicians, etc.) and developments in real income of the whole population can be seen in Table 9. According to these figures, real income of the "others" group decreased between 1949 and 1955, but in 1955 real income per capita was still higher in this group than in any of the other two groups. At the same time, the decrease in the proportion of this group in the population reduced the average real income of the population, whereas the shift from the lowest income group, from the peasants to the workers' and other employees' group, increased it. These shifts by and large canceled each other, and the increase in per capita real income of the population as a whole appears to be 5.4 per cent. This increase can be ascribed exclusively to the increase in the proportion of the working force in the population from 41.5 to 45.0 per cent.[44] If real income is calculated per head of the active population, a reduction of 2.8 per cent is experienced.[45] This last figure is accepted here as representative of changes in living standards, since the increase in per-capita real income for the population as a whole was accompanied by a diminution of leisure.

For the sake of comparison with data on real consumption in the national income accounts, the increase in per-capita real con-

44. Population data are given in SE, p. 57:

	Active Population	Dependents	Together
1949	3,993	5,627	9,620
1955	4,416	5,389	9,805

45. These developments have been examined by F. Vági, who reaches the following conclusion: "For years the standard of living increased only in those families where the number of workers grew. At the same time the standard of living of other families—the majority of them—stagnated more or less below the 1949 level. As a result of the low level of earnings of the husband, the wife was forced to work, although her labor power would have been needed in the household" ("The Purchasing Power and the Commodity Supply of the Population," Yearbook, p. 309).

sumption has also been estimated from the statistics on the standard of living. Since the real consumption of the peasantry rose more than its real income, the increase in per-capita real consumption of the population has been higher than the rise in real income, and in 1955 it amounted to 107.7 per cent of the consumption per capita in 1949.[46] The discrepancy between this

TABLE 9. *Per-Capita Real Income of the Population in 1949 and 1955*

	1949				1955		
	Propor-tion in the Population	Share in Real Income	Real Income per capita as the Per-centage of Real Income per cap-ita of the Population (2) : (1)	Index of Real Income per capita (1949 = 100)	Real Income per capita in 1955 as a Per-centage of Real Income per cap-ita of the Population in 1949 (4) : (3)	Propor-tion in the Population	Real Income (5) : (6)
	(1)	(2)	(3)	(4)	(5)	(6)	(7)
Workers and other employees	43.3	48.2	111.3	104.9	116.8	50.5	59.0
Peasants	48.1	40.1	83.4	107.8	89.9	44.2	39.7
Others	8.6	11.7	136.0	93.0	126.4	5.3	6.7
		100.0					105.4

Source: National Accounts, p. 9; Tables 7 and 8. The index of real income per capita of the "others" group has been calculated from its percentage share in the population and in total real income in 1949 and 1955.

figure and the 19 per cent increase in per-capita real consumption shown in the national income accounts indicates an upward bias in the latter.[47]

Up to this point we have dealt with changes in real wages and real incomes between 1949 and 1955. In regard to real wages of workers and other employees, data are available also for 1938–55. According to the figures of Table 10, reduction in real wages between 1938 and 1955 appears to be greater than in 1949–55: whereas real wages in 1949 amounted to 98 per cent of the 1938

46. In the estimation of per-capita consumption of the population the method used in calculating the data of Table 9 has been applied. In conformity with official statistics (*National Accounts,* p. 58), the assumption has been made that—with the exception of the peasantry—the entire personal income is consumed. In 1949 the per capita real consumption of the peasantry was 91.5 per cent of its per-capita real income (*SE,* p. 296).

47. Cf. above, pp. 210–11.

level, the index of real wages on the 1938 basis stood at 87 in 1955.

The presented estimates show changes in real wages and real incomes. The absolute level of the standard of living can be indicated if the purchasing power of wages is estimated. Such a calculation was made by the United Nations Economic Commission for Europe on the basis of monthly need in various foodstuffs. The cost of a "food basket" containing the minimum nutritional requirements for an adult person (2,800–3,000 calories and 100 grams each of protein and fats) [48] has been calculated and

TABLE 10. *Changes in Real Wages between 1938 and 1955*

	Monthly Earnings in Forints (1938 : in Pengös)	Index (1938 = 100)	Cost of Living Index	Correction for Quality Deterioration and Disguised Price Increases	Index of Real Wages (without Correction under 4) (2) : (3)	Index of Real Wages (with Correction under 4) (5) : (4)
	(1)	(2)	(3)	(4)	(5)	(6)
1938	104	100	100	100	100	100
1949	606	583	563	95	103	98
1955	1082	1040	1022	85	102	87

Source: Data on wages for 1938 are given in *Facts and Figures*, p. 342; for 1949 and 1955 in *SE*, p. 296. The index of the correction for quality deterioration is given in *Prices*, p. 70. For measuring price changes between 1938 and 1949, the geometric average of the Laspeyres and Paasche indices (the former gives 595.8, the latter 531.9: Drechsler, *SSz*, No. 7 (1958), pp. 629–30) has been calculated in order to take account of the shift in consumption habits. The price change between 1938 and 1955 has been estimated by a chain index, use being made of the previously applied implicit price index for measuring changes in the cost of living between 1949 and 1955.

compared with average earnings. The composition of the food basket was taken from a Polish source, and it corresponds largely to the Hungarian diet. It has been found that in Hungary on prices existing at the beginning of 1956 (consumer prices were virtually unchanged between 1955 and 1956) the cost of a subsistence food basket was 353 forints a month per adult person. In 1955 the average wage of workers and other employees

48. The food basket contains the following quantities per day: rye bread, 0.400 kilograms; wheat bread, 0.100 kilograms; wheat flour, 0.050 kilograms; pork, 0.100 kilograms; beef, 0.050 kilograms; veal, 0.050 kilograms; eggs, 2 per week; lard, 0.025 kilograms; butter, 0.025 kilograms; milk, 0.500 liter; potatoes, 0.500 kilograms; sugar, 0.100 kilograms; vegetables, 0.200 kilograms; pulses, 0.080 kilograms: *Economic Bulletin for Europe*, No. 2 (1956), 38.

amounted to 1,082 forints; consequently three baskets could be bought with the monthly wage. If the ratio of expenditure on food to expenditure on other items is calculated on the basis of the findings of household statistics,[49] and these items are added to the cost of the food basket, the need for 740 forints per adult person is estimated. In other words, the average earnings of one wage earner was not sufficient even for the needs of two adults. This explains the increase in proportion of the active population between 1949 and 1955.

In connection with changes in real wages and incomes we also have to consider various social benefits, of which three groups can be distinguished:

1. The first group comprises those benefits which are included in wages. These are paid vacation, paid holidays, and paid lunch-time. Since these items appear in the wage figures, they are not considered separately.

2. Various nonwage benefits, such as children's allowances, sick pay, medicaments, clothing allowances, and contribution to the cost of meals consumed at the working place belong to the second category. These items are included in personal income but not in the wage figures. Between 1949 and 1955 nonwage benefits increased the real wage index by 0.7 per cent.[50] There are no data on changes between 1938 and 1949, but it is known that the last-mentioned two types of nonwage benefits were found only seldom in 1938. In my estimate, this factor may add about 5 or 6 per cent to real wages in the planning period if the comparison is made with 1938.

3. The third group includes budget expenses on cultural, social, and medical purposes. These items are not contained in the personal income figures. In 1955 they amounted to 7.7 per cent of personal income and were said to increase the index of per-capita real income (on the 1949 basis) by 4 per cent.[51] Actually, this figure exaggerates the improvement, since in 1949 part of these expenditures was not included in the budget but was financed from other sources. An even smaller part was included in the 1938 budget, hence there is no reliable basis for making comparisons. Nevertheless, it is likely that, comparing

49. Vági, *Yearbook*, p. 316.
50. See above, n. 40.
51. *National Accounts*, p. 12.

1955 with 1938, this factor adds approximately 3 or 4 per cent to the 1955 real wage index.

The housing situation shows a less favorable picture. The Five Year Plan envisaged the construction of a considerable number of apartments: according to the original version of the plan 180,000 dwellings should have been built, 220,000 according to the augmented plan. Actually, the construction of 103,000 apartments was finished during the 1950–54 period, and more than 20 per cent of these were not new dwellings but partition of larger apartments or repair of dwellings damaged during the war.

TABLE 11. *Construction of Dwellings between 1950 and 1955*

	New Apartments	Partition, Repair	Total
1950	17,269	7,400	24,669
1951	13,494	4,248	17,742
1952	13,747	2,936	16,683
1953	13,272	3,521	16,793
1954	23,010	4,201	27,212
1955	26,113	5,413	31,526

Source: *SE*, p. 348. For 1950 only the total number of dwellings built has been published. The breakdown of this figure was estimated on the basis of the breakdown in 1951.

The figures of Table 11 show that after a reduction in the number of dwellings built in 1951–53, there was an upswing beginning with the New Course. Yet even the relatively higher figures for 1954 and 1955 fell short of actual need, estimated at 54,000 new apartments per year. This figure includes 37,000 dwellings for population increase and 17,000 for replacement.[52] Actually, the population increased by 7.1 per cent between January 1, 1949, and December 31, 1955, but the number of apartments rose by only 3.9 per cent in the same period.[53] To evaluate the housing situation, the reduction in the number of rooms per apartment should also be taken into account. The increase in the number of occupants per room (Table 12) shows the deterioration of housing conditions in 1955 in comparison with 1938 and 1949.

On the basis of the above considerations—changes in real wages and real incomes, social benefits, and housing—the standard of living in 1955 appears to be slightly lower than in 1938 and 1949.

52. K. Miltényi, "Some Questions of Our Population Policy," *DE*, No. 1 (1958), 19.
53. A. Mód, "Why Do Eloquent Figures Keep Silent?" *SSz*, Nos. 3–4 (1957), 284.

These results are in sharp contrast with the planned increase of the standard of living. In the original version of the Five Year Plan the standard of living was planned to increase by 35 per cent between 1949 and 1955 and was to reach 185 per cent of the

TABLE 12. *Changes in the Average Density of Occupation*

| | Number of Inhabitants | |
	Per 100 Dwellings	Per 100 Rooms
1930	392	259
1941	382	257
1948	365	257
1955	373	264

Source: K. Miltényi, "Some Questions of Our Population Policy," *DE*, No. 1 (1958), 19.

prewar living standard.[54] The augmented version of the plan projected a 50–55 per cent increase in living standards which would allegedly have corresponded to a more than twofold increase in comparison to the prewar standard of living. It should be added that in the years between 1949 and 1955, the standard of living was lower than in either 1949 or 1955.

WHAT DO THE SUCCESS INDICATORS SHOW?

We stated in Chapter 1 that the actual performance of an economic system may be evaluated by using five success indicators: static efficiency (efficiency in resource allocation), dynamic efficiency (the hypothetical growth rate of national income under identical resource use and saving ratio), actual growth rate, consumer satisfaction, and distribution of income. On the foregoing pages we have examined the workings of Hungarian planning with a view to these success indicators. In this section we present a summary of our findings.

Static Efficiency

Static efficiency (efficiency in resource allocation) is achieved if the final bill of goods is produced with least-cost production methods. It has been established that the use of scarcity prices

54. The differences between these figures show the erroneous estimation of changes in living standards between 1938 and 1949.

(prices expressing the scarcity of resources in regard to given targets) is necessary to make a rational choice among alternative production methods. Planning on the basis of physical allocation of resources, as in Hungary, dispenses with the use of scarcity prices in resource allocation and calculates production requirements mostly under the assumption of constant technological coefficients. Yet even if production coefficients are modified in the face of shortages and surpluses in certain resources, this is only an imperfect substitute for scarcity prices, since all possible alternatives of resource use cannot be considered in physical terms.

Physical planning cannot lead to an efficient allocation of resources but, theoretically, consistency among planning decisions (the absence of shortages and surpluses in resources, intermediate and final products) can be achieved. This purpose is served by drawing up an input-output table in which physical balances are expressed in value terms and consolidated in a balance sheet demonstrating the interdependence of the various sectors in the economy. In Hungarian planning consistency requirements have not been satisfied either. No input-output table has been prepared, and the physical balances, although certainly useful to indicate broad proportions in the economy and to check gross errors, do not ensure the compatibility of planning decisions. Reasons are: lack of consistency between the physical and the aggregate value balances, neglect of indirect input requirements in drawing up physical balances, and the lack of balances for commodities comprising about one-half of the national product. Further imbalances between the supply of and demand for resources and products arise in the practical application of economic balances because of various factors, such as absence of links between physical balances and enterprises' plans, lack of compatibility between the plans of different enterprises, changes and modifications effected during the planning period, and insufficient reserves.

Disequilibria resulting from lack of consistency among planned targets deteriorate efficiency. In Hungarian planning, efficiency has also been impaired through use of arbitrary prices in the limited field of decision-making where comparison of production, investment, and export alternatives has been made. Further inefficiencies occur because of the so-called quantitative point of view and because of bargaining in the planning process.

In a centralized system of planning, the collection of information and centralized decision-making inflicts an additional burden on the economy in the form of the cost of a bureaucratic apparatus and lags in the decision-making process. In Hungary, ideological and political considerations also contributed to excessive centralization. Nevertheless, the enterprises find leeway in the formal system of comprehensive regulations. In view of its material interest, the enterprise's activity is keyed to the maximization of bonuses. Various practices are used to maximize bonuses, some of which conflict with the interests of the national economy and lead to quality deterioration, production of unneeded commodities, etc. In the absence of competition among producers, administrative methods are not sufficient to check these practices.

The factors described above have led to inefficiencies in resources allocation in Hungarian planning; there is one factor which partly counteracts these inefficiencies: the virtually full employment of resources throughout the period under consideration. This certainly appears as an advantage of the Hungarian economy compared to a capitalist economy with a high rate of unemployment, although in the latter the resources actually employed are presumably used more efficiently.

Dynamic Efficiency

Dynamic efficiency shows the growth possibilities of an economy, given its initial resources and saving ratio. In a system of physical planning, centralized decision-making is advantageous for achieving certain goals which, in turn, may serve the growth of the economy. Furthermore, economic balances can be used to achieve consistency among investment decisions, and the planning authorities may redirect resources in view of their social productivity. On the other hand, the absence of scarcity prices in physical planning obstructs rational choice among alternative investment possibilities.

In the Hungarian economy, the neglect of investments for consumption purposes has contributed to a high growth rate. This objective has been served also by reallocating the labor force from low productivity sectors, such as agriculture and handicraft, to sectors of higher productivity, such as manufacturing and construction. This reallocation has been accompanied by appropriate investments to provide the laborers of the latter sectors with necessary tools and equipment. On the other hand, the excessive development of industries in which Hungary is at a disadvantage with her trading partners and the neglect of industries in which she has comparative advantage pull in the other direction. Dynamic efficiency has also been impaired by a certain lack of consistency among investment decisions. Investment plans were mostly forint plans, the real content of which had frequently not been specified until construction was begun.

Besides lack of consistency in investment decisions, further shortcomings have been experienced in the efficiency of investments. Calculations on investment efficiency have not been used either in allocating investment funds among sectors or in choosing among investment projects. Such calculations have been prepared, however, on divers occasions to compare the efficiency of technological variants of a particular investment project, but the irrationality of the price structure and absence of an interest rate have impeded making rational decisions.

Deficiencies arising in the realization of investment projects have also impaired dynamic efficiency. Lack of technological plans; lack of incentives on the part of investors, design bureaus, and contractors to reduce costs in investment activity; and frequent shortages in construction materials should be mentioned in this connection.

A further factor that has had a disadvantageous effect on dynamic efficiency is laggardness in technological change. All in all, it appears that in the Hungarian economy the shortcomings encountered in regard to dynamic efficiency carry greater weight than the favorable factors.

Growth Rate

Whereas dynamic efficiency has been defined as the hypothetical growth rate of national income under given resource use and saving ratio, the actual growth rate is influenced also by the planning authorities' actions in overruling consumer preferences in regard to saving versus spending and work versus leisure. In other words, shortcomings in static and dynamic efficiency can be counteracted in a planned economy if the central authority decides to speed up growth by increasing the rate of investment or by direct and/or indirect compulsion to more work. Both methods have been widely used in Hungary: in contrast to the 10 per cent saving ratio in the postdepression years of the thirties, about 35 per cent of national income was invested during the period of planning. It has been seen that the results were very disproportionate to the sacrifices made: the growth rate of national income was 4.8 per cent in 1933/34–1937/38 and 5.6 per cent in 1949–55. An increase in work performed has been achieved by the rise of the proportion of the active population. Whereas in 1949 41.5 per cent of the population was in the labor force, this percentage increased to 45.0 by 1955. About one-fourth of the increase in national income can be attributed to this factor. (Besides the numerical increase of the working force, a rise in labor hours per worker can also contribute to raising the amount of work performed. No statistical data have been published in this regard, but experience indicates that no change has taken place.)

In connection with the growth rate of national income, the meaning of this indicator in physical planning should be given consideration. In an economy where prices reflect (alongside resource scarcities) consumer preferences, the rate of growth will show the increase of national income in correspondence to individual preferences. Now, since—apart from occasional malinvestments, external effects, and collective consumption—output can be regarded as rational under consumer sovereignty, the rate of growth of national income gives a good indication of how the welfare of the population changes.

If the final bill of goods is determined by the planners' preferences, the prices of commodities may reflect the valuation of the planners. This is certainly so in a system of price planning, but in physical planning the arbitrary nature of prices robs the national income figures of much of their meaning. This latter problem has been mentioned in the first section of this chapter, where we reached the conclusion that for the Hungarian economy the 1949 prices seem to be usable without committing great errors in the measurement of national income. The rationality of outputs is another problem. The question arises: Can the outputs—the quantities which, weighted at 1949 prices, form the national income of 1955 in Hungary—be accepted as rational?

Theoretically, if the planners' preferences are accepted as a guide, outputs must be regarded as rational no matter how they differ from the hypothetical bill of goods which would correspond to consumer preferences. But one can rightly ask whether production in 1955 and the direction of development between 1949 and 1955 corresponded to the objective conditions of the Hungarian economy. It is contended here that serious deficiencies can be found in this respect. The construction of Sztálinváros and the development of the material-intensive branches of machine industry might have corresponded to the planners' preferences at a certain point of time on the basis of correct or incorrect evaluation of the international situation, of trade possibilities, etc.; but if due regard is paid to objective conditions as they appeared in 1955, a considerable part of production and investment seems to be misdirected, and the welfare value of a significant part of national income can be regarded as nil. This category comprises a considerable fraction of the investment apportioned to heavy industry, which becomes superfluous as soon as Hungary proceeds to reallocate production according to the principle of comparative advantage. The excess costs experienced in the carrying out of investment projects and the production of unneeded commodities which inflate the inventories belong to the same category. Thus the growth of the Hungarian economy as indicated by the figures presented in the first sections of this chapter appears to be partly fictitious. We lack sufficient information to estimate the numerical value of these items, but some indication can be found in the writings of Hungarian economists.

F. Jánossy wrote before the outbreak of the Revolution on the accomplishments of the Five Year Plan: "The standard of living has hardly improved during the period of the first Five Year Plan; our investment possibilities were not significantly better at the end of the Five Year Plan than at the beginning; the condition of fixed capital has deteriorated in many areas; our foreign debts have been not reduced but increased." [55] In an article written immediately after the Revolution the following statement is made: "The attainment of production levels with the structure of production before October 23 [1956] would in itself not mean consolidation, since even at that time such tendencies were prevalent in the national economy which, in the absence of a basic

55. *ME*, July 20, 1956, p. 3.

change in economic policy, would have led to economic bank-ruptcy in a few years." [56]

It is difficult to establish how the continuation of economic policy of the years before the Revolution would have led to "economic bankruptcy." The outbreak of the Revolution does not permit us to determine in what degree errors in economic policy and deficiencies in planning contributed to the transitional de-cline of production levels after October 1956 and in what degree the re-establishment of former production levels can be ascribed to policy changes. Nevertheless, our discussion suggests that the structure of the Hungarian economy as found in 1956 presented difficulties in the way of further growth.

In view of this conclusion we have to qualify our former evaluation of the reallocation process in the Hungarian economy. It is suggested here that although the reallocation of the labor force accompanied by appropriate investments certainly contrib-uted to the high growth rate in 1949–55, a balanced develop-ment of the various sectors coupled with intensive cultivation in agriculture might have been desirable for future growth.[57]

Consumer Satisfaction

Consumer satisfaction can be indicated by the living standards of the population, by changes in work performed, and by the correspondence of the goods produced to consumer preferences.

We have seen that real income calculated per capita of the active population decreased by 2.8 per cent between 1949 and 1955. Yet in the evaluation of the achievements of this period it is not sufficient to compare the living standards of these two years; we must consider developments in the standard of living in the period as a whole. Calculations on corrected per-capita real income have not been worked out for intervening years; never-theless, the official data on real wages of workers and other em-ployees and real incomes of peasants show that the standard of living was throughout the period at a level considerably lower than in either 1949 or 1955.[58] On the basis of these data we can

56. S. Ausch and M. Gerö, "On the Danger of Inflation," *KSz*, Nos. 11–12 (1956), 1320.

57. On questions of agricultural policy, see Appendix B.

58. Exceptions are 1950 for workers and other employees, 1950 and 1951 for peasants. (Table 7.)

estimate that in 1950–55 real income per head of the working population was on the average about 10 per cent lower than in 1949.

As a result of the increase in the proportion of the working force in the population, per-capita real income for the population as a whole increased by 5.4 per cent between 1949 and 1955. But this increase cannot be considered an improvement, since it corresponds to a diminution of leisure which appears as consumer *dis*satisfaction. It should be added that the increase in the active population-dependents ratio has been brought about largely as a result of indirect pressure through decreasing real wages.[59] Consequently, real income per capita of the active population appears to be a better indicator for evaluating changes in consumer satisfaction. It is also noted that for 1950–55 as a whole not only real income per capita of the active population but also per-capita real income of the entire population appears to be on a lower level than in 1949.

In regard to consumer satisfaction, a further important consideration is the correspondence of the goods produced to consumer preferences. In physical planning, the production of consumer goods is largely determined by the planning authorities. This situation imposes a restraint on the consumers, since the purchasable quantity of individual consumer goods is given. In Hungary several commodities, such as textiles and shoes of good quality, or tropical fruits, were not available for the consumer, and in many everyday commodities (meat, dairy products, shortening, flour, etc.) frequent shortages were experienced. The population purchased also the inferior and less desired products as substitutes—however imperfect—for the desired goods. This non-availability of certain commodities and replacement of high quality goods by inferior products have further reduced consumer satisfaction.

Distribution of Income

Dispersion of incomes has been considerably reduced since World War II. This development can be regarded as desirable, but—at the same time—certain deficiencies of the present wage system should also be noted. These are insufficient differentiation

59. Cf. above, n. 45.

between salaries of leading employees and of those performing routine work, inadequate adjustment of the salary scale for experience, and neglect of differences in the quality of individual performance.[60]

Conclusion

In Chapter 1 we emphasized the need for a preference scale in regard to the success indicators. The question has been posed: What is more important, efficient resource allocation or growth, dynamic efficiency or an equitable distribution of income? Alternatively, for example, with regard to the growth of the Hungarian economy one could say that the hardship forced on the population by the high rate of investment is deplorable; yet others may assert that the high saving ratio was desirable for the sake of future satisfaction. These questions involve a comparison (and evaluation) of individual preferences, which will not be attempted here. Nevertheless, we can reach meaningful conclusions also if we shun interpersonal comparisons.

It has been established that the shortcomings and deficiences encountered with respect to the allocation of resources and the planning and realization of investments as well as laggardness of technological change had a restrictive effect on the growth of national income in Hungary. In view of these inefficiencies a serious sacrifice had to be imposed on the population in the form of increased saving and work. Without these measures only a fraction of the actual growth rate would have been achieved. If the saving ratio was not higher than in the postdepression years of the thirties, the planning period would have exhibited a growth rate much lower than in the thirties. It should be added that part of the growth of national income in the 1949–55 period entailed a misdirection of resources. It can be surmised that in a free enterprise framework—if the same rate of investment were achieved through forced saving—a higher growth rate could have been attained.

60. Kornai, pp. 75–80.

Appendix A: The Working of a Price System

A DEMONSTRATION of how the price mechanism brings about an efficient allocation of resources is given here. Efficient resource allocation (static efficiency) has been defined as a situation where the output of any commodity can be increased only by reducing the output of another commodity, with production conforming to the community's preferences.[1] We now turn to the conditions of efficient resource allocation.

By "cost of production" the layman usually means money expenses or expenses in physical units, such as labor hours, land use, etc. But from the economic point of view, cost is the loss of possible alternatives (alternative or opportunity cost). Costs are opportunities foregone by using productive resources for the production of commodity A instead of commodity B. In an economy where only two goods, for example beer and bread, are produced, the cost of an additional pound of bread is expressed in terms of gallons of beer, since by increasing the production of bread by one pound we forego the use of resources for manufacturing, say, two gallons of beer. In a money economy we shun the cumbersome usage of expressing the cost of a given good in terms of all the other goods and express cost in money terms instead. Nevertheless, the essence of cost measurement remains the same: cost is alternative (opportunity) cost; it expresses opportunities foregone.

Let us examine a simple case of money economy where land and labor are the only factors of production (inputs) and bread and beer are the only commodities produced (outputs). Our model will be presented as follows.

The Participants of the Economic Process

Resource-holders supply the factors of production inelastically —that is, a change in the price for services of land and labor will

1. See above, p. 7.

not result in an alternation of the quantity of factors of production brought on the market. The number of resource-holders is sufficiently large to ensure that the quantity of factors supplied by any one of them does not affect the market price of land and labor, and they take the market price as given.

Producers manufacture two commodities: beer and bread. Any producer may engage in the production of one or both commodities. The production possibilities for any producer can be expressed in the form of a production (transformation) function. The production function expresses the transformation possibilities of inputs into outputs, and the possibility of substitution between factors and between products.

It is assumed that the proportions of land and labor are not the same in the production of the two commodities. For example, bread requires relatively more land and less labor: it is land-intensive, while beer is labor-intensive. The technological coefficients in production (the quantities of land and labor used for producing any of the commodities) are variable. For example, if there is an increase in the number of laborers, labor will become cheaper and there will be a tendency to substitute labor for land in the production of both commodities. In other words, the technological coefficients are partly determined by the availability and price of the productive factors.

The number of producers is sufficiently large to ensure that a single producer cannot affect the market prices of the inputs and outputs; he regards these prices as given.

Consumers are the resource-holders who consume their income obtained by selling the services of land and labor. The consumers desire to consume our two commodities, bread and beer. The demand functions (schedules) of consumers indicate the quantity of particular products demanded at different prices. The demand functions of individual consumers summed up give the demand functions of the society for our two commodities. Perfect certainty and absence of market failures are assumed throughout.[2]

Behavioral Assumptions

Producers aim at profit maximization—that is, they endeavor to maximize the difference between total revenue from the sale

2. See above, p. 8.

of the commodities and total cost incurred in producing them. In view of our assumption that the individual producer cannot affect market prices, and assuming that there is a rise in the additional cost due to an additional unit of output, profit maximization is achieved at the point where the price of an additional unit of output equals the cost of production of this additional unit *and* for further units of output the price would not cover additional costs. This is the famous "price equals marginal cost" rule. To give an example: If the cost of the first ton of bread is $300, of the second $310, of the third $320, and of the fourth $330, and the price of a ton of bread is $320, our producer will produce no more than 3 tons of bread, since he would lose $10 on the fourth ton. At this point his profits are maximized in the amount of $30.

Under the above assumptions the "price equals marginal cost" rule can also be expressed as follows: an additional unit of input will be used up to the point where the revenue obtained from the increase in value of output due to the last unit of this input still covers the remuneration paid to the factor of production.

Investments are made in the production of the commodity bringing profit, and producers withdraw if they incur losses. Thereby investments tend to have an equilibrating effect.

Consumers aim at maximizing satisfaction out of given income. They reshuffle their consumption expenditure until they reach the point where nothing can be gained from further exchange. At this point the last dollar spent gives the same satisfaction in the consumption of both commodities.

Equilibrium and Efficiency

Equilibrium is reached when there is no incentive to reshuffle production or consumption any more. At this point, resources are allocated efficiently, since if any factor could be used more profitably in producing another commodity, the profit motive would induce the entrepreneur to change his production plan. Similarly, if any two consumers could gain from further exchange, commodities would be exchanged between them. In (general) equilibrium, production corresponds to consumers' demand, and it is no longer possible to increase the production of any commodity without reducing the production of another. The price system and the behavioral assumptions of our model lead, through a continuous reshuffling of production and consumption, to an efficient position. The resulting prices are so-called scarcity prices, which means that (1) the prices of the factors of production reflect the scarcity of resources in view of consumer demand for commodities for whose production the resources are used; and (2) the prices of the commodities reflect consumer demand, resource scarcities, and transformation possibilities, and express the alternative cost of producing one commodity instead of another.

Under the assumption of given resources the pricing of the factors of production can be regarded as a process of "imputation." Consumer demand determining quantities of consumption goods to be produced constitutes the indirect demand for productive factors. Given the indirect demand for the factors of production and their quantity, factor prices are determined at the point where the quantity demanded equals the quantity supplied.

Our results are essentially unchanged if we introduce more commodities, more factors of production, and intermediate products (for example, grain), and if we assume that the supply of the factors of production reacts to changes in their prices. In this generalized case our system will consist of the following components:

1. the demand functions of consumers, indicating the quantity of particular commodities demanded at various prices;

2. the transformation functions of producers, expressing transformation possibilities from resources into intermediate products (from land and labor to grain) and from intermediate products into final commodities (from grain to bread) and, furthermore, indicating the possibilities for substitution between factors, between intermediate products, and between final commodities;

3. supply functions of the factors of production, indicating the quantity of particular factors supplied at various prices.

These functions can be regarded as part of a mathematical equation system, the equations being solved by the market through a reshuffling of production and consumption until equilibrium is reached where resources are allocated efficiently. Besides achieving static efficiency, our model of pure competition is also conducive to progress, since every producer will attempt to cut costs by introducing innovations and thereby increasing profit. Hence profit maximization is not only a powerful means to accomplishing efficient resource allocation in a static situation but also a dynamic force.[3]

In our model the efficient allocation of resources was achieved with the assistance of the price system and the profit motive in harmony with consumer preferences. But the price system and the profit motive can help in allocating scarce resources efficiently among *any given ends*. It is conceivable that a central authority will decide the final bill of goods, distribute them among consumers (for example, by rationing), and demand the production of these goods on the market. The individual producers, confronted with this demand, will bid for the contracts, will organize production with a view to maximizing profits, and will thereby achieve an efficient allocation of resources among given ends. Factor prices are still scarcity prices, but now they reflect resource scarcities in regard to the final bill of goods determined by the central authority rather than by consumer sovereignty. This situation may be approximated in a free enterprise economy in wartime if military production is organized along the lines of private enterprise and consumer goods are allocated by some form of rationing. The efficiency of the price system and consumer sovereignty are not inseparable: not only are efficient allocation of resources and the abrogation of consumer sovereignty compatible, but it is conceivable that consumer sovereignty would be retained and, instead of a price system, physical allocation of resources would be used, disregarding considerations of efficiency.

We can conclude that the concepts of scarcity and efficiency are relative notions: resources are scarce, and allocation is efficient in regard to alternative final uses, whether these uses are determined by the consumers or by a central authority. In all these cases the price system expresses the alternative cost of producing one commodity instead of another on the basis of the valuation of consumers or of a central organization, and the use of these scarcity prices ensures the choice of least-cost production methods.

3. For qualifications, see above, pp. 11–12.

Appendix B: Collectivization in Agriculture

AGRICULTURAL POLICIES IN THE POSTWAR PERIOD

THE IMPORTANCE of agriculture in the Hungarian economy warrants a separate treatment of it. In the thirties, 49 per cent of the population was engaged in agricultural pursuits, in 1949 48 per cent, and in 1955, 44 per cent; [1] the percentage of national income stemming from agriculture was 36 in 1936–37 and 30 in 1955.[2]

Prewar Hungary was characterized by extensive cultivation and an uneven distribution of landownership. Large estates and dwarf holdings were predominant, and about 35 per cent of the agricultural population were landless peasants. Sweeping changes were brought about by the 1945 land reform, which affected 3.2 million hectares, about one-third of the country's land area. Large estates over 576 hectares were expropriated, holdings between 57.6 and 576 hectares were reduced to 57.6 hectares, or, in the case of peasant-proprietors, to 115 hectares. Some 642,000 families (landless or land-poor) received an average allotment of about 3 hectares, the remaining 1.3 million hectares (including 0.8 million hectares of forests) being retained for public use.[3]

The comparative distribution of landholdings, before and after the second World War, is given in Table 13. It should be noted that a considerable proportion of the dwarf farms belonged to industrial workers and craftsmen who cultivated their land plots in their spare time. Healthy development in the distribution of holdings is indicated by the increase in the average area of small farms from 3.8 to 5.0 hectares and in the average size of medium

1. *National Accounts*, p. 9.
2. Above, p. 25; *SE*, p. 39.
3. *Magyar statisztikai zsebkönyv (Hungarian Statistical Handbook)*, 1948, Budapest, 1949.

farms from 10.8 to 12.0 hectares. In 1946 the large holdings, with few exceptions, were state farms.

After the land reform, the course of future development of agriculture had to be decided. The predominance of small farms and the high density of the agricultural population pointed in the direction of intensive cultivation. The idea was not new; in the thirties it had become widely held that in Hungary one of the major preconditions for increasing national income and living

TABLE 13. *Distribution of Landholdings*

	1935				1946			
	Number		Area		Number		Area	
Farm Size (in hectares)	(in thousands)	Percentage	(1,000 hectares)	Percentage	(in thousand)	Percentage	(1,000 hectares)	Percentage
Dwarf farms (–2.85)	1,185	72.5	930	10.1	1,406	68.1	1,637	17.9
Small farms (2.85–5.7)	204	12.5	842	9.2	388	18.8	1,932	21.1
Medium farms (5.7–28.5)	218	13.3	2,380	26.1	247	11.9	2,935	32.0
Large farms (28.5–)	27	1.7	5,002	54.6	25	1.2	2,663	29.0
	1,634	100.0	9,164	100.0	2,066	100.0	9,167	100.0

Source: Hungarian Statistical Handbook, 1948.

standards was the promotion of labor-intensive crops. The plan was advanced that Hungary should concentrate on horticulture, vegetables, industrial crops, daily products, and livestock. It was intended to transform Hungarian agriculture along the lines of the Danish pattern.[4] Intensive cultivation seemed to be necessary not only to increase the income of the population as a whole but also to ensure the viability of the small farms, since before the war many holders of small land plots had had to supplement their meager incomes by working part time for the great landowners. Yet political considerations steered the course of development in a different direction.

Lenin contended that the economy of a socialist state stands with only one foot on a firm basis if private agriculture exists side by side with socialized industry, and both he and Stalin emphasized the need for collectivization. Subsequently, the collectivization campaign transformed Soviet agriculture into its

4. I. Kovács, *Agrárpolitikai feladatok (The Tasks of Agricultural Policy)* (Budapest, 1946), pp. 33–35.

present form. The Hungarian policy-makers faithfully followed the Soviet example and endeavored to establish large state and collective farms in place of private holdings. Development of intensive cultivation had to give way to collectivization, with emphasis on extensive farming.[5] In the shaping of agricultural policy differences in natural endowment between the two countries were neglected. Hungary, with her population density of 280 persons per square mile, faces different problems from those of the Soviet Union, with a density of 24 per square mile. In the latter, land being abundant, extensive farming may be economical, as it is on the great plains of the United States or in Australia. On the other hand, land being scarce in Hungary, high productivity of land is the proper objective. Furthermore, the Hungarian soil and climate are suitable for horticulture, viticulture, etc., and markets can be found for these products.[6] These arguments had little effect on the policy-makers, and the decision was for collectivization.

THE SOCIALIST SECTOR

During the first years after the second World War the Hungarian Communist leaders denied that their purpose was to establish collective farms in Hungary. Mathias Rákosi said: "The new farmers are frightened with rumors that the Communists will establish kolkhozes . . . We do not want kolkhozes but strong and prospering small farms."[7] Ernö Gerö was even more specific in 1947: "It does not follow from the fact that the Soviet peasant needs the kolkhoz that it is also needed by the Hungarian peasant. The history, customs, and traditions of the Hungarian peasantry differ from the history, customs, and traditions of the Russian peasant . . . We would be silly and insane if we did not take into account that our peasantry wants to prosper by way of consolidating private property and individual farming."[8]

---

5. For comparison: in 1955, 57.2 per cent of income of the individual farmers and 37.7 per cent of income of collectives came from agricultural activities other than crop cultivation (*National Accounts,* p. 117).

6. The need for intensive cultivation was emphasized again immediately before and after the Revolution: *SzN,* October 18, 1956; *KSz,* Nos. 11–12 (1956), 1286; ibid., No. 7 (1957), 546, 711.

7. *SzN,* October 16, 1945.

8. Ibid., January 19, 1947.

These pronouncements were quickly forgotten when the drive for collectivization was launched in 1948. The first collective farms [9] were established at the beginning of 1949 and the following years witnessed the forced collectivization campaign. Some representative figures on the collective farms are presented in Table 14. The fluctuation in the figures is a clear indication of

TABLE 14. *Collective Farms in Hungary*

End of the Year	Number of Collectives	Area of Collectives (1,000 hectares)	Membership (thousands)	Percentage of the Active Population in Agriculture
1949	1367	182	36.4	1.7
1950	2185	445	119.5	5.7
1951	4625	1002	310.5	15.1
1952	5110	1502	369.2	19.1
1953	4536	1144	250.0	13.1
1954	4381	1083	230.0	11.8
1955	4816	1314	305.5	15.3
1956	2089	597	119.3	5.9

Source: SE, pp. 57, 187; *SHK,* No. 1 (1957), 34.

changes in the vigor of collectivization policy. As we have seen in Chapter 2, a tough policy was followed until 1953, when the New Course halted forced collectivization and permitted the dissolution of collective farms if the majority so wished. Although in some areas these directives were not carried out, the membership of the collectives decreased by almost 40 per cent. In 1955 the return to the Stalinist line had as a corollary the renewal of the drive for collectivization. Further efforts to collectivize were made in the first half of 1956. By September 1956 the number of collective farms (4,857) had almost reached the 1952 peak, and, the area of these farms had risen to 1,459,000 hectares.[10] Parallel with the increased efforts to collectivize, discontent in the countryside mounted sharply. As Z. Tildy, former president

9. The following types of collective farms were established: *Type I,* Collective plowing and sowing of plots grouped in land compounds; individual harvesting; cost of plowing and sowing burdens each member according to the land contributed; the crop belongs to him after the reduction of this cost. *Type II,* Collective plowing, sowing, harvesting, and threshing; proportionate distribution of net receipts according to the land contributed. *Type III,* Both land and means of production common property; each member paid according to work units; no land rent. In Hungary, the last-mentioned two types are of main importance. In the following no distinction will be made among these farm types.

10. *SHK,* No. 1 (1957), 34.

of the Hungarian Republic, said, "I know that to speak about collectives is, unfortunately, the most unpopular thing in Hungary." [11] The real attitude of the Hungarian peasantry toward the collectives became manifest during the Revolution. It has been estimated that about 90 per cent of the collective farms were expected to disband, and after the Kádár government was placed in power by the Soviet army, in spite of the efforts to maintain collectivization, more than 60 per cent of the members chose the road to private farming. By the end of 1956 membership was less than at the end of 1950, and had fallen to less than one-third of the peak figure reported in 1952.[12] Psychological reasons and the profit motive are primarily responsible. The Hungarian peasant is characterized by his strong individuality; hence his dislike for the kolkhoz. If he entered a collective as a result of direct or indirect coercion by the state, the peasant was inclined to work less, since he felt no direct connection between his work and his remuneration. Instead, he concentrated effort on the household plot allotted to him and endeavored to increase, for example, his poultry production. It has been reported that this disinterest in collective work resulted not only in reduction of working hours but also in deterioration of the quality of work performed. The management of the collectives also left much to be desired. The chairman (nominally elected by the members but often actually chosen by the district's Party secretary) was selected primarily through political considerations. In many large collective farms these positions were filled by industrial workers sent from the towns by the Party, who were politically reliable but had neither knowledge nor experience in agricultural work.[13] This policy may have served political objectives, but it is not likely to have been conducive to economical production on the collective farms.

Alongside the efforts to collectivize individual holdings, the

11. SzN, October 19, 1956.

12. Most of the remaining members were landless peasants for whom the collective farm established on, for example, former kulak holdings was attractive. On this point see N. Spulber, "Collectivization in Hungary and Romania," in I. T. Sanders, ed., Collectivization of Agriculture in Eastern Europe (University of Kentucky Press, 1958), p. 154.

13. In 1954, 400 former industrial workers were put in leading positions (Facts and Figures, p. 242).

so-called socialist sector was increased by raising the number and area of the state farms. Most of these were established in 1950–52, mainly on land expropriated from the kulaks or abandoned by small farmers. The growth of the state farms is indicated by Table 15.

TABLE 15. *State Farms in Hungary*

Middle of the Year	Area of State Farms (thousand hectares)	Percentage of Agricultural Land
1949	177	1.2
1950	642	6.3
1951	973	6.6
1952	1441	9.7
1953	1698	11.4
1954	1700	11.4
1955	1640	11.1

Source: SE, pp. 154–57. These figures do not include the state farms engaged in forestry, which constitute an additional 13 per cent of agricultural land in state management during the period under consideration.

Before the war the state farms served special purposes, such as horse-breeding and production of improved grains. The new state farms concentrated on field crops to take the place of production on the former giant estates. Frequent complaints were raised against the inefficiency of state farms. Poor standard of management, inadequate wage system, and lack of incentive were mentioned as the main causes of the shortcomings.[14] In the selection of managers political considerations played a much greater role than in industry. The agricultural specialists who formerly worked on the large estates were not hired; agronomists trained in short courses assumed many of the leading positions. The piece-rate wage system was not a felicitous choice either; it resulted in work of lower quality and disproportionate wages, because of differences in soil conditions and the help received from the supervisor in evaluating work performance.[15]

All this is not meant to depreciate the role of state farms in Hungarian agriculture. They have an important role, especially in the production of cereals, whose cultivation is more efficient

14. Cf. ibid., pp. 227–28, 235.
15. For a discussion of incentives for management see above, pp. 132 ff.

in large units than on small plots. In my opinion, coexistence of state farms and private holdings with intensive cultivation could serve as a basis for a thriving agriculture in Hungary. This, however, would require improvement in the economical operation of state farms.

In evaluating the actual performance of the socialist sector, the contribution of the various agricultural sectors to national income can be of use. Table 16 shows the net product per acre in the state, collective, and private sectors in 1955 expressed in 1954 prices. The figures indicate the superiority of individual

TABLE 16. *Net Product per Acre in 1955*

	State Farms (without forestry)	Collective Farms	Individual Farms	Together
	(forints, in 1954 prices)			
Crops (including horti- culture, vineyards)	2,186	2,510	3,003	2,559
Livestock	1,602	1,606	2,482	1,896
Other	28	16	20	17
Together	3,816	4,132	5,505	4,472

Source: SE, p. 109. It should be noted that the price weights used in effecting the calculations cited have not been disclosed, and changes in price ratios may substantially modify the results. In this table and on the following pages, agricultural production is evaluated on a per acre basis. Labor and capital inputs will be considered at the end of this Appendix.

farming in the category of both crops (in general) and livestock-raising. As to the first, the productivity of the state sector was higher in cereals, but this was more than outweighed by the superiority of individual farming in intensive cultivation.[16] Individual farmers achieved these results at rather heavy odds. The socialist sector was given the advantage in allotment of credits, apportionment of artificial fertilizers,[17] and allocation of machine work.[18] Other circumstances influencing productive activity on the private farms will be considered in the next section.

16. *SE,* 174.

17. In 1956 the following quantities of artificial fertilizer were allotted to the various sectors (kilograms per hectare): state farms, 55.4; collective farms, 31.7; private farms, 4.2. *SHK,* No. 1 (1957), 40.

18. In 1956 approximately one-third of the agricultural machines belonged to the state farms (with 13 per cent of arable land); the remaining two-thirds were operated by the state-owned machine stations. Some 24 per cent of machine work performed by these machine stations was done for private farmers who worked 60 per cent of the arable land: *SHK,* No. 1 (1957), 38–39; *SE,* pp. 154–57.

The Private Sector

If we wish to examine the impact of agricultural policy on the individual farmer, the following problems deserve consideration: the forced collectivization, the fight against the kulak, the planning of agricultural production, the system of compulsory delivery, and the so-called consolidation of holdings. These problems will now be taken up in turn.

First, the policy of forced collectivization. The individual peasant could never be sure when a new campaign would compel him to join a collective farm. In view of this uncertainty, the farmer was reluctant to enlarge his productive activity.[19] The peasant was especially unwilling to undertake investments, since he was afraid that their benefits would not be reaped by himself.[20] Changes in the amounts spent on the means of production mirror the shifts and turns in the policy of collectivization. Available data show a steady decline in the proportion of the peasants' income spent on means of production between 1949 and 1953, from 17.2 to 10.2 per cent. In absolute figures, calculated on unchanged prices, the decrease per farmer was 39 per cent. The New Course brought about an improvement in 1954, but another decline took place in 1955.[21]

The impact of the policy of forced collectivization on the individual peasant can also be seen from changes in the area left fallow (Table 17). The data indicate a remarkable correlation between the intensity of collectivization and the area of fallow land.[22] Both the increase in the fallow area and the reduction in the purchase of means of production show that the policy of forced collectivization interfered with productive activity on the individual farms.[23]

19. The official Party paper writes on the morning of the outbreak of the Revolution that the regime's agricultural policy has led to "uncertainty in the villages which constitutes a hindrance to an increase in agricultural production" (*SzN*, October 23, 1956).

20. S. Ausch and M. Gerö, "On the Danger of Inflation," *KSz*, Nos. 11–12 (1956), 1321.

21. F. Vági, "The Purchasing Power and the Commodity Supply of the Population," *Yearbook*, pp. 307–8.

22. A similar conclusion is reached in *Facts and Figures*, p. 171.

23. In regard to the impact of forced collectivization on the individual peasant, reference should also be made to a statement by Imre Nagy in 1953, which also is pertinent for 1955–56: "The too rapid development of the cooperatives and the

The Soviet example was imitated also in the fight against the kulak—in spite of significant differences between the Russian and Hungarian situations. In the Soviet Union the kulak class was still an important economic and political power in the twenties and their liquidation was regarded as a precondition of collectivization. In Hungary the kulaks did not constitute a political force of any importance, and their economic power was less than in Russia. In Hungary peasants possessing more than 13–14 hectares of land were considered kulaks. The most industrious part of the peasantry belonged to this group, the majority of whom acquired or increased their holdings by their own efforts. The kulaks employed one or two laborers and worked the land

TABLE 17. *Changes in Agricultural Land Left Fallow*

Year	Hectares	Index
1949	43.806	100
1950	42.541	93
1951	48.563	111
1952	84.750	193
1953	62.107	142
1954	45.480	104
1955	67.240	153

Source: SE, p. 179.

themselves. Their knowledge of efficient techniques of cultivation was considerably higher than that of the average peasant, and the surplus of their production over their own consumption needs constituted an important source of the agricultural products sold on the market. The number of kulaks in 1947 can be estimated at about 60 to 70 thousand; their land may have amounted to 20–21 per cent of the cultivated area.[24]

The fight against the kulak was begun in 1948 and developed parallel to the drive for collectivization. The results of this campaign can be seen in changes in livestock in the hands of the kulak and in their landholdings. Faced with confiscation, the kulaks disposed of most of their livestock. Data on a sample consisting of 600 kulak farms show that in 1949 the number of cattle and

violation of the voluntary principle undoubtedly contributed to the unfavorable development in agriculture" (*For a Lasting Peace, for a People's Democracy*, July 17, 1953).

24. An estimate based on data published in the *Hungarian Statistical Handbook*, 1948.

horses per farm was 4.6, against 14.9 in 1935.[25] During 1950–53 restriction of the kulak often changed into liquidation, and the number of kulak holdings decreased by one-third, while their arable land diminished by two-thirds.[26] These circumstances contributed to the increase in fallow land noted above: because of uncertainty in agriculture, a considerable part of these lands remained uncultivated.[27]

The New Course eased the situation. In 1954, however, voices were raised against the too lenient policy toward the kulak. Rákosi announced that while prior to 1953 "the right policy of restriction of the kulak frequently slid into liquidation of the kulak, since last June [1953] the opposite extreme has been experienced in several places: the fight against the kulak has greatly diminished, and he is now treated like a middle peasant." [28] After the repudiation of the New Course, the strengthening of the class war against the kulak again came to the foreground.[29]

In considering the economic effects of this policy, besides the loss in production due to the decline in kulak holdings, its impact on the middle peasant should be emphasized. The so-called kulak limit was highly flexible. Because of changes in policy in general and also because of personal factors or a change in the person of the district Party secretary, some people were requalified several times as middle peasants only to have the kulak tag pinned on them again a year later. Instead of the official limit of 14.3 hectares (and there were many exceptions to this limit), frequently peasants possessing 9–10 hectares were also put on the kulak list. Consequently, the middle peasant could never feel himself removed from this danger. This uncertainty was reinforced on the

25. A. Mód, "The Kulak Question in the Mirror of Statistics," SSz, No. 12 (1949), p. 397.

26. Gazdasági életünk egyes kérdései a közgazdaságtudomány tükrében (Some Problems of Our Economic Life in the Mirror of Economic Science) (Budapest, 1954), p. 411.

27. According to Imre Nagy, "the measures taken against the kulaks, which assumed a nationwide character and went beyond the policy of restricting the kulaks, meant, in addition, that the government, year after year, had to worry more and more what to do with the so-called reserve-land, abandoned or handed over to the state, and which remained uncultivated because of the uncertainty in agriculture and because of the difficult conditions for cultivating the land" (For a Lasting Peace, for a People's Democracy, July 17, 1953).

28. SzN, May 25, 1954. Those farmers were considered "middle" peasants who owned more than 5–6 hectares but not more than 13–14.

29. Editorial in TSz, Nos. 2–3 (1955), 7; see also SzN, February 27, 1955.

official side as well. Rákosi admonished that "if the middle peasant becomes a kulak, the regulations on the restriction of the kulak will become applicable against him." [30] This policy has certainly discouraged the middle peasant from developing his productive activity.

Detailed planning in agriculture has also considerably affected the individual peasant. The sown area of various crops was planned for the whole country as well as on county, district, and village levels.[31] On the basis of these plans, individual peasants were compelled to devote certain percentages of their holdings to the production of various cereals, sunflowers (for producing vegetable oil), and—for some years—cotton. The compulsory cultivation of cotton was part of the drive for autarky when an attempt was made to acclimate cotton, natural rubber, peanuts, and other hitherto uncultivated industrial crops in Hungary. The Five Year Plan prescribed that "measures have to be taken that the raw-material demands of the Hungarian textile industry should be satisfied to a larger extent by home-grown cotton. It is to be endeavored that by the last year of the Plan period 100,000 hold should be planted with cotton." [32] The failure of cotton cultivation resulted in losses for both the individual peasant and the national economy.[33] Aside from the mandatory cultivation of cotton, economical production suffered also from the percentage allotments of the planting of several other crops, for the possibility of specialization was diminished thereby and some crops were sown even if the soil was more suitable for other produce.

Another method to ensure cultivation of certain crops was compulsory delivery. The relative importance of this method for particular crops can be seen in Table 18. The figures indicate that the relative importance of compulsory delivery changed with revisions of agricultural policy. In general, at the end of the period compulsory delivery obligations had a higher share in production than in 1950. The situation is similar with regard to pigs and dairy products, including poultry and eggs. If the peasants' own consumption is taken into account, not much

30. *SzN*, May 25, 1954.

31. *Some Problems of Our Economic Life*, p. 126.

32. *The Five Year Plan of the Hungarian People's Republic*, p. 33. One hold = 0.576 hectares = 1.42 acres.

33. Because of the disheartening results only 725 hectares of cotton were sown in 1955, and harvest was practically nil: *SE*, p. 174; *SHK*, No. 5 (1957), 73.

remained for the free market after the compulsory delivery obligations had been satisfied. (The share of the peasantry in food consumption may correspond to its relative share in the population—44 per cent at the end of the period.)

TABLE 18. *Compulsory Delivery of Selected Agricultural Products*
(in percentage of production)

	1950	1951	1952	1953	1954	1955
Wheat	42.6	45.6	56.0	50.0	47.0	54.4
Rye	49.3	47.2	55.0	51.8	43.7	57.5
Bread grains	44.4	46.0	55.7	50.3	46.3	55.0
Barley	21.6	27.4	41.8	28.5	24.5	20.3
Corn	9.4	16.1	23.2	13.5	12.6	15.5
Potato	16.5	17.0	27.9	17.3	17.8	20.7

Source: SE, p. 234.

As compulsory delivery obligations increased, there was an increasing divergence between delivery and free market prices. On the 1949 basis, by 1955 prices paid for compulsory delivery had increased by 13 per cent, prices paid by the state for purchases outside the compulsory delivery system had risen by 110 per cent, whereas free market prices showed a 234 per cent increase. The average increase in the prices of agricultural produce was 144 per cent.[34] In examining the effects of the compulsory delivery system, the following considerations are of importance:

1. The existence of the compulsory delivery system had a psychological effect on the peasantry. Most of the farmers were not aware that if this system had been abolished, their income might have remained unchanged if calculated on the newly established average prices. Rather, the comparison was made with existing free market prices, and the farmers concluded that the state, through low delivery prices, had curtailed their income. It has been contended that such considerations are likely to have impeded the development of agricultural production.[35]

2. The wide discrepancies between state and free market prices magnified the fluctuations of the peasantry's income: in bad years nothing remained for sale on the free market after compulsory delivery obligations had been fulfilled, whereas in good years the earnings were extremely high. Official data show that, for example,

34. *Prices*, p. 7.
35. K. Szabó, "The Role of the Free Market in the New Course," *TSz*, Nos. 8–9 (1954), 44.

the real income of the peasantry decreased by 56 per cent between 1951 and 1952 and rose again by 63 per cent between 1952 and 1953.[36]

3. The high delivery quotas left little possibility for the farmer to adjust his production according to the conditions of his soil.

4. The steeply progressive delivery quotas endangered the viability of medium and kulak farms.

In view of these considerations, the impact of the compulsory delivery system seems to have been disadvantageous to economical production in agriculture. During the Revolution compulsory delivery obligations were abolished, and the new Communist government has not reinstated this unpopular system. Nevertheless, a land tax was levied in kind, and threshing fees also have to be paid in kind to the state machine stations.[37]

The situation of individual farmers was also greatly affected by the so-called land consolidation. It was intended to consolidate the holdings of state and collective farms by regrouping their land in one piece. Land consolidation did not mean exchange of land plots for land of identical quality; rather, the authorities gave the better lands to the socialist sector, at the expense of the individual farmer. This policy was also used to compel the individual peasant to enter the collective farms. Official statistical data based on a sample comprising four counties show that, in exchange for their original holdings, the private farmers received land of lower quality and at a greater distance from their domicile.[38] In many districts land plots were regrouped again and again in succeeding years. The extent of land consolidation can be seen if the areas affected by the land reform of 1945 and by the regroupings of 1949–56 are compared. In the former case, 3.2 million hectares were redistributed, in the latter case 5.2 million—almost 60 per cent of agricultural land—were regrouped.[39]

It has been said that the "regrouping and particularly the absence of compensation considerably reduced the will to produce

36. *SE*, p. 296.

37. *NSz*, April 6, 1957; *SzF*, March 24, 1957.

38. The reduction in quality (expressed in net land value) was, on the average, 15 per cent, whereas the distance from the domicile rose by 42 per cent. L. Borbély, "The Role of the 1949–55 Land Regroupings of Farm Plots and Their Impact on Our Agriculture," *SSz*, No. 6 (1957), 456.

39. Ibid., p. 452.

on the part of the individual peasants." [40] Because of the danger
of regrouping, the individual farmer was not only disinclined
to make investments but also reluctant to use the necessary
quantity of fertilizer on his land. The data of Table 19 supply
evidence of the impact of land consolidation on productivity,
indicating a high correlation between the intensity of regrouping
and the change in the yield of wheat production. Changes in
livestock were similarly correlated with land consolidation. In
counties with extensive regrouping the number of livestock decreased by 8 per cent in the above period; in the case of little
regrouping the reduction was only one per cent; whereas in
counties where regrouping of land did not occur at all livestock
increased by 12 per cent.[41]

TABLE 19. *Land Consolidation and Productivity*

Proportion of Regrouped Area in Total Agricultural Area of Counties	Yield of Wheat Production in 1953–55 as a Percentage of the Yield in 1949–52
30–40	114
40–50	106
50–60	102
60–80	98
80–100	94
AVERAGE	102

Source: L. Borbély, "The Role of the 1949–55 Regroupings of Farm Plots and Their Impact on Our Agriculture," *SSz*, No. 6 (1957), 452.

In addition to the factors mentioned above, production on
private farms was influenced by imposition of high taxes, un-
availability of credits, and neglect of the individual farmer's
fertilizer and machine needs, as mentioned in the previous section.
In 1954, evaluating the situation of the private farmers, Zoltán
Vas put the matter rather bluntly: "Instead of money, machines,
and investments, we wanted to achieve our goals by harassing
and coercing the peasantry." [42] The situation was not materially
different on the eve of the Revolution. An editorial in the
Közgazdasági Szemle concluded:

> With regard to agriculture, it became manifest long ago that
> the forcible collectivization effected in spite of the announced

40. Ibid., p. 457.
41. Ibid., p. 453.
42. *SzN*, October 27, 1954.

principles of voluntariness . . . , the artificial sharpening
of the class war in the villages, the economic overburdening
of the peasantry, the continual land consolidation, etc. have
been harmful not only to the peasantry but also to the productive forces of agriculture, and have led to extensive cultivation in a country with a high density of agrarian population.[43]

Production Results

In the foregoing sections we have examined the effects of
agricultural policy on various groups of producers. We shall now
turn to the actual production results of Hungarian agriculture.[44]
We intend to rely primarily on physical data, since estimation
of the net contribution of agriculture to national income is
greatly influenced by the choice of price weights and by the
methods employed in the calculation of the value of materials
used up in agriculture. Nevertheless, physical data have deficiencies of their own in regard to harvest estimates and livestock
figures.[45]

We begin with a comparison of the employment of land in
various uses before the war and at the end of the period under
consideration (Table 20). It appears that the reduction in arable

TABLE 20. *Use of Land in Hungary*

	1935	1956	1935	1956
	(*1,000 hectares*)		(*percentage*)	
Arable land	5,606	5,400	60.3	58.0
Gardens,vineyards	321	368	3.4	3.9
Meadows, pastures	1,646	1,452	17.7	15.6
Forest	1,132	1,291	12.1	13.9
Productive land	8,705	8,511	93.5	91.4
Nonproductive land	604	801	6.5	8.6
TOTAL	9,309	9,312	100.0	100.0

Source: A. Kiss, "Changes in Intensive Cultivation during the Last Hundred
Years, 1857–1957," *SSz*, Nos. 1–2 (1958), 28–29.

43. *KSz*, Nos. 11–12 (1956), 1286.
44. With regard to agriculture, production results up to 1956 will be taken into
account, since the harvest was gathered before the outbreak of the Revolution.
45. On problems of harvest estimates in Hungary and other eastern European
countries see *Economic Survey of Europe in 1951*, pp. 222–25. On the quality of
livestock cf. below.

land and in meadows and pastures has been due to the disincentive effects of various measures described in the foregoing sections. Other things being equal, these reductions lessened the available quantity of food products partly directly, partly indirectly, through their impact on livestock raising. The favorable increase in the area of gardens and vineyards (actually there has been a small reduction in vineyards and a large increase in gardens) is likely to be primarily the consequence of the land reform.

Table 21 presents a comparison between sown areas, yields,

TABLE 21. *Sown Areas, Yields, and Harvests*
(Areas in million hectares, yields in quintals per hectare)

		1911–15	1936–40	1952–56
Bread grains	Area	2.23	2.21	1.83
	Yield	12.5	13.7	13.3
	Harvest	2.79	3.01	2.44
Coarse grains	Area	1.78	1.87	1.72
	Yield	15.1	18.4	17.8
	Harvest	2.66	3.44	3.06
Potatoes	Area	0.246	0.288	0.222
	Yield	80.1	81.0	85.7
	Harvest	1.94	2.31	1.91
Sugar beets	Area	0.060	0.049	0.114
	Yield	248.5	212.0	174.4
	Harvest	1.50	1.04	1.99

Source: Data for 1911–15 and 1936–40 are from *Economic Bulletin for Europe*, No. 2 (1955), p. 92. Data for 1952–55 are from *SE*, pp. 171–76, and for 1956 from *SHK*, No. 1 (1957), 32–33. It should be noted that the total area of the crops under consideration amounted to about 75 per cent of total arable land in the examined periods.

and harvests of the main crops in 1911–15, 1936–40, and 1952–56. If compared to the 1936–40 period, a deterioration in yields is apparent in bread grains, coarse grains, and sugar beets, whereas potato yields show an improvement. The sown area has been reduced for bread grains, coarse grains, and potatoes and increased for sugar beets. The absolute decrease in the harvest of bread and coarse grains and of potatoes appears considerable. The discrepancies are magnified if the harvests of different periods are reckoned per capita of population. The data of Table 22 indicate that in regard to harvest per capita the last period scores worse by comparison not only with 1936–40 but also with 1911–15, the exception being sugar.

TABLE 22. *Harvests per Capita of the Population*

	KILOGRAMS		
	1911–15	*1936–40*	*1952–56*
Bread grains	356	328	251
Coarse grains	350	375	316
Potatoes	248	252	199
Sugar beets	191	113	204

Source: Population figures given for 1911–15 are from *ASH*, p. 1; for 1936–40 and 1952–55 from *SE*, p. 3; and for 1956 from *SHK*, No. 1 (1957), 3.

Harvest figures show the availability of certain crops; in the evaluation of productivity of crop cultivation a comparison of changes in yields in various countries can be of use. The data of Table 23 show parallel increases of yields in various West European countries and a widening gap in yields between these countries and Hungary. Similar discrepancies can be observed

TABLE 23. *Yields of Bread Grains in Various Countries*

	WHEAT			RYE		
	1934–38	*1951–55*	*Index*	*1934–38*	*1951–55*	*Index*
	(quintals per hectare)			(quintals per hectare)		
Denmark	30.4	37.5	124	17.7	24.9	141
Netherlands	30.2	37.7	124	22.8	28.2	124
Belgium	26.9	33.4	124	24.0	27.8	116
England	23.1	29.2	126	16.2	22.8	141
West Germany	22.0	27.6	125	18.4	24.2	131
Hungary	14.0	13.9	99	11.5	11.4	99

Source: Data are from B. Csendes, "The Development of the Production of Bread Grains in Hungary before and after the Liberation," *Yearbook*, p. 360, except for Hungary, where the 1934–38 data are from *ASH*, p. 88, and the postwar figures (which in the case of Hungary refer to the 1952–56 period), are from sources of Table 21.

also with regard to barley, corn, potatoes, and sugar beets.[46] It becomes apparent that the relative position of Hungarian crop cultivation has greatly deteriorated during the postwar period.

The decrease in the area of meadows and pastures, shown in Table 23 in one figure was approximately the same percentage for each, if taken separately. Whereas in 1938 the area of meadows was 645 thousand and that of pastures 965 thousand hectares, the corresponding figures for 1955 are 560 and 913 thousand hectares. The data available on the yield of the meadows show

46. K. Garamvölgyi, "Problems of Planned Development in Agriculture," *KSz*, No. 5 (1957), 537.

a decrease from 28.4 quintals of hay per hectare in 1938 to 25.0 quintals in 1955.[47] These changes, alongside the reduction in the available quantity of coarse grains, indicate a shrinkage in the fodder base of animal husbandry.

Changes in the quantity of livestock can be seen from Table 24. The figures indicate that animal husbandry made great

TABLE 24. *Livestock in the Prewar and Postwar Periods*

Date	Cattle	Cows	Hogs	Sows	Horses	Sheep	Poultry
			(i n t h o u s a n d h e a d s)				
1938: March 1	1,882	917	5,224	602	886	1,629	21.919
1950: Feb. 20	2,222	1,064	5,542	638	712	1,049	—
1956: March 1	2,170	891	6,056	479	729	1,930	22.779
			(p e r t h o u s a n d i n h a b i t a n t s)				
1938: March 1	204	99	568	66	98	177	2.432
1950: Feb. 20	237	113	591	67	75	112	—
1956: March 1	218	91	608	48	73	194	2.280

Source: Data on horses, sows, and poultry are for February 28, 1935, instead of March 1, 1938. Sources for 1938, *MGIH*, No. 44 (1939), 83; for 1935, 1950, and 1956, *SE*, p. 184. There are no data on the stock of poultry in 1950.

strides in the years following the land reform of 1945. Yet after the collectivization campaign began, the number of cattle decreased; and the sharp fall in the number of cows and sows does not augur well for future reproduction either. With regard to cattle, hogs, and sheep, the 1956 figures compare favorably with prewar data. Nevertheless, it has been reported that the quality of livestock was considerably lower in 1956 than during the thirties. Whereas in 1930–35 the average weight of slaughtered cattle was 469 kilograms, it decreased to 410 kilograms by 1954 and to 408 by 1955. In the same years the average weight of slaughtered calves declined from 73 kilograms to 59 and finally to 57.[48] Similar changes are said to have occurred in regard to pigs.[49] In the case of sheep—in spite of the 18 per cent increase in stock—wool production declined by 30 per cent between 1938 and 1955.[50]

It is likely that the main causes for unfavorable developments in animal husbandry are the policies examined in the foregoing sections and the insufficient fodder base of livestock raising.

47. Data for 1938 are from *ASH*, pp. 82, 93; for 1955, from *SE*, p. 180.
48. *Facts and Figures*, p. 257.
49. M. Ribiánszky, "On the Agricultural Program," *AT*, Nos. 1–2 (1957), 3.
50. Garamvölgyi, p. 539.

These deficiencies resulted, on the one hand, in a shift of the composition of the diet from animal to vegetable foods,[51] and, on the other hand, in the deterioration of export possibilities for Hungarian animal husbandry.[52] Frequent shortages in meat, lard, and dairy products have been experienced during recent years.[53] According to official data, per-capita meat consumption was 41.4 kilograms in 1935 and only 35.9 in the especially good agricultural year of 1955. If 1950–52 and 1953–55 are compared, the corresponding figures are 34.6 and 32.5.[54] The consumption of milk and dairy products presents a similar picture: whereas in 1934–38 the average yearly consumption of these products was 102 kilograms per inhabitant in milk equivalents, the corresponding figure for 1950–55 was 92.7. During the latter period, consumption per capita amounted to 112 kilograms in 1950 and 87 in 1955.[55]

We mentioned previously that the contribution of agriculture to national income is influenced by the choice of price weights and by the methods used in estimating the value of materials used up in production. In the absence of relevant information on these methods we can hardly do more than present the official value figures here. The figures of Table 25 indicate the inferior per-

TABLE 25. *Contribution of Agriculture to National Income*

Year	Index of the Net Value of Agricultural Production	
	1938 = 100	*1949 = 100*
1938	100	—
1949	84	100
1950	94	112
1951	112	137
1952	70	83
1953	97	115
1954	92	110
1955	107	127
1956	89	106

Source: National Accounts, p. 100.

51. D. Kovács, "Food Consumption in Hungary in 1950–55," *KSz*, No. 1 (1958), 91–93.
52. See below, p. 267.
53. Kovács, p. 100.
54. I. Szlamenszky, "The Main Economic Aspects of the Hungarian Poultry and Egg Production," *KSz*, Nos. 11–12 (1956), 1374.
55. Kovács, p. 91.

formance of Hungarian agriculture when compared to prewar production. The improvement between 1949 and 1956 is not impressive if we take into account that in 1949 the after-effects of the
second World War were still noticeable.

These conclusions, like most of our discussion of the production results in agriculture, have been based on the implicit assumption of the constancy of labor and capital inputs. At this point
we shall introduce, however, a consideration of changes in labor and
capital in agriculture as shown by the available figures. In regard to
labor, we shall rely on data concerning agricultural population as
a whole, since the difficulties in estimating the working population in agriculture are well known. Agricultural population in
1949 was approximately one per cent less than during the thirties,
whereas a further one per cent decrease has taken place between
1949 and 1955.[56] In contrast to the slight decrease in labor inputs,
there has been an increase in the use of capital. Measured in 1,000
HP, the stock of agricultural machines increased from 611.9 to
858.9 between 1935 and 1957, the 1949 figure being 501.7.[57]
Taking into account changes in the number of plow animals,
driving power per 100 hectares (in horsepower) appears to be
5.8 in 1935, 5.1 in 1949, and 6.2 in 1957.[58] If these figures are regarded as representative of changes in capital stock, the conclusion can be reached that the reduction of the agricultural labor
force since the thirties has been more than counterbalanced by
increased use of capital, and the increase of the combined amount
of labor and capital inputs was still greater between 1949 and
1955. On the basis of the increase of labor and capital inputs
taken together, the performance of the Hungarian agriculture
in the planning period appears to be even less favorable than
shown in Table 25.

56. The figure used for the thirties is an average of data from the 1930 and 1941
Censuses; for 1949 and 1955 see *National Accounts*, p. 9.
57. Kiss, *SSz*, Nos. 1–2 (1958), 28–29. Data for 1955 are not available.
58. Ibid.

Appendix C: Developments in Foreign Trade

FOREIGN-TRADE POLICY

FOREIGN TRADE is of great importance in the Hungarian economy. Hungary is one of the poorest countries in raw materials: 100 per cent of her needs in cotton, rubber, and metals (other than aluminum), 90 per cent of coking coal, 80 per cent of iron ore, and 60–70 per cent of wool and sawn timber must be imported. Balanced development of the economy requires that Hungary participate in the international division of labor. Still, imitation of Soviet economic policies meant the rise of autarkic tendencies. Besides ideological and political rationalizations, spurious economic arguments were also set forth to demonstrate that autarky and, in general, reduction of imports was desirable. It was held that "the primary task of socialist foreign trade is to procure, through import, those producer goods and consumer goods which are not produced and not available in necessary quantity at home. To fulfill this task effectively, foreign trade must start with an estimate of the national economy's real import needs." [1] The idea of comparative cost does not appear; instead of a comparison of relative costs (domestic and foreign), "absolute" import needs are claimed to be the basis of foreign trade activity.[2] Others have maintained that imports should be reduced at all costs and that it is injurious to the interests of an industrially less developed country if foreign trade amounts to a high share of national income.[3]

The fallacies in the theories of autarky were exposed during the New Course. Imre Nagy said that "it is necessary to change the one-sided nature of the development of the national economy.

1. E. Illyés, "The Role of Foreign Trade and the Present Tasks in Its Planning," *TSz*, No. 5 (1954), 96.
2. Ibid., p. 102.
3. On these views see T. Liska and A. Máriás, "Efficiency and the International Division of Labor," *KSz*, No. 1 (1954), 80–81.

There is no justification for industrial autarky," because it means "economic isolation," it "overburdens the strength of the country" and "predetermines rejection of the favorable opportunities" in foreign trade.[4] In the theoretical field a scholarly article by T. Liska and A. Máriás argued for the need for participation in the international division of labor on the basis of comparative advantage.[5] Yet after the repudiation of the New Course the old views were voiced again.[6] Among others, it was asserted that the socialist countries should be "emancipated from the influence of the world market" and strange views were professed also in regard to foreign trade inside the Soviet orbit; the contention was that "the socialist market is an *organized* market; this fundamentally excludes the validity of the principle of comparative cost on the new world market. The principle of comparative cost can be valid only in the framework of the anarchy of production." [7] Notwithstanding these views, further development of heavy industry rendered it necessary to step up imports. In other words, the attempts to establish autarky in the material-intensive industries involved an increase in foreign trade through import of materials unavailable in Hungary but indispensable for the development of heavy industry. The inferior performance of agriculture also entailed a need for higher imports, and these, in turn, required more exports. The data of Table 26 show that after

TABLE 26. *Foreign Trade, in Percentage of National Income*

1929	40.8
1938	28
1949	24.7
1950	25.8
1951	23.5
1952	29.8
1953	33.1
1954	37.2
1955	41.0

Source: T. Kiss, "The Interrelationships of National Income and Foreign Trade in our Country," *KSz*, No. 6 (1957), 645.

4. *For a Lasting Peace, for a People's Democracy*, July 17, 1953.

5. *KSz*, No. 1 (1954), 82–93. For an abbreviated English translation see *Economic Survey for Europe* (1954), pp. 131–35.

6. On autarky in heavy industry cf. Chapter 6, n. 33.

7. G. Göncöl, "The Marxist Theory of Foreign Trade," *KSz*, No. 11 (1955), 1293–94. Italics in original.

a temporary retardation in the growth of foreign trade, the share of trade in national income has grown intermittently since 1951. Nevertheless, as will be seen at a later point, the increase in foreign trade was accompanied by a deterioration in efficiency.

Another aspect of foreign-trade policy is the change in the direction of trade. After the second World War, as political power came more and more into the hands of the Communist party, a tendency has become manifest to cut down trade with the West to an unavoidable minimum. In 1938 more than 70 per cent of imports came from the capitalist countries; this percentage decreased to 50 by 1949 and to 24 by 1952 (cf. Table 27). A similar

TABLE 27. *Direction of Foreign Trade*
(percentages)

	EXPORTS				IMPORTS			
	Soviet Union	People's Democracies	Capitalist Countries	Under-developed Countries	Soviet Union	People's Democracies	Capitalist Countries	Under-developed Countries
1938	0.1	13.4	78.7	7.8	0.1	23.8	71.5	4.6
1949	24.9	27.0	43.0	5.1	21.4	24.8	50.1	3.7
1950	28.9	37.1	28.9	5.1	24.5	32.1	38.4	5.0
1951	32.6	36.1	25.7	5.6	25.5	40.4	27.1	7.0
1952	33.5	39.9	21.6	5.0	26.6	45.8	24.0	3.6
1953	31.2	47.5	16.7	4.6	30.1	43.1	23.7	3.1
1954	32.7	40.9	21.4	5.0	28.6	39.4	27.4	4.6
1955	25.1	41.4	25.8	7.7	18.6	36.3	37.7	7.4

Source: Statistical Yearbook, 1949–55. SE, pp. 258–67.

reduction is apparent in exports to these economies and in trade with underdeveloped countries. The share of the Soviet Union and the people's democracies reached its highest point in 1953. After 1953 the share of foreign trade with capitalist and underdeveloped countries increased at the expense of the Soviet orbit. This latter change appears to be due to the inability or unwillingness of some countries in the Soviet orbit to contribute to the increase in foreign trade in the other countries of the bloc,[8] and to the lessening of restrictions in East-West trade on both sides of the Iron Curtain.

It is interesting to note that growth in the share of trade with

8. Imre Nagy reports that in January 1955 the Soviet Union informed Hungary that she "was willing to guarantee only 50 per cent of the 1954 import volume and only 36 per cent of the items on our want list for 1955" (*Imre Nagy on Communism*, p. 190). Similar cuts were imposed also by other people's democracies (ibid.).

underdeveloped countries surpassed the prewar level in 1955. This increase is part of the policy of the Soviet bloc to enlarge economic relations with underdeveloped countries. In regard to the future, it is likely that trade relations will continue to be greatly influenced by political considerations.

CHANGES IN THE COMPOSITION OF FOREIGN TRADE

The composition of Hungarian foreign trade in 1938, 1949, and 1955 can be seen in Table 28. On the export side we find a significant increase in the share of machinery, equipment, fuel, and raw material exports, but a reduction in the export of live-stock and food. In regard to imports, the increase in import of raw materials, fuels, and food was accompanied by a reduction in import of consumer goods. For 1949 and 1955 the further break-down of these items is not given in official statistics; the following discussion must therefore be based on information provided by various articles published in Hungarian journals, the authors of which apparently had access to unpublished material.

Agricultural Products

Table 28 shows the development of foreign trade in livestock and food. Adding export and import of materials of agricultural origin, such as medicinal plants and hemp (classified among raw materials in Table 26), foreign trade in agriculture shows the following changes: the share of agricultural exports in total exports

TABLE 28. *Composition of Hungarian Foreign Trade*
(*percentages*)

	EXPORTS			IMPORTS		
	1938	*1949*	*1955*	*1938*	*1949*	*1955*
1. Machinery, equipment, tools, and precision products	17.2	17.4	29.4	12.5	17.4	11.4
2. Fuels and raw materials	10.2	22.2	23.9	48.4	76.4	67.6
3. Livestock	17.4	6.7	2.9	—	0.1	0.1
4. Food	37.3	36.5	27.6	6.8	3.4	17.5
5. Other consumer goods	17.9	17.2	16.2	32.3	2.7	3.4
	100.0	100.0	100.0	100.0	100.0	100.0

Sources: for 1938, *ASH*, pp. 156–57; for 1949 and 1955, *SE*, pp. 256–57.

declined from 60.3 per cent in 1938 to 35.2 per cent in 1955, whereas during the same period the share of agricultural imports rose from 14.6 to 21.6 per cent. The reduction in agricultural exports extends over the whole field of agriculture: cereals, livestock, seeds, fruits, wines, etc.[9] The causes of this phenomenon can be traced back to the inferior performance of Hungarian agriculture in the period of planning, described in Appendix B. The decrease in the production of many agricultural commodities necessitated also an increase in imports.

Machinery

The hiatus created by the decline of exports in agricultural products was partly filled by the increasing export of machinery. In 1950–55 machine exports rose by 160 per cent.[10] This increase is the sign of developing heavy industry. Even so, this development has been criticized on various grounds. It has been pointed out that for Hungary the export of machinery is not economical and does not solve the country's foreign trade problems, since the materials of heavy industry must be procured from abroad. In 1954 about 57 per cent of imports served heavy industry and 56 per cent of exports consisted of heavy industrial products.[11] It has been charged that in developing the machine industry no attention was paid to the fact that many of its products can be produced under more favorable conditions in other countries of the Soviet orbit.[12] Lack of specialization and insufficient technical development have also been noted.[13] Because of such shortcomings, these products could hardly find markets in the West, and the possibilities of their export to the Soviet bloc also show signs of decline. Tatár observes that "the prices of the capitalist world market exert an increasing influence on the price level of the socialist world market, reducing it, because the socialist coun-

9. *SE*, pp. 268–71. I. Dobi, chairman of the Presidential Council of the Hungarian People's Republic urged at the end of 1956 that "we have to regain the lost markets for Hungarian fruits, wine and seed" (*EH*, December 30, 1956).

10. I. Tatár, "Actual Problems of Our Foreign Trade," *KSz*, No. 2 (1957), 194–95.

11. T. Kiss, "The Interrelationships of National Income and Foreign Trade in Our Country," *KSz*, No. 6 (1957), 655.

12. Illyés, *TSz*, No. 5 (1954), 91.

13. J. Bognár, "Problems of Our Foreign Trade," *KSz*, Nos. 8–9 (1957), 841–42. It has been pointed out that the weight of exported machines is 1½ to 2 times the weight of competing machinery (*Facts and Figures*, p. 317).

tries are not willing to take our machinery at higher than world market prices.[14] These factors have resulted in a serious decline in the demand for Hungarian machinery since 1955.[15] It is likely that—especially in the very material-intensive branches of machine production—Hungary will not be able to meet foreign competition.

Raw Materials

The development of the material-intensive branches of heavy industry necessitated a sharp increase in the importation of raw materials. In 1955 four times as much coal and coking coal and three times as much iron ore was imported as in 1938.[16] There was a similar increase in metals, lumber, etc. In addition, the increase in textile exports required a doubling of cotton imports.

Electrical Instruments; Precision Mechanics

It will be recalled that the labor-intensive branches of heavy industry, such as the production of electrical instruments and precision mechanics, have received few of the investment funds allotted to heavy industry. This policy, coupled with insufficient development in technology, has brought about a deterioration in the competitive position of these industries of long tradition. Precision instruments, telecommunication equipment, and vacuum techniques are most frequently mentioned as examples. It is widely held that the development of these labor-intensive sectors would be more economical for Hungary than the production of heavy machinery, since the former fields are those in which Hungary has a comparative advantage over countries better endowed with industrial raw materials.[17]

Light and Food Industries

An increase in the export of light industrial products followed the war, although having reached its peak in 1953 this export has shown a decline. Increased export activity was carried out

14. Tatár, *KSz*, No. 2 (1957), 189.
15. Ibid., pp. 196–97.
16. *SE*, pp. 262–67.
17. Bognár, pp. 841–42; Kiss, pp. 653–54; Tatár, p. 196.

mostly with an unchanged machine stock, and this fact has been a hindrance to further development after 1953.[18] An improvement in the export position of Hungarian light industry requires both substantial investment and technological improvements, since in the absence of these changes its competitive position will deteriorate further. These conditions apply also to the food industry.[19]

Consumer Goods

The unfavorable developments in Hungarian foreign trade have led to curtailment of consumer good imports. This decrease extends over both industrial products (woollen cloth, luxury goods, books, records, etc.) and foodstuffs (coffee, cacao, tropical fruits, etc.). These measures have reduced the range of goods available to consumers and thereby contributed to the reduction of consumer satisfaction.

It can be concluded that unsatisfactory production results in agriculture, forced development of import-intensive heavy industry, and insufficiency of investments and technological change in labor-intensive industries have jointly caused a deterioration in Hungary's foreign-trade position. And these developments could not be sufficiently counterbalanced by curtailment of the import of consumer goods. Hungarian economists characterized the situation as follows: "the more we have increased export and the more we have reduced the not indispensable import, the greater have become our foreign exchange difficulties," [20] and "import has come to serve less and less the direct or indirect satisfaction of our domestic needs, but more and more we have imported to be able to export in order to secure further import." [21]

Export of goods manufactured from imported materials is not disadvantageous if higher productivity in the manufacturing process compensates for higher cost of material procurement. The

18. Tatár, p. 198.

19. Kiss, pp. 653–54.

20. S. Balázsy, "Remarks on the Efficiency of Foreign Trade," *KSz*, No. 3 (1957), p. 303.

21. A. Mód, "Overcoming Inflation—Our Reserves and Prospects," *KSz*, No. 6 (1957), 607. A similar opinion has been expressed by Tatár: "A desperate race has developed between import and export, which has resulted in a series of forced measures. The management of the national economy has consequently been characterized by confusion and improvisation" (pp. 194–95). See also *Facts and Figures*, p. 291.

data of the next section indicate that this has not been true for Hungary.

EFFICIENCY OF FOREIGN TRADE

In Chapter 4 we disregarded foreign trade; trade relations were not considered until Chapter 6. The impact of foreign trade on domestic prices will be discussed briefly here. If a planned economy enters into trade relations with other countries, prices of traded commodities should reflect not the scarcities of the country taken in isolation but the scarcities of the world economy. If we assume that the country in question cannot affect world market prices, an optimum situation cannot be achieved until domestic prices of these commodities equal prices on the world market, allowance being made for transportation costs.[22] In such a situation those commodities will be produced in each country where there is a comparative advantage over other countries.[23] Adherence to these rules will ensure optimization in foreign trade.[24] The Hungarian economy has fallen far short of a trade optimum. The reasons for inefficiency in foreign trade can be seen primarily in the following factors: deficiencies in foreign-trade policy of the regime and of the organization of foreign trade, neglect of efficiency calculations in trade, and irrationality in the price structure. The foreign-trade policy of the planning period has already been discussed. We turn now to the other factors.

Foreign trade is conducted by specialized state trading companies in Hungary. These companies are in contact, on the one hand, with the foreign importer and exporter, and, on the other, with the domestic producer or user. To evaluate the operation of the organizational structure in foreign trade we must examine various factors affecting the behavior of the producer, user, and trading firms.

In a competitive economy, production for export serves the same function as production for domestic use: the results of productive activity are not realized until the commodities are sold. Consequently, the material interest of the producer induces

22. Participation in the international division of labor will also affect the prices of nontraded goods through changes in the prices of traded commodities.

23. For qualifications see Chapter 6, n. 13.

24. P. A. Samuelson, "The Gains from International Trade," *Readings in the Theory of International Trade* (Philadelphia, Blakiston, 1950), pp. 239–52.

him to cater to the foreign buyers' needs and to explore the possibilities of increasing sales by changing the quality or other properties of the product, by modifying the conditions of sale, etc. In the Hungarian economy the objective of the producing enterprise is to maximize bonuses by fulfilling the production and profit plans; it is not concerned with the foreign purchasers' (or the domestic users') satisfaction. The results of the production process are realized as soon as the manufacturing has been finished, and the plan fulfillment is not affected by the fact that foreign buyers may not take the product. Furthermore, the price received for the commodity has no relation to the price paid by the foreign importer [25] but is determined in the same way as the price of any other commodity in domestic use. For example, there are possibilities of increasing producer prices of nonstandardized products, the producers of which are said to have used a "moving price scale," that is, the originally stipulated price has frequently been raised during the period of manufacture.[26] In pursuance of bonus maximization, producing enterprises have made use of certain manipulations, described in Chapter 5, in regard to exported commodities.[27] A Hungarian economist has characterized the results of this behavior of the producer toward exports: "The producers are not interested in marketing. As a result, production frequently does not proceed appropriately and does not fulfill the requirements set by the foreign purchasers." [28]

Interest in plan fulfillment can be observed in the trading companies also. As exporters they fulfill their plans if foreign-exchange proceeds show an increase. Consequently, the price charged by the producer is not their concern. Neither are the trading companies interested in the profitability of exports, since the loss indicated by the difference between the price paid to the producer and the forint equivalent of the sale proceeds is borne by the state budget. Thus the plan fulfillment of the trading com-

25. For years the prices attained in selling the exported commodities were regarded as classified material and were not even communicated to the producing enterprises (Tatár, p. 199).

26. Ibid., p. 200.

27. It has been mentioned, for example, that commodities of greater weight than required have been manufactured for export purposes in order to overfulfill the production plan (*SzN*, December 27, 1955).

28. E. Varga, "Foreign Trade Monopoly and the Independence of the Enterprises," *GF* (March 31, 1957), p. 4. A similar conclusion is reached by Bognár, p. 852.

pany may be served by selling the commodities at unduly low prices if, demand being elastic, foreign-exchange proceeds are increased thereby.[29] The trading companies as importers have the task of procuring the required commodities. They have no material interest in attaining low prices, as the domestic users are also sheltered from world market prices by the practice of setting low domestic prices for imported materials.

These shortcomings of the organizational structure of foreign trade in Hungary have been frequently deplored. In addition, weak cooperation between industrial enterprises and firms engaged in foreign trade [30] and the "unusual slowness and inflexibility of foreign-trade organs" [31] have also been noted. It has been recognized that the material interest of the producer, user, and trading enterprise is not conducive to efficiency in foreign trade.[32] To remedy this situation, in 1956 six enterprises received the right to trade directly with foreign companies.[33] The results are to be seen, but absence of appropriate calculations of the efficiency of exports together with irrationalities in the price structure continue to be a hindrance to more economical foreign-trade activity. To these latter questions we now turn.

We have indicated before that trading with foreign countries is efficient if the trade is based on the principle of comparative advantage. In a centrally planned economy this objective can be achieved if prices are scarcity prices and if calculations are made of the efficiency of alternative possibilities in export and import. The problems of efficiency in foreign trade have been greatly neglected in the Hungarian economy. The prevailing policy can be characterized by saying that imports have been designed to serve primarily the development of heavy industry, and that in

29. *Facts and Figures*, p. 292. The undue lowering of export prices is mentioned by Tatár, p. 200. Illicit price reductions by the foreign representatives of trading companies have also been reported, for instance, in connection with Hungarian goose export to West Germany.

30. *KSz*, No. 5 (1958), 534.

31. *Imre Nagy on Communism*, p. 192.

32. To quote an official Hungarian publication on the results of this behavior: "Foreign trade instead of directing (at least in part) production, has become excessively dependent on industry: it had (and has) to sell what industry produces, notwithstanding the often changing direction of demand in foreign markets . . . and the quality requirements for various commodities" (*Facts and Figures*, p. 317).

33. *KSz*, No. 5 (1958), 534.

exporting the main goal has been the increase in foreign-exchange earnings to pay for these imports, with hardly any attention paid to the cost to the economy of exporting various commodities. S. Balázsy states that "for a long time nobody had examined, on a scientific basis, the problems of efficiency in foreign trade . . . After the 1953 Party resolutions . . . more and more economic functionaries [began to make such calculations. But] these calculations lacked a theoretical basis . . . and were mostly discontinued after a short time." [34] If such calculations were made, they were based on the net foreign-exchange earnings/production cost ratio. Since in production cost only labor costs (direct and indirect) are included and the scarcity value of fixed and circulating capital is disregarded, these calculations give a distorted picture of the efficiency of trade alternatives.[35] Yet disregard of the rate of interest is only one aspect of the irrationality of the price structure as a whole. The unreliability of calculations of the efficiency of foreign-trade alternatives has been given strong expression by Tatár. According to him, "as a result of the complexity of the price system, the dictated character of prices, and the rigid separation between producer prices and prices in foreign trade, at present actually nobody, no organization, can ascertain whether an export product is profitable or unprofitable for the country." [36] Hence, there is no satisfactory way to determine what proportion of the mounting deficit in Hungarian foreign trade is real and what is imaginary—that is, due to incorrect valuation of exports and imports.[37] Nevertheless, the substantial increase in the foreign-trade deficit valued on plan prices between 1949 and 1955 (cf. Table 29) indicates that the greater part of this loss is a real loss, caused by the inefficiencies of Hungarian foreign trade discussed above.[38] The loss in foreign trade, measured in domestic prices,

---

34. Balázsy, p. 304.

35. T. Liska, "Experimental Calculations on the Efficiency of Investments and of Our Participation in the International Division of Labor," *KSz*, No. 5 (1956), 520–21.

36. Tatár, p. 199. A similar opinion is expressed in *Facts and Figures*, p. 291, and by J. Fáy, "The Foreign Trade Aspects of the New System of Producer Prices," *SSz* (1956), 952.

37. Péter, p. 119.

38. Assuming equality between exports and imports expressed in foreign-exchange forints (foreign-exchange proceeds and payments multiplied by the exchange rate), loss in foreign trade expressed in domestic forints (excess of the value of exported goods over those imported) may ensue as a result of three factors: (1) deterioration

has reached about 50 per cent;[39] in 1955 one unit of exports bought 37.1 per cent less in imports than in 1949.[40]

Despite the deterioration of efficiency in foreign trade, the quantitative expansion in exports has resulted in a positive balance of

TABLE 29. *Loss in Hungarian Foreign Trade*
(million forints)

	1949 Prices	1954 Prices
1949	524	•
1950	740	•
1951	1180	•
1952	2266	•
1953	3358	•
1954	3602	7453
1955	•	8522

Source: SE, p. 38. The loss in foreign trade is arrived at by expressing imports and the corresponding exports in domestic prices.

trade in recent years. The figures of Table 30 show that the positive trade balance is a product of the high export surplus with the countries of the Soviet orbit and of the deficit with the capitalist and underdeveloped countries. It should be noted that the largest part of the Hungarian surplus in trade with the former countries has gone into paying obligations of (at least partly) uncertain origin to the Soviet Union. This is indicated by the fact that in spite of the cumulative positive balance of trade amounting to 1.6 billion foreign-exchange forints in 1950–55, the deficit in the balance of payments is said to have increased steadily between 1951 and 1955,[41] and the external short-term debt has risen from 1.7 billion foreign-exchange forints in 1953 to 3.1 billion in 1956.[42]

---

in the efficiency of foreign trade, (2) changes in the assortment of exports and imports, and (3) deterioration in the terms of trade. No data have been published on the terms of trade of Hungary. Nevertheless, in view of the arguments given above, it is likely that the greater part of the deterioration shown in domestic prices can be attributed to inefficiencies and to changes in the composition of trade resulting from the errors committed in foreign-trade policy.

39. T. Morva, "The Trade and Payments Balances and Their Connection with the National Product and Income Balances," *KSz*, No. 10 (1958), 1043.

40. Figures are based on data in *Economic Survey of Europe in 1957*, chap. 6, p. 29.

41. *Facts and Figures*, pp. 309–14.

42. *Economic Bulletin for Europe*, No. 2 (1957), 80. A negative balance in invisible transactions might also be partly responsible for this deficit.

TABLE 30. *Hungarian Foreign Trade in 1949–55*
(in million foreign-exchange forints)

	Trade with the Soviet Bloc			Trade with Other Countries			Foreign Trade Total		
	EXPORTS	IMPORTS	BALANCE	EXPORTS	IMPORTS	BALANCE	EXPORTS	IMPORTS	BALANCE
1949	1708	1562	+146	1585	1820	−235	3294	3382	−88
1950	2544	2099	+445	1313	1608	−295	3857	3707	+150
1951	3189	3047	+142	1456	1578	−122	4645	4625	+20
1952	3815	3770	+45	1383	1438	−55	5198	5208	−10
1953	4645	4050	+595	1259	1481	−222	5904	5531	+373
1954	4538	4094	+444	1626	1925	−299	6164	6019	+145
1955	4753	3445	+1308	2394	2829	−435	7147	6274	+873

Source: SE, p. 255.

Bibliography

Hungarian Newspapers
   Esti Hirlap (Evening Gazette)
   Népszabadság (Freedom of the People)
   Szabad Föld (Free Land)
   Szabad Nép (Free People)

Hungarian Periodicals
   Agrártudomány (Agricultural Science)
   A Magyar Gazdaságkutató Intézet Helyzetjelentései (Economic Reports of the Hungarian Institute for Economic Research)
   Demográfia (Demography)
   Gazdasági Figyelö (Economic Observer)
   Gazdaságstatisztikai Tájékoztató (Bulletin of Economic Statistics)
   Közgazdasági Szemle (Economic Review)
   Müszaki Élet (Technical Life)
   Pénzügy és Számvitel (Finances and Accounting)
   Pénzügyi Szemle (Financial Review)
   Statisztikai Havi Közlemények (Monthly Bulletin of Statistics)
   Statisztikai Szemle (Statistical Review)
   Statisztikai Tájékoztató (Statistical Bulletin)
   Századok (Centuries)
   Társadalmi Szemle (Social Review)

Books and Other Publications Dealing with the Hungarian Economy
   Adatok és adalékok a népgazdaság fejlödésének tanulmányázásához (Facts and Figures for the Examination of the Development of the National Economy), 1949–55. Budapest, Central Statistical Bureau, 1957.
   A Magyar Dolgozók Partja III. Kongressusának jegyzökönyve (Minutes of the Third Congress of the Hungarian Working People's Party). Budapest, 1954.
   A Magyar népgazdaság fejlödésére vonatkozó adatok (Data on the Development of the Hungarian National Economy). Budapest, Hungarian Institute for Economic Research, 1938.
   A Magyar Tudományos Akadémia Közgazdaságtudományi Intezetének Évkönyve (Yearbook of the Economic Institute of the Hungarian Academy of Science). Vol. *1,* Budapest, 1957.
   Annuaire statistique Hongrois, 1938. Budapest, 1940.

Anyagellátási ismeretek (The System of Material Allocation). Budapest, 1954.

Áralakulás Magyarországon 1938-ban és 1949–1955-ben (Prices in Hungary in 1938 and 1949–1955). Budapest, Central Statistical Bureau, 1957.

B. Balassa, *Épitöipari önköltségvizsgálat (Cost Audit in the Construction Industry)*. Sztálinváros, 1956.

B. Balassa and I. Bakonyi, *Munkahelyi tájékoztató az épitöiparban (Workshop Administration in the Construction Industry)*. Sztálinváros, 1955.

B. Csikós Nagy, *Árpolitika az átmeneti gazdaságban (Price Policy of the Transitional Period)*. Budapest, 1958.

Gazdasági életünk egyes kérdései a közgazdaságtudomány tükrében (Some Problems of Our Economic Life in the Mirror of Economic Science). Budapest, 1954.

E. Gerö, *The Position of the Hungarian Economy and the Tasks of its Development* (in English). Budapest, 1953.

E. Gerö, *The Results of the First Year of the Five Year Plan and Our Future Tasks in Building a Socialist Economy* (in English). London, 1951.

E. C. Helmreich, ed., *Hungary*. New York, Praeger, 1957.

G. Kemény, *Economic Planning in Hungary, 1947–49*. London, Royal Institute for International Affairs, 1952.

J. Kornai, *A gazdasági vezetés tulzott központositása (The Excessive Centralization of Economic Management)*. Budapest, 1957.

I. Kovács, *Agrárpolitikai feladatok (The Tasks of Agricultural Policy)*. Budapest, 1946.

M. Krémer, *A szállitási szerzödések és a népgazdasági tervezés (The Procurement Contracts and National Economic Planning)*. Budapest, 1955.

P. Kürthy, *Utmutató az egységes termék és árjegyzék használatához (Guide to the Use of the Uniform Product and Price List)*. Budapest, 1950.

O. Lukács, *Iparstatisztika (Industrial Statistics)*. Budapest, 1953.

Magyar statisztikai zsebkönyv (Hungarian Statistical Handbook), 1948. Budapest, 1949.

M. Matolcsy, *Mezögazdasági munkanélküliség Magyarországon (Agricultural Unemployment in Hungary)*. Budapest, 1933.

M. Matolcsy and S. Varga, *The National Income of Hungary 1924/25–1936 37*. London, King, 1938.

Imre Nagy on Communism. In Defense of the New Course. New York, Praeger, 1957.

Népgazdasági mérlegek, reáljövedelmek (National Accounts, Real Incomes), 1956. Budapest, Central Statistical Bureau, 1957.

G. Péter, *A gazdaságosság és jövedelmezöség jelentösége a tervgazdálkodásban (The Importance of Efficiency and Profitability in Planning).* Budapest, 1956.

I. T. Sanders, ed., *Collectivization of Agriculture in Eastern Europe.* Lexington, University of Kentucky Press, 1958.

L. D. Schweng, *Economic Planning in Hungary since 1938.* New York, Mid-European Studies Center, 1951.

N. Spulber, *The Economics of Communist Eastern Europe.* Cambridge, the Technology Press of M.I.T., 1957.

Statisztikai Évkönyv (Statistical Yearbook), 1949–55. Budapest, Central Statistical Bureau, 1957.

Tervgazdasági ismeretek (The System of Planning). Budapest, 1952.

The Five Year Plan of the Hungarian People's Republic (in English). Budapest, 1950.

The Hungarian Three Year Plan (in English). Budapest, 1947.

Üzemgazdaság (Business Economics). Budapest, 1950.

Author Index

Subject Index

Accounting prices, 92–93, 95

Agriculture, 25 ff., 34, 37, 39–40, 61, 75, 184, 231, 244 ff., 267–68; distribution of landownership, 244–45; collectivization, 247–48, 250; state farms, 249–50; private farms, 251 ff.; compulsory delivery, 254–56; land consolidation, 256–57; production results, 258 ff.

Bargaining, 56, 79 ff., 107–8

Bonuses, 61, 82, 108, 132 ff., 188–89, 191–92, 203, 207, 231; conditions of, 134 ff., 149; practices of management, 140 ff.; changes in assortment, 142–44; falsifications, 145; temporal adjustment of records, 145–47; clash of interest inside of the maximizing unit, 147–49, 160–61; special bonuses, 149 ff.

Bureaucracy, 53, 84 ff.

Buyers' competition, 130–31, 165–67

Capital goods, use of, 162–64

Collective consumption, 9, 20, 210–11

Complementarity effect, 15, 21

Construction, 61, 87, 106–7, 109, 137, 189 ff., 231

Consumer goods: planning of, 19, 47 ff., 55, 110 ff., 117; pricing of, 47–49, 94, 98, 105–6, 112 ff.; assortment of, 111–12, 115, 155

Consumer preferences, 7, 10, 16, 18 ff., 44 ff., 111, 232, 235

Consumer satisfaction, 5, 16 ff., 47, 54, 229, 235–36

Consumer sovereignty, 3, 16, 18 ff., 44 ff.

Consumption, 209–11, 215, 224–25

Cost of living index, 221–23

Depreciation, 162, 209, 211–12, 214

Distribution of income, 5, 17–19, 223, 236–37

Domestic trade, 29, 89, 111–12, 144

Dynamic efficiency, 5, 10 ff., 50, 199 ff., 216–17, 229, 231–32

Economic balances, 48, 50, 52–53, 56, 63 ff., 230; physical balances, 48, 50, 52, 63–64, 66, 69, 78, 95, 110, 175, 230; synthetic balances, 48, 65–66, 102

Efficiency, 4 ff., 44 ff., 56, 88 ff., 239 ff., 271–73

Enterprise. See Firm

Equilibrium: general, 5, 51 ff., 241–42; statistical, 52–53, 65–67; partial, 50, 66, 70, 74, 78–79

Expectations, 8, 12

External effects, 3, 9, 12

Firm: plans, 28–29, 58 ff., 64, 69 ff., 82–83, 94, 124; plan fulfillment, 74, 83, 107, 112–13, 134 ff., 164; distinguishing characteristics, 124–25; role in the economy, 127–28; and inventory policy, 159–61, and material procurement, 75–77, 155 ff.

Foreign trade, 61, 71, 75, 95, 125, 172–73, 234, 264 ff.; policy, 264–66, composition of, 267 ff.; and efficiency, 271 ff.

Free enterprise system, 1 ff., 7 ff., 44–45, 92, 130, 132, 218–19

Full utilization of resources, 9, 199–200, 271

Growth rate, 5, 13 ff., 55, 215 ff., 229, 232 ff., 237

Handicraft, 33, 36, 231

Housing, 228–29

Incentives, 62, 79, 107–8, 129–30, 132, 164 ff., 189–90, 202–3

Income. See Distribution of income, National income

Increasing returns, 3, 8

Industry: organization, 57, 123 ff., 200, 217–19; production, 25, 30, 33. See also Industries

Industries, 25 ff., 178 ff., 231; heavy, 31, 33, 36, 38–40, 42, 59, 75, 90, 120, 133, 178; light, 33, 36, 38, 40, 61, 75, 87, 90, 105, 120, 133, 156, 183–84, 213, 269–70; food, 33, 36, 38, 105, 120, 270; mining, 26–27, 35, 90, 180–81, 201; iron and steel, 27, 32, 37, 55, 90, 180–82; chemical, 36, 183, 201; local, 36; machine, 36, 87, 90, 146, 184, 201–2, 234, 268–69; leather and shoe, 88, 105, 146–47; textile, 105, 109, 160, 202; elec-

YALE STUDIES IN ECONOMICS